**SAGE** was founded in 1965 by Sara Miller McCune to support the dissemination of usable knowledge by publishing innovative and high-quality research and teaching content. Today, we publish more than 850 journals, including those of more than 300 learned societies, more than 800 new books per year, and a growing range of library products including archives, data, case studies, reports, conference highlights, and video. SAGE remains majority-owned by our founder, and after Sara's lifetime will become owned by a charitable trust that secures our continued independence.

Los Angeles | London | New Delhi | Singapore | Washington DC

# THE PROTECTION OF GEOGRAPHICAL INDICATIONS IN INDIA

# THE PROTECTION OF GEOGRAPHICAL INDICATIONS IN INDIA

A New Perspective on the
French and European Experience

## DELPHINE MARIE-VIVIEN

www.sagepublications.com
Los Angeles • London • New Delhi • Singapore • Washington DC

Copyright © Delphine Marie-Vivien, 2015

All rights reserved. No part of this book may be reproduced or utilized in any form or by any means, electronic or mechanical, including photocopying, recording, or by any information storage or retrieval system, without permission in writing from the publisher.

First published in 2015 by

**SAGE Publications India Pvt Ltd**
B1/I-1 Mohan Cooperative Industrial Area
Mathura Road, New Delhi 110 044, India
www.sagepub.in

**SAGE Publications Inc**
2455 Teller Road
Thousand Oaks, California 91320, USA

**SAGE Publications Ltd**
1 Oliver's Yard, 55 City Road
London EC1Y 1SP, United Kingdom

**SAGE Publications Asia-Pacific Pte Ltd**
3 Church Street
#10-04 Samsung Hub
Singapore 049483

Published by Vivek Mehra for SAGE Publications India Pvt. Ltd., typeset in 10/13 pt Berkeley by PrePSol Enterprises Pvt. Ltd., Haryana and printed at Chaman Enterprises, New Delhi.

**Library of Congress Cataloging-in-Publication Data Available**

**ISBN:** 978-93-515-0273-9 (HB)

**The SAGE Team:** Rudra Narayan, Alekha Chandra Jena, Anju Saxena and Rajinder Kaur

*To Eric, my husband, and to my three children,
Louis, Gabriel and Blanche-Saraswathi, who often accompanied
me to meet Indian artisans and farmers, creating
irreplaceable bridges between cultures.*

Thank you for choosing a SAGE product!
If you have any comment, observation or feedback,
I would like to personally hear from you.

Please write to me at **contactceo@sagepub.in**

**Vivek Mehra,** Managing Director and CEO, SAGE India.

## Bulk Sales

SAGE India offers special discounts
for purchase of books in bulk.
We also make available special imprints
and excerpts from our books on demand.

*For orders and enquiries, write to us at*

Marketing Department
SAGE Publications India Pvt Ltd
B1/I-1, Mohan Cooperative Industrial Area
Mathura Road, Post Bag 7
New Delhi 110044, India

*E-mail us at* **marketing@sagepub.in**

## Get to know more about SAGE

Be invited to SAGE events, get on our mailing list.
*Write today to* **marketing@sagepub.in**

This book is also available as an e-book.

# Contents

| | |
|---|---|
| *List of Abbreviations* | ix |
| *Foreword* by Dev S. Gangjee | xi |
| *Preface* | xiii |
| *Acknowledgements* | xv |
| *Introduction* | xvii |

**Part I: Globalization, Geographical Indications and the 'Indian Identity'**

1. India and Globalization, Opportunities and Risks — 3

2. An Analysis of the Diversity of Legal Concepts Underlying GIs — 25

3. GIs on Handicraft Goods in India Compared to France/Europe — 69

4. Indian GIs for Agricultural Goods? Uniqueness Justified by Natural and Historical Factors — 110

**Part II: The Peculiarities of the Role of the State for the Protection of GIs in India, Compared to France and Europe**

5. The Influence of WTO on the Role of the State in the International Protection of GIs — 145

6. The Decline of the Role of the State in France and Europe — 159

7. The Interventionism of the Indian State — 178

8. The Legitimacy of the Involvement of the Indian State     200

**Part III: An Essay on the Particularism of GIs as Intellectual Right**

9. An Intellectual Right Characterized by the Dismemberment of the Right to Use     247

10. A Collective Right to Use Tinted with Public Law     255

*General Conclusion*     266
*Bibliography*     271
*Index*     280
*About the Author*     289

# List of Abbreviations

| | |
|---|---|
| AIAMA | All India Agarbathi Manufacturers' Association |
| AOC | *appellation d'originecontrôlée* |
| APEDA | Agricultural and Processed Food Products Export Development Authority |
| APTDC | Andhra Pradesh Technology Development & Promotion Centre |
| BEDF | Basmati Export Development Foundation |
| BJP | Bharatiya Janata Party |
| CDI | Craft Development Institute |
| CII | Confederation of Indian Industry |
| DHS | Distinctiveness, Homogeneity and Stability |
| DSB | Dispute Settlement Body |
| DTA | Darjeeling Tea Association |
| EC | European Community |
| ECJ | European Court of Justice |
| FAME | Federation of Aroma/Agarbathi Manufacturing Enterprise |
| FISME | Federation of Indian Micro and Small & Medium Enterprises |
| GDP | Gross Domestic Product |
| GI | Geographical Indication |
| INAO | National Institute of Appellations of Origin |
| IPAB | Intellectual Property Appellate Board |
| IPF | Intellectual Property Facilitation |
| IPRs | Intellectual Property Rights |
| ISO | International Organization for Standardization |
| KHMPPT | Kashmir Handmade Pashmina Promotion Trust |
| KK | Kanyakumari |

| | |
|---|---|
| KSDL | Karnataka Soaps & Detergents Ltd |
| KSHDC | Karnataka State Handicraft Development Corporation |
| KSIC | Karnataka Silk Industries Corporation |
| LPG | Liquefied Petroleum Gas |
| NABARD | National Bank for Agriculture and Rural Development |
| NIIP | National Institute of Intellectual Property |
| NIIST | National Institute of Interdisciplinary Science and Technology |
| OHIM | Office for the Harmonization in the Internal Market |
| OJEU | Official Journal of the European Union |
| OSYU | Open Source Yoga Unity |
| PDO | Protected Designation of Origin |
| PGI | Protected Geographical Indication |
| PIC | Patent Information Centre |
| TGI | Tribunal de Grande Instance |
| TIFAC | Technology Information, Forecasting and Assessment Council |
| TRIPS | Trade-Related Aspects of Intellectual Property Rights |
| TSG | Traditional Specialty Guaranteed |
| TTD | Tirumala Tirupati Devasthanam |
| UNIDO | United Nations Industrial Development Organization |
| USPTO | United States Patent and Trademark Office |
| WIPO | World Intellectual Property Organization |
| WTO | World Trade Organization |

# Foreword

In an increasingly globalised world, place continues to matter. Geographical indication (GI) protection is the legal regime which most directly acknowledges this special significance of place. As Article 22.1 of the WTO's TRIPS Agreements declares: GIs are signs 'which identify a good as originating in the territory of a Member ... where a given quality, reputation or other characteristic of the good is essentially attributable to its geographical origin'. Typical regional products such as Darjeeling, Champagne or Parmigiano-Reggiano exemplify this link. In this exceptionally well-researched monograph, Delphine Marie-Vivien sets out to investigate the history as well as practical operation of this link between product and place, which sets GIs apart as a distinct legal category. She does so through a revealing comparative study of the GI regimes in France (as well as the European Union) and India.

The principal contribution this book makes is therefore to enrich our understanding of this link. The author advances the argument that this link has undergone a conceptual transformation. It was historically premised on the notion of *terroir* and emphasised natural factors such as soil and climate, which in turn influenced product quality. However, the greater interest in crafts and textiles in the Indian context—and here the Indian case study represents other developing countries' perspectives—shifts the focus to human or cultural factors and the know-how associated with such products. Its second significant contribution is to compare and contrast the nature of state involvement in the GI recognition, certification as well as protection process. Third, it fills a major gap in the scholarship in this area by exploring the controversial question of the proprietary nature of GIs. GIs are considered to be intellectual property rights, which are in turn generally understood as rights associated with private property. However, the interest in GIs is inevitably collective, with all the producers in the region of origin having a stake in the product. This book addresses this difficult question: the extent to which collective interests can be accommodated within a property framework, based on the distinction between a right to own and a right to use (i.e. beneficial enjoyment).

Delphine Marie-Vivien is uniquely well placed to write such a book. Having worked on GIs (and conducted extensive fieldwork) in both France and India for over a decade, she draws on historical insights, a nuanced understanding of international as well as domestic legal rules, an attentiveness to economic policy and a practical awareness of the politics surrounding GIs as well as implementation projects which results in a book which is both a pleasure to read and contains many new insights. With GIs increasingly prominent in international policy debates as a vehicle for achieving development policy goals, this book should be read by all those who have an interest in the protection as well as regulation of traditional products.

**Dev S. Gangjee**
Associate Professor in Intellectual Property
Faculty of Law, University of Oxford, Oxford

# Preface

This book has been written from a PhD dissertation, defended in France and fully available in French at http://tel.archives-ouvertes. fr/docs/00/58/73/07/PDF/Marie-Vivien_thA_se_IG_Inde2010. pdf. The thesis has been drawn not only from theory but also from observation of practice, thanks to a three-year stay in India as visiting researcher at the National Law School of India University, Bengaluru, between 2005 and 2008, which made it possible to understand the complexity of GI products, to extensively investigate the GI application files for consultation in the GI office in Chennai, and to meet the people concerned: producers, artisans, farmers, public authorities, applicants, lawyers, scholars and experts.

# Acknowledgements

My deep gratitude goes to the unfailing support of my husband, Eric, his confidence, his patience and dedication not only throughout this work but also during the last 20 years.

I want to thank Centre de coopération internationale en recherche agronomique pour le développement (CIRAD) and especially Hubert Devautour and Denis Sautier, who offered me the opportunity to engage in research after years of activity as a legal adviser and allowed me to go on an assignment to India. This work research in India has been achieved through the projects Biodivalloc, funded by French Agence Nationale de la Recherche (ANR), and SinerGI, funded by the European Union (EU).

My gratitude and memories go to multiple Indian colleagues of the National Law School of India University (NLSIU) in Bengaluru, in particular Sudhir Krishnaswamy and Rahul Singh; of the University of Agricultural Sciences in Bengaluru, particularly P. Chengappa; to practitioners and lawyers involved in the protection of geographical indications (GIs), including Latha Nair, Subodh Kumar and Zaheda Mulla; and finally to producers such as Narayanan Unny who helped me to understand the complexity of India.

I sincerely thank Dev Gangjee, University Lecturer in Intellectual Property at the Faculty of Law at Oxford, for his precious insights and his continuous support towards writing this book and thus making available the results of the thesis in English. I also want to thank Yogesh Pai, Assistant Professor at Delhi University, who reviewed the manuscript with highly appreciated comments.

I warmly thank my colleagues from CIRAD and particularly Estelle Bienabe and Didier Chabrol, for their listening, their advice and their time. I thank Laurence Bérard, anthropologist at Centre national de la recherche scientifique (CNRS), for her help in the formulation of my thinking.

I also express my gratitude and appreciation to Marie-Angèle Hermitte, my PhD supervisor, for her unconditional presence despite the distance, her encouragement and her teachings.

# Introduction

Basmati rice, a product with an aroma as unique as the taste of Roquefort cheese, is the only rice exempted from the ban on exports issued by the Indian government on 1 April 2008 following the food crisis. Does the cause lie in the fact that the quantities produced are excessive or that Indians are tired of Basmati rice?[1] Definitely not! The special status of this elongated, aromatic rice is explained by because 'Basmati' being a potential geographical indication (GI) of a famous rice having qualities attributable to its geographical origin and benefiting from an added value in the market.[2]

GIs identify a good as originating in a region where a given quality, reputation or other characteristics of the good is essentially attributable to its geographical origin.[3] This definition of the World Trade Organization (WTO) Agreement on Trade-Related Aspects of Intellectual Property Rights (TRIPS) protects a very old concept, first legalized in France and Europe. However far we go back in history, numerous products differing widely from each other gained in reputation when they bore the name of the region from whence they came. It could be minerals (marble), art objects (bronze or terracotta), cloth (silk), perfume (incense) and

---

[1] The registration of Basmati as a GI is still pending, following oppositions regarding the definition of the geographical area in India and the issue of a transborder GI with Pakistan.
[2] Refer to http://apeda.com/apedawebsite/six_head_product/cereal.htm consulted 1st May 2010.
[3] Art. 223 of the Agreement on Trade-Related Intellectual Property Rights (TRIPS).

agricultural products (honey).[4] Legal rules protecting GIs have been there for centuries in Europe. For example, French king John's decree of 1351 demonstrates a first rudimentary official defence of quality: 'It is decreed that no wine merchant can mix two wines together. Disregarding this law can entail a loss of wine and a fine'.[5] Laguiole cheese dates back to early antiquity; the cheese-making process as well as how the mountains are to be used and farmed were fixed by the monks of Aubrac monastery since the XII century.[6] Since the XV century, Roquefort cheese has been the subject of a royal charter, granted to the inhabitants of Roquefort. In it they are conferred the monopoly over the maturing process which was carried out in well-guarded cellars.[7] In the Middle Ages, guild trademarks were normally used to indicate the geographical origin of products. Many are still used today such as 'Murano glass', named after the island where it was manufactured, next to Venice.[8]

GIs indicate the rootedness of the product in the local environment which confers upon it a quality, characteristics or a reputation, in such a striking manner that the name of the product itself includes a reference to the place of origin. But GIs are more than just about where the product comes from. They reflect 'historical echoes and collective practices' grounded in a specific milieu. This makes them objects having a qualitative link with their origin.[9] Products reputed because of their geographical origin, 'local symbols', are increasingly desirable objects, even though the current epoch of globalization could lead to believe that they are going to disappear. On the contrary, this desire is a result of globalization which does not entail the disappearance of

[4] *Une Réussite Française: L'appellation D'origine* Contrôlée (INAO, 1985). 11.
[5] Mr Baron Le Roy's report, President of the l'Institut National des Appellations d'Origine (National Institute of Appellations of Origin) *1er Congrès De L'origine, Tenu En Pays D'auge À Deauville Du 25 Au 27 Juin 1948* (Caen: BNICE et INAO, 1992). 12.
[6] The report of M. le Docteur Ayrinchac, President of the Fédération des Labels du Massif Central, ibid. 35.
[7] Marie-Hélène Bienaymé, 'L'appellation D'origine Contrôlée', *Revue de* Droit Rural, no. 236 (1995). 420.
[8] Bernard O'Connor, *The Law of Geographical* Indications (London: Cameron May, 2004). 21.
[9] Laurence Bérard and Philippe Marchenay, *Les Produits De Terroir, Entre Cultures Et Règlements* (Paris: CNRS Edition, 2004). 41.

'local and regional products' but rather their emergence or reconstitution.[10] Indeed, origin-based products reflect cultural identity, and while economic growth is on the rise and populations are migrating beyond cultural frontiers, they display a tendency to use their cultural identity as a rampart. This cultural identity is expressed by origin products, which, however, are under threat. Local traditional products are vulnerable to the risk of the opening of frontiers: the delocalization of production dilutes or refutes the close link between products and their origin and the waning of lifestyles which supported these traditional products because of the arrival of new products.

The example of India is particularly meaningful with its pre-1991 economic policies, based on the Swadeshi movement and self-sufficiency, sought to avoid too deep an involvement in global exchanges because that would have inevitably compromised its independence.[11] The fear of loss of independence explains that India sought to legally protect products reflecting its cultural identity, which were liable to be tampered with by globalization, through a commitment to GIs. GIs are thus an expression of the right to be different, 'allowing the preservation of localization in the context of globalization'.[12]

Often attached to underprivileged producers, the aim of GIs is to boost their earning by adding value to their products and making them remunerative enough to cover the cost involved in respecting traditional production methods.[13]

Globalization is also a legal issue. Thus, national laws are increasingly under pressure from international laws. GIs are incorporated into the TRIPS Agreement as a result of the internationalization of the appellation of origin, the forefather of GIs, protected as such since the beginning of the 20th century in France. In the internationalization of laws, GIs

---

[10] Virginie Amilien, 'A Propos De Produits Locaux', *Anthropology of Food*, no. 4 (2005). 1.

[11] For a complete study on India's participation in global commercial exchanges, see Gilles Boquérat, 'Le Swadeshi À L'épreuve De L'ouverture', in *De La Mondialisation Au Développement Local En Inde*, ed. Frédéric Landy and Basudeb Chaudhuri (Paris: CNRS Editions, 2002). 27–41.

[12] Producers from all over the world requested WTO to progress on the issue of the extension of protection to all products, see the communication of Origin, www.origin-gi.com.

[13] Bienaymé, 'L'appellation D'origine Contrôlée'. 422.

have the particularity of being both cultural and economic conducting to a conflicting internationalization. Confronting the tradition of the 'Old World' countries, with a long history behind them, whereby it is customary to use names of places to designate the products which have originated there, is the tradition of the 'New World' countries, populated by migrants who have brought along the names of their villages in their travelling bags and name the fruits of their farms accordingly, though they are situated thousands of kilometres away. However, this traditional stance of 'New World' countries is evolving because of the producers' new aspirations, thus coming closer to the GI concept.

India has a strong cultural identity founded on its plurimillenary history and offers numerous products which are locally rooted. India defends the idea that 'the Indian tradition in the area of "material know-how" is as legitimate as any other tradition and can play a major role in nation building'.[14] Moreover India, as other Southern countries, is an emerging country which demonstrates a growing capacity to defend its interests in the international arena and particularly in different WTO forums. India's experience of protecting GIs at national level influences their protection at international level and thus needs to be understood.

The Indian scenario where the Geographical Indications of Goods (Protection and Registration) Act (GI Act) of 1999 has been implemented following the TRIPS Agreement is fascinating to analyze in the light of the French and the European experience which are the cradle of legal protection of GIs, representing Old World countries. India, also an Old World country due to its ancient culture, only recently enriched with a *sui generis* legal framework for the protection of GIs is a 'new country of the Old World'.

In France, the modern regime for the protection of appellation of origins was set up in 1905,[15] surely linked to its history of viticulture. The French definition of appellation of origin became more sophisticated over time, evolving from a simple defining of production zone boundaries to the development of specifications which describes in detail product characteristics, production method and the link between

---

[14] Marie-Claude Mahias, 'Les Sciences Et Les Techniques Traditionnelles En Inde', *L'Homme* 37, no. 142 (1997). 105.

[15] Dion, R., *Histoire de la vigne et du vin en France, des origines au XIXème siècle* (Paris: Flammarion, 1977).

the product and its geographical origin. In 1992, drawing largely on the French tradition, the European Community (EC) introduced homogeneous protection in all European territory,[16] restricted to agro-food products and founded on the principle of mutual recognition of surviving national norms.[17] Since 1992, European regulation has been amended twice, in 2006 and 2012.[18]

The literature provided four justifications concerning the development of public protection policies and the promotion of GI in France and in Europe. They are the fight against unfair competition, the control of agricultural markets via rights granted to producer, rural local development and safeguarding of natural and cultural heritage.[19] GIs are a major element in European agricultural policies in the context of surplus production of food products which has given rise to the implementation of a quality economy alongside a quantity economy. It is not certain, that in the global agricultural context in the beginning of the 21st century, we will observe the same trend. But in the domain of handicraft, the situation of India participating in globalization seems comparable to the European situation of agricultural surplus. This is especially true in the case of textiles, where the demand for traditional saris is undermined because of cheaper imitations or Western products, threatening the long ancient trade of cloth and textile. India is thus in a transitory phase between tradition and modernity. The state in which India was in the beginning of the 21st century is often compared to the awakening of an elephant, an echo of the awakening of the dragon, symbolizing China

[16] Regulation (CEE) no. 2081/92, 14 July 1992 on the protection of designation of origin and geographical indications of agricultural goods and foodstuff.

[17] Schmidt-Szalewski J., 'La protection des noms géographiques en droit communautaire', JCP, éd. E, 1997, Chr. N°703 ; Pollaud-Dulian F., 'Appellations d'origine', Répertoire de droit communautaire, Paris, Dalloz.

[18] Council Regulation (CE) No. 510/2006 of 20 March 2006 on the protection of geographical indications and designations of origin for agricultural products and foodstuffs, OJEU L 93, p. 12, replaced by Regulation (EU) No. 1151/2012 of 21 November 2012 on quality schemes for agricultural products and foodstuffs, OJEU L 343/1.

[19] Bertil Sylvander, Gilles Allaire and Giovanni Belletto, 'Les Dispositifs Français Et Européens De Protection De La Qualité Et De L'origine' (paper presented at the Symposium international 'Territoires et enjeux du développement régional', Lyon, 9–11 mars 2005): 1–22.

about 10 years ago. This awakening challenges the reputation of India as being unshakeable for centuries, with ancient cultural and religious traditions still propagated by a diverse and multitudinous population. These traditions are supposed to attract visitors seeking spirituality from the so-called modern West. The emblematic figures of the 'non-violent' fight for independence, such as Gandhi and the search for a third way, Nehru's defence of non-aligned countries, have created a unique image of the political and economic regime in India, that of social democracy.

Meanwhile, India has been changing since 1990, with a gross domestic product (GDP) reaching a two-figure growth rate, and its entry into the global arena has given rise to a contrasting reality. On the one hand, the Indian middle class, which has benefited from the opening of India to foreign capital and high-tech sectors in the area of new information technology, is on the rise. On the other hand, the situation of the underprivileged, farmers and artisans possessing the knowledge and skills for manufacturing products, the bearers of Indian cultural identity, is increasingly precarious.

The practice consisting of naming products based on the production place is well established in India. This is striking in the case of fruits and vegetables species which do not often have names which are different from the geographical name of their place of origin. In 1999, just at the time the long legal battle on Basmati rice was coming to an end (India contested an American multinational company which had applied for patents for new Basmati rice varieties), India adopted the GI Act.[20] The Indian GI Act requires that all GI applications shall describe the 'uniqueness' of the product, the history, the method of production and shall be examined by a panel of experts. Since then India has been one of the most dynamic countries among Third World countries, registering GIs at the national level, with 248 GIs registered as for June 2015[21] and also in Europe where Darjeeling tea is a registered GI since 2011. Each Indian participant feels concerned, whether it be government bodies actively involved in the protection of Indian heritage, intellectual property lawyers whose expertise serve in documenting the products and their regions or universities convinced about the benefits of intellectual

---

[20] Geographical Indications of Origin of Goods Act, 1999.
[21] Out of which there are 226 GIs for Indian products and nine GIs for foreign products. See http://ipindia.nic.in/girindia/.

property rights.[22] Only the producers are often unaware of the existence of GIs or what is in India 'GI tag'.

The analysis of GIs in India reveals characteristics which contrast with the French and European experience. This comparison enables us to understand how the legal tool of GI can be internationalized and how this internationalization can influence the vision of countries which are cradles of GIs protection like France and Europe and help in discovering the legal nature of GIs. Understanding this process can add new facets to the international protection of GIs, which, it is commonly admitted, is far from being complete.

First, the thesis shows that India has grasped the opportunity offered by the TRIPS Agreement to extend GI protection to non-agricultural products, whereas in France and Europe, only agricultural and agro-food products are eligible for GI protection. The GI concept provides a suitable framework for the protection of handicraft, the jewel of Indian cultural identity, especially in the area of textiles where the mastery of sophisticated know-how is a must, against the threat of globalization. GIs have been registered to designate a sacred metal mirror as well as hand-woven silk and sculpted wooden objects, and their use is all the more seductive because of the absence of any legal framework dedicated to the protection of traditional knowledge and know-how at the international level. The original Indian experience of using GI for non-agricultural products, thus not linked concretely to the soil, challenges the nature of the link between a product and its geographical origin. Can we refer to a *terroir* as in the case of French appellations of origin? Is the link with the origin only through the knowledge and skills of producers sufficient? It seems that the criteria of how ancient the know-how is will be a deciding factor to justify the uniqueness of the product. History is what incites this link between the product and its place of origin, and this is also true for GIs for agricultural products obtained from very old varieties. The similarity with the European PGI is striking and will lead to consider the Indian choice of granting GIs to handicraft goods to be a valid one, a consideration very recently adopted by the French

---

[22] See for example, Samaddar, S.G. and A.B. Samaddar (2010). 'Koma Chaul—A Potential Candidate for Geographical Indication'. *Journal Of Intellectual Property Rights* 15(May): 2214–2219.

government which introduced in the French Law on consumption passed on 17 March 2014 the creation of GIs for non-agricultural goods.

Second, another vital element which emerges from the Indian experience is the preponderance of the State's role. Many Indian GIs are registered in the State's name or in the name of its bodies and authorities or at least with the State's support. In India, the protection of GI is carried out by the State and is a top-down process. It contrasts with the French and European history of the protection of GIs, which after many failed attempts resulted in the choice of conferring the preponderant role to producers: it is thus a bottom-up process. Nevertheless, in France and Europe, the intervention of the State in the examination of the specification's technical content and the monitoring of the system of control confers GIs with certain aspects of public law advocated by the Old World countries.

The Indian situation can be explained by the registration of certain GIs for symbolic products which are hardly vulnerable to the threat of usurpation, and shall be protected by the State because they are representatives of Indian cultural identity. Moreover, farmers and artisans are underprivileged sections of population whose interests the State shall defend in accordance with the tradition of interventionism, specific to India. The intervention of the Indian State is, however, legitimate only if the State complies with the obligation of the GI Act that the applicant of the GI shall represent the producers. The same criteria of the representation of producers by the GI applicant have shaped the French reform of the appellation of origin and GIs legislation in 2006. Yet more and more voices are calling for less intervention of the State in India.

Finally, the Indian Act which provides for the separation between the proprietor of the GIs and the registered users challenges the legal nature of GIs regarding both their collective character and their public nature. In light of the few registered authorized users in India which emphasizes wrongly the need to be proprietor on the one hand and the absence of proprietor in French and European Law on the other hand, we will argue in favour of the idea that GIs are a right of use, and not a property right.

These conclusions of the thesis have been drawn not only from theory but also from observation of practice, thanks to a three-year stay in India in 2005–2008, which made it possible to understand the complexity of GI products, to extensively investigate the GI application files for consultation in the GI office (analysis of the GI specifications published by the

GI Registry in the *Journal of Geographical Indications*, documents provided by the applicant and examined by the GI Registry and the consultative group available in the 40 GI files consulted at the GI Registry, documents provided during oppositions also consulted at the GI Registry), and to meet the people concerned: producers, public authorities, applicants, lawyers, scholars and experts (interviews with concerned parties provided data for 25 GIs). The research was then continued until 2015.

# Part I
# Globalization, Geographical Indications and the 'Indian Identity'

The modern legal protection of GIs originated in the south of Europe, more specifically in France, and was later adopted by countries which signed the Lisbon agreement, a World Intellectual Property Organization (WIPO) treaty with an open membership policy. It was finally internationalized because of the WTO's TRIPS Agreement, which came into effect in 1995.[1] All WTO members had to implement legal means to protect GIs. India began doing this with the GI Act of 1999. Thus for India, the GI Act was the consequence of the WTO, a vehicle for contemporary globalization. This exogenous legal institution found an unexpectedly favourable echo in India though, because it corresponded to the Indian preoccupation of protecting its culture and identity when it opted for an open-market economy and began participating in modern global trade, thus exposing its traditional products to the risk of usurpation–imitation. Though it coincided with the Basmati case, the GI law was linked to the WTO's agenda and could thus be qualified as a legal tool for protecting GI post-TRIPS Agreement. However GIs, as of today, are

[1] J. Audier, Accord ADPIC. Indications géographiques, Office des publications des Communautés européennes, Luxembourg, 2000, p. 1/47.

the result of a long and tumultuous journey, with many hurdles on the way, leading to a rather loose definition of GI. In France, the cradle of the appellation of origin act took almost half a century to arrive at the current legal definition. And in Europe, the diverging traditions between the Northern and Southern countries of the Old Continent gave birth to two legal tools: PDO and PGI. As a result, GI protection, founded on different concepts in France, Europe and India, lacks uniformity at the international level.

In India, the use of GI to protect all types of products, agricultural, handicrafts, manufactured and natural, is unique. In France, for example, even though certain appellations of origin could have been used to protect non-agricultural products, the legal protection of GI developed because of the need to monitor the production of food and agricultural products. At the European level, only agricultural or food products[2] are protected by the 510/2006 regulation on designation of origin and GIs, along with wine and alcoholic beverages, monitored by the texts of the common wine market[3] association. The Indian experience lends a deeper insight into the nature of the link between the product and its geographical origin, especially in the case of handicrafts.

The common denominator of all Indian GIs is their reference to history, which indicates the 'uniqueness' of the product, the value of the know-how involved and the reputation of the production zone. Indian history is multilayered, spanning thousands of years of traditional knowledge, including knowledge of indigenous plant varieties and the more recent knowledge of agro-products imported by colonizers. In addition to the historical element which establishes the link between products and their origin, natural factors can also exert an influence similar to the French appellation of origin. Thus, the Indian experience makes us aware of the wide diversity of links to the origin.

---

[2] Products are listed in annex I of the European Community Treaty and in annexes I and II of the European Regulation no. 510/2006. These annexes may be amended in order to extend or reduce the list of products eligible for the registration of PDO and PGI as soon as there are agricultural products or foodstuff.
[3] Previously, the production of wines and spirit was regulated by specific rules aiming to build a common market for wines.

# 1
# India and Globalization, Opportunities and Risks

## The Internationalization of GIs at WTO

The concept of the appellation of origin was best known in Southern Europe, where the diversity and richness of nature, soil and gastronomic traditions have given birth to local products, wine being the perfect illustration. The dissemination of this demanding concept was difficult at the international level, with the limited signatories of the Lisbon Agreement for the Protection of Appellations of Origin and Their International (1958) under the Paris Convention on the Protection of Intellectual Property (1883), creating a special union between signatory countries with the objective of protection of appellations of origin recognized and protected as such in the country of origin in all signatory countries, and the softer definition of geographical indication was included in the WTO agreement.

## GI, an Intellectual Property Right Backed by the 'Old World'

The developed countries through the intellectual property rights sought to protect their innovations, copied in developing countries, while the Southern countries argued that copying was justified in the dynamics of development. India, placed in the category of developing countries, referred to as 'Southern countries', and at the time of the Uruguay Round negotiations barely an emerging market, adopted a traditional stance of opposition against developed countries, referred to as 'Northern countries' in the negotiation on intellectual property rights. This was even more pronounced during the negotiations concerning patents.

India's contribution lies in pleading for more flexibility and exceptions in the Intellectual Property Rights agreement, such as the possibility of compulsory patent licences.

The subject of GIs, on the contrary, has created a rupture in developed countries, between Old World and New World countries, concerning the antiquity of their history.[1] It is around this issue that the differences between the Old World and the New World crystallized, the Old World headed by the EU and the New World by the United States.[2] Besides this cultural difference, the New World countries, especially the United States,[3] which is at the head of them all, are generally characterized by a different legal culture. These differences came to light during the TRIPS negotiation and led to an unsatisfactory compromise. This divide continues to generate debates and negotiations at WTO.

*Cultural and Legal Differences between the Two Worlds*

The Old and the New World disagree regarding GIs on two fronts: the relation to history and culture and the choice of legal/political systems. To this can be added the different manner in which the agriculture industry is organized, whence the GI concept emerged.

The New World was built by European migrants. Leaving their land behind, they carried with them their traditional knowledge, skills and seed stock. They continued their farming activities in the new land and used the same terms that they used in their country of origin to designate their produce. For the New World, this reality justified their use of a GI, even though the country of its origin was elsewhere. They thus do not consider that there is any intention of fraud or misappropriation

---

[1] Gangjee, D., *Relocating the Law of Geographical Indications* (Cambridge: Cambridge University Press, 2012).
[2] Watal, *Intellectual Property Rights in the WTO and Developing Countries*, 11.
[3] See Tim Josling, 'The War on Terroir: Geographical Indications as a Transatlantic Trade Conflict', *Journal of Agricultural Economics* 57 (2006).

in using well-known indications.⁴ The reason behind this clash can be found in the history of wine, wherein lies the cultural and historical differences between countries where originally vines were cultivated (the Mediterranean basin) and who are for using the names of their territories to designate wines which are exclusively produced there, and the new countries of immigrants, where the newly arrived winegrowers use the original appellation for newly planted vines on their territory. Moreover, the New World group go even further by saying that the producers of the Old world who would like to take back these names are 'parasites' seeking to take advantage of New World producers' commercial success.⁵ The New World countries thus argue that GIs are 'historical and geographical accidents'.⁶ For the Old World countries, however, GIs are not historical accidents but reflect history continued and reinvigorated ceaselessly by producers who have remained in their country of origin. The reputation of a product may be based on decades or even centuries of creativity through which traditional knowledge has been not only maintained but adapted and improved.⁷ It is not an accident of geography, but rather a characteristic of ecosystems, which can certainly change and call into question a GI that does not produce the same special qualities it did before, and of other places that might prove capable of creating it.

The second factor dividing the two worlds concerns the political regime and the economy most appropriate for the protection of GIs, especially regarding the role given to the State. The political regime built by immigrants, who have tasted freedom, seeks to be less bureaucratic than European countries. Benjamin Franklin's pamphlet of 1784 meant for potential emigrants states that America has few government posts to offer and especially no superfluous posts, contrary to the situation in

---

⁴ IP/C/W/386, 'Implication of Article 23 extension', in Communication from Argentina, Australia, Canada, Chili, El Salvador, United States, Guatemala, New Zealand, Paraguay, Philippines, Chinese and Tawain (8 November 2002): 7.
⁵ TN/C/W/25, 'Issues related to the extension of the protection of geographical indications provided by Article 23 to products other than wines and spirits', in Note Secrétariat (18 May 2005), paragraphe 38.
⁶ Ibid., 12.
⁷ Bulgarie, IP/C/M/38, § 125; Switzerland, 7 February 2005.

Europe.⁸ The system of appellation of origin monitored by the State in France and the EU is thus considered to be bureaucratic and disturbing by New World countries.⁹ According to Professor of Law J. Hughes, it is perceived as undermining the fundamental rights of winegrowers to choose the appellation they wish to identify their products.¹⁰

Such divide of the role of the State leads to two systems which were at loggerheads during the GATT negotiations: on the one hand, the system of certification marks or collective marks, such as in the United States, and on the other hand, the *sui generis* system of appellation of origin (completed later by GIs), as in France and Europe.¹¹ In the first case, the trademarks are examined by a trademark office to check if the logo/symbol/sign is available without going into the rules of use. Moreover, the applicant has to meet certain criteria (Constitution of an association, controlling capacity). The quality standards are decided by the market, which is to say that a product is either successful with consumers or not. This system is completed with the protection of the geographic origin through the tort of passing off, similar to steps taken in case of unfair competition against practices which intend to make consumers believe that the products are of another company.

In the second case, a GI is applied for by a group of producers and includes a list of specifications describing the method of production for achieving quality. It is examined by ad hoc committees such as the National Institute of Origin and Quality in France or the European Commission's Directorate-General for Agriculture.

The two different concepts were accentuated during the TRIPS Agreement negotiations. The name of the category created, GI, reflected the compromise between the two concepts. This terminology came up during the WIPO negotiations in the 1970s. It did not exist in the French law, which only knew appellation of origin and indication of source.

---

[8] Pamphlet 'To Those Who Would Remove to America' quoted in Justin Hughes, 'The Spirited Debate over Geographic Indications', *Law Review* (2003): 50.
[9] Ibid., 48.
[10] Ibid., 49.
[11] European Community or Communities (EC) will be used in the same manner as European Union (EU), even if it is the EC which has signed GATT and is a member of WTO.

Under Article 22.1 of the TRIPS Agreement, GIs are indications which identify a good as originating in the territory of a member, or a region or locality in that territory, where a given quality, reputation or other characteristic of the good is essentially attributable to its geographical origin. It is quite clear that GIs include appellations of origin,[12] but the existence of 'natural and/or human factors' is not specified in the text, contrary to the Lisbon Agreement definition of appellation of origin[13] and the EU proposal.[14] This definition does, however, clearly exclude rules of origin or indications of source which do not refer to a good's quality, reputation or characteristic, but only to its place of production.

The Brussels proposal which set forth the criteria of a 'reputation based on a given quality or other characteristics' did not mention the three alternative criteria of the final definition: 'specific quality, reputation or another characteristic'. The personalization of the reputation criterion signifies that this criterion is enough to receive a GI, excluding the necessity of product quality or characteristic. Even if it is difficult to imagine that reputation is not founded on a specific quality or characteristic of a product, the final draft of the TRIPS Agreement makes provisions for the official recognition of a GI for a product lacking a specific quality or characteristic, but well known because of 'other things'. This GI definition is at the base of the PGI definition, one of the two legal tools for the protection of origin in the EU, besides designation of origin.

How far the range of protection should be extended was the question that raged during the most heated debates between the Old World and New World countries. These debates continue today with the question of the 'extension of additional protection', which is not granted under

---

[12] Proposals from EC and USA included this precision.
[13] Art. 2 of the Lisbon Agreement, 'appellation of origin means the geographical name of a country, region, or locality, which serves to designate a product originating therein, the quality and characteristics of which are due exclusively or essentially to the geographical environment, including natural and human factors'.
[14] GI definition in the EC proposal of 7 July 1988, MTN.GNG/NG1/W/126, was: 'Geographical indications are, for the purpose of this agreement, those which designate a product as originating from a country, region or locality where a given quality, reputation or other characteristic of the product is attributable to its geographical origin, including natural and human factors'.

the text to other goods than wine and spirits, although certain countries would like to see it extended to cover all products.

The EU and Swiss proposals provided for a level of protection similar to that formulated in the Lisbon Agreement, which corresponds to the additional protection granted by the TRIPS Agreement to wine and spirits according to Article 23.[15] This level of protection ensured that GIs are protected against all types of use. It is thus not possible to use a GI for products not originating in the place indicated by the GI, even though the consumer is not misled as to the true origin of the product, or even if it is used with expressions such as kind, style, imitation and the like. The United States, however, did not wish for this kind of protection. They wanted to protect only the acts which could mislead the public, and that too only in relation to wines. On the other hand, the group of developing countries' proposal made provisions for protecting GIs only against use liable to mislead the public.[16]

In 1994, a final compromise was made and, depending on the type of products, different rights were granted. The level of Lisbon protection called 'additional protection' (or 'absolute protection') in the TRIPS Agreement, proposed by the EU and Switzerland, was granted only to wines and alcoholic beverages/spirits. The level of protection proposed by the United States and the developing countries was granted to all products. Thus, Article 22.2 of the TRIPS Agreement, which applies to all products, prevents the use of any means in the designation or presentation of a product, that indicates or suggests that the product originates in a geographical area other than the true place of origin in a manner which misleads the public as to its geographical origin, and any use which constitutes an act of unfair competition within the meaning of Article 10b is of the Paris Convention (1967).

---

[15] Art. 3 of the Lisbon Agreement provides that protection shall be ensured against any usurpation or imitation, even if the true origin of the product is indicated or if the appellation is used in translated form or accompanied by terms such as 'kind', 'type', 'imitation' or the like.

[16] Shri Ashwani Kumar, the then minister of state in the Ministry of Commerce and Industry, 'Lok Sabha Unstarred Question No 3824 to Be Answered on 16.05.2006 G I Certificate', ed. Government of India, Ministry of Commerce and Industry (2006), 1–57.

Article 23.1, which only applies to wine and spirits, stipulates that using a GI to identify wines not originating from the place indicated by the geographical origin in question, or to identify spirits not originating in the place indicated by the geographical origin in question, should be prevented. This is the case even when the real origin of the product is mentioned or when the GI is used in translation or accompanied by expressions such as kind, type, style, imitation or the like.

For example, according to Article 23.1, the indication 'Napa Valley of France' should be prohibited and the indication 'sparkling Champagne like wine produced in Chile' too, because Article 23 applies to all use of GI for goods not originating from the place indicated by the geographical origin even if there are additional details to inform consumers about its true origin. The indication 'Roquefort cheese made in Australia' or 'Indian style Basmati rice' for rice grown in Texas cannot be prevented though, because consumers, who are attentive to details, have access to information on the real origin of the product.[17]

To prevent such uses, the protection conferred by Article 22 requires that elements proving consumers have been misled be provided. This can be difficult to demonstrate in the case of certain exportable products whose GIs are not well known internationally. For example, it should be demonstrated that consumers of exported products know that Roquefort cheese is made in a small village in the south of France.

The same dual regime applies to the protection of GIs against trademarks filed after the recognition of the GI. In this way, Article 22.3, which applies to the full ensemble of possible products, contains the obligation for the refusal or invalidation, either at the level of the governmental office (if permitted by the legislation), or at the request of an interested party, of the registration of a trademark that contains a GI or is constituted by such an indication, for products that do not originate in the indicated territory if that usage of the mark for such products is of a nature that would induce the public to be mistaken in its true place of origin.

---

[17] For a detailed study, see Felix Addor and Alexandra Grazzioli, 'Geographical Indications beyond Wines and Spirits: A Roadmap for a Better Protection for Geographical Indications in WTO/TRIPS Agreement', *The Journal of World Intellectual Property* 5, no. 6 (2002): 878–895. See also examples cited in O'Connor, *The Law of Geographical Indications*, 57.

Wines and spirits are further protected by Article 23.2 which stipulates that the registration of a trademark for wines (or spirits) which contains or consists of a GI identifying wines or spirits shall be refused or invalidated, ex officio or if the legislation so permits or at the request of an interested party, with respect to such wines or spirits not having this origin.

The GI Chapter of the TRIPS Agreement is currently incomplete because of the difficulty in reaching a compromise. This is revealed through the numerous exceptions in the GI protections. These exceptions, defended by the New World countries, preserved their established rights gained through previous right of use. These exceptions are different depending on whether a product falls into the category of wines or spirits and whether the previous usage was based on a trademark or not. For wines and spirits, following Article 24.5, all previous usages can be continued in two situations: either the usage dates back to 10 years before the TRIPS Agreement came into effect, and in this case, whether the usage is honest or not does not have to be proved, or the usage is honest. For other products, according to Article 24.4, only the previous usage as a trademark can benefit from this exception and can thus be continued (with the same alternative criteria of a usage dating back to 10 years before the TRIPS Agreement came into effect, or an honest practice).

A last exception concerning GI protection is that the indications which have become generic, that is, which have become common names to designate products, cannot benefit from GI protection.[18] This decision can be only taken by the country where protection is sought, and once this decision has been made, it irrevocably blocks the access to GI protection. Ultimately, GATT negotiations did not lead to a conclusion concerning the creation of an international GI registry along the lines of the Lisbon Agreement model. This point has been left for future negotiations.

*The Abiding Rift*

The differing views of the Old and New Worlds continue to be perpetrated through the current negotiations on establishing a multilateral system

---

[18] For a complete study on generic denominations, see Renaud François, 'Les Dénominations Génériques' (Université Robert Schuman de Strasbourg, 2002) and Jacques Audier, 'Indications Géographiques: Le Virus "*Générique*"', *Propriétés Intellectuelles*, no. 8 (2003): 252–260.

of notification and registration of GIs for wines and the possibility of extending additional protection to all other products.[19]

Many new countries are presently involved in the negotiations on the extension of protection which have attracted many non-wine-producing countries, among which are several developing countries.[20] Here too the countries are divided along the same rift between the Old World and the New World. The Old World countries, in order to better define their common cause, identify themselves as 'GI friends', lending an emotional connotation to their attachment to GI. India can be definitely qualified as an Old World country because of its history dating back to thousands of years. In fact, India asserts this identity, preferring though the terms of Old and New 'cultures'.[21]

The EU[22] and Switzerland, the traditional defenders of the extension of GI protection, have also been joined in their coalition by the new countries of the EU, several central European countries and countries of the former Soviet Union (Turkey, Cyprus, Kyrgyzstan), some African countries (Guinea, Kenya, Madagascar, Nigeria), Morocco, several Asian countries (India, Pakistan, Sri Lanka, Thailand) and Jamaica (for its 'Blue Mountain' coffee), who also advocate for the extension of additional protection to all products.

India has always been in favour of the extension of protection, with the Basmati rice and Darjeeling tea[23] cases being the motivating factors. Since 2006, China, an important emerging country, has also become a

---

[19] The negotiations on the multilateral system of notifications provided in Art. 23.4 and the negotiations on the extension of the additional protection to all products have been mandated by the Doha Declaration, §12 and 18.

[20] See Sergio Escudero, 'International Protection of Geographical Indications and Developing Countries', South Centre, *TRADE Working Papers*, South Centre (2001), 1–57.

[21] See Sunjay Sudhir cited in *Intellectual Property Watch*, 11 July 2000, Kaitlin Mara.

[22] The EU joined the negotiations on the extension quite late, following the communication TN/C/W/21/Rev.1 proposed by Switzerland and the developing countries in December 2004, after having alleged that the only issue under negotiation was the multilateral system of notification for wines and spirits (IP/C/W/107).

[23] Kasturi Das, 'International Protection of India's Geographical Indications with Special Reference to "Darjeeling" Tea', *The Journal of World Intellectual Property* 9, no. 5 (2006): 459–495.

'GI friend'. The opponents of the extension of additional protection are New World countries such as Argentina, Australia, Brazil, Canada, New Zealand, Chile, Colombia, El Salvador, Ecuador, Guatemala, Panama, Paraguay, Philippines, Dominican Republic, Chinese Taipei and the United States, who have hardly any reputed products or none at all besides wine.

Even though quite a large number of new countries have joined the discussions and despite the progress made, the line of demarcation between the New World and the Old World has not budged.

This configuration can change since the New World producers have gradually begun to want their local products to benefit from the same protection as those of the Old World such as the wine producers of the Napa Valley in the United States. We can cite the example of the rather successful action of the 'Napa Valley' wine producers who fought for linking this appellation to the wine produced in the region. Indeed, the California Supreme Court ratified the California law which reserved the 'Napa Valley' appellation for wine containing at least 75 per cent grapes coming from the Napa region. The Supreme Court thus proclaimed that the law did not go against the freedom of expression or trade between the states of the United States. This regulation came under attack by a company which bottled wine in the Napa Valley region but used grapes which came from elsewhere.[24]

Moreover, the balance can tilt in favour of the protection of GIs in future negotiations through an ingenious blend of North–South interests combined with Old–New World interests. Indeed, many WTO members who are against the extension of additional GI protection and also against setting up a GI register among the Southern countries with high biodiversity are for introducing a new obligation in the field of patent rights: the disclosure of the origin of genetic resources[25] in patent applications, in

---

[24] See the case *Bronco vs Jolly, 04-945*, Supreme Court of California, Jean Christophe Boze, 'L'affaire Bronco En Californie: Pas De "Napa" Sur L'étiquette Sans Raison De Napa Dans Le Vin', *Revue de Droit Rural*, no. 333 (2005): 22–25.

[25] See the report of the General Director of WTO, TN/C/W/50, 9 June 2008, and TN/C/W/52, 19 July 2008 commented in William New, 'Modalities Drafted for WTO Geographical Indications, Biodiversity Amendment', *Intellectual Property Watch*, 15 July 2008. See also Sumit Chakravarty, Gopal Shukla, Suman Malla and C.P. Suresh, 'Farmers' Rights in Conserving Plant Biodiversity with Special Reference to North-East India', *Journal of Intellectual Property Rights* 13, no. May (2008): x.

order to negotiate a fair share of the benefit resulting from the use of genetic resources, as per the Rio Convention on Biodiversity. The disclosure of the origin is often perceived by countries with a great range of biodiversity but a small number of patents as a means to take advantage of their assets, namely, their genetic resources. Thus the EU, northern Old World country, GI friend, with low biodiversity is ready to disclose the source of their genetic resources in patents in exchange of better protection of GIs. It remains to be seen if the Southern countries with great biodiversity but located in the New World are ready to make concessions on GIs in return for a sharing of benefit resulting from the use of genetic resources. India, a Southern country of the Old World, a GI friend, with a great biodiversity range has everything to gain from such a proposition. Yet recent consultations organized by the WTO in 2011[26] concluded that countries supporting the extension of the additional protection to all products[27] are not signatories of the proposal to the disclosure of genetic resources in patent applications and vice versa.[28] Thus, India has preferred to follow Brazil position and to give priority on the issue of protection of biological diversity.

## India, a New Country of the 'Old World'

India is a country with a past stretching back to thousands of years, interspersed with long periods of colonization and the cradle of numerous handcrafted creations and agro-crops, which come under the GI Act. India in the 21st century is an emerging country, in the throes of change, striding forward economically as well as culturally, moving directly from the Middle Ages into the computer era. Due to a long history of colonization which bled the country dry, India turned towards an interventionist economy where the Indian State played a major role. The numerous GIs registered in the name of the State or its bodies are an inheritance of the

---

[26] See the report of the General Director of WTO, WT/GC/W/633 TN/C/W/61, 21 April 2011.
[27] See communication of Albania, China, Croatia, Géorgia, Guinéa, Jamaïca, Kenya, Liechtenstein, Madagascar, Suisse, Sri Lanka, Thaïland, Turquey and European Union, TN/C/W/60, 19 April 2011.
[28] See communication of Brazil, China, Colombian, Equator, India, Indonesia, Peru, Thailand, ACP group and African group TN/C/W/59, 19 April 2011.

mixed economy policies implemented since Independence, still present, in spite of the liberalization process which began in 1991. Development in India was not initiated from outside, but the result of a slow restructuring of the private sector industry, especially around the domestic market.[29] This explains why a lot of GIs are registered for products at destination of the Indian market.

This evolution, though far from uniform, has given India renewed confidence in its history and values. At the same time, however, globalization threatens numerous products which are flag bearers of its culture and heritage. Paradoxically India has implemented the GI Act, a product of globalization, to protect its identity reflecting its long history and its wide population diversity. Amartya Sen describes this delightful blend: The four colours of the skin of the inhabitants of the land—white, brown, black and yellow—mingle together enviably there. Languages issued from all the major linguistic families cohabit there.[30] The organization of an independent Indian Republic, equipped with a powerful State, was perceived as a means to cement this pluralistic society.[31]

Sixty years after Indian independence, the phase of nation building is almost over, but regional political parties defending their state's language and culture and seeking more political autonomy have become increasingly popular and powerful. The question of local identities in the heart of the national identity has raised its head and a kind of sub-nationalism has emerged from this movement. The GI issue in this context has assumed another dimension, on the ground with the backing of local culture, rooted in a specific region, GIs can lead to the fragmentation of the national identity since they are the advocates of regional identities. In fact, there is a sort of competition between different states concerning the number of GIs registered.

Contemporary India does not hesitate to point out the superiority of its history[32] as illustrated by the advertising campaign for a new media

---

[29] Ibid., 195.
[30] Amartya Sen, *The Argumentative Indian: Writings on Indian Culture, History, and Identity* (London: Penguin Books, 2005), p. 348.
[31] Ruet, 'Réformes Et Nouvelle Économie Politique En Inde', p. 191.
[32] See the comments on the art of Ajanta (close to Mumbai) described as having influenced numerous temples in Tibet and Sri Lanka according to Singh, *L'etat Et Les* Arts En Inde. 54.

agency, Daily News Analysis, based in Bangalore: 'We used to export cardamom, now we export CEOs'. It is ironic that ultimately GIs, which are often based on this type of rhetoric about faithfulness to Indian culture, will indeed be used to protect cardamoms!

## Protection against the Decline of Traditional Products

Since globalization, the competition the Indian products face from foreign products and more particularly Chinese products increased considerably. The handicraft sector in India employs the highest number of people after the agricultural sector.[33] The example of saris, for which numerous GIs have been registered, perfectly illustrates the twofold evolution of a change in dress habits and the mass infiltration of machines in the handicrafts sector.

The sari, the national dress of women in India, also represents one of its most dazzling weaving traditions. But life styles and dress habits have started changing. In many towns and also in semi-rural zones, young women and women working outside their homes prefer to wear *salwar-kameez*, or even Western clothes instead of saris. Even in areas where saris are still the main item of clothing, the local markets are flooded with machine-produced synthetic saris, following the end of the Multifiber Agreement in 2005, signalling the end of quota restrictions.[34] For connoisseurs, compared to hand-woven silk or cotton saris, these saris are of very bad quality, but for many women, the shining chemical colours, the new material and lower prices are much more advantageous. However, there is another market for very sophisticated, expensive saris, since saris continue to be worn on important occasions or festivals. For millions of weavers who depend on the basic, local market, however, the future is bleak.[35] Indeed, for handicraft products other than those for everyday use, new markets have been developing. To make these special

---

[33] M.N. Panini, 'Trends in Cultural Globalisation', *Economic and Political Weekly* 34 no. July 31 (1999): 3912.
[34] Multifibre Agreement, 1974–1994.
[35] Maureen Liebl and Tirthankar Roy, 'Handmade in India', in J. Michael Finger and Philip Schuler (eds), *Poor People's Knowledge: Promoting Intellectual Property in Developing Countries* (World Bank/Oxford University Press, 2004), p. 58.

products, craftsmen had to adapt to high standards set by consumers, but it allowed them to preserve their specialized technical knowledge and maintain their way of life.[36]

In the domain of agriculture, however, the WTO negotiations for removing obstacles against trade of agricultural products are at a standstill, with India's refusal to expose its farmers to the risk of globalization, since they are not sufficiently prepared to compete against the inflow of imported products, and not competitive enough in exports vis à vis other emerging countries.[37]

Indeed, agriculture is an essential constituent of the Indian economy. It represents about a quarter of GDP and employs two-thirds of the country's active population. Most of the cultivated lands are made up of small holdings because of postcolonial agrarian reform which set limits to farm size.

During the Green Revolution of the 1970s, improved high-yielding varieties were developed and cultivated with the use of pesticides, fertilizers and irrigation systems. A spectacular number of new plant and seed varieties were developed, and alongside regular evolved varieties and hybrid varieties, transgenic varieties were introduced, provoking a lot of controversies. The main concern was not so much that traditional seed varieties, and along with them the genetic diversity of cultivated species could disappear, but that the cultivation of these new varieties (improved, hybrid, transgenic) went hand in hand with the use of new, expensive inputs and the necessity of purchasing seeds each year from seed companies. Protests against these innovations came from anti-globalization groups, including Intercontinental Caravan, which raised their voices against GMOs.[38]

M.D. Najundaswamy, president of Karnataka's farmer's association, who launched the idea of the Caravan, declared that his mission was 'to fight against the perversion of Indian culture'. He advocated a return to traditional Indian civilization, native, generally signifying authenticity and living in autarky.[39] Even though farmers' problems are also there and mostly due to structural inequalities of caste, class, region and sex in the

---

[36] Ibid., 70.
[37] 'L'Inde Agricole: Entre Forces Et Faiblesses' (Momagri, Mouvement pour une organisation mondiale de l'agriculture, 2008), p. 5.
[38] Ibid., 179.
[39] Ibid., 199.

agrarian sector, globalization is perceived as a real threat.[40] The registration of GIs is thus used as a strategy for promoting local varieties.

## The Fight against the Counterfeiting of Indian Products in the 1990s

In the 1990s, India became aware that its products were being usurped. These usurpations had to do not only with denominations of geographic origins, but also genetic resources and traditional knowledge which had been the objects of patent filings, acts which were characterized by many in India as acts of 'biopiracy'. The most emblematic cases are those of Basmati rice and Darjeeling tea.

### Basmati Rice

First, India protested against the American patent on improved rice varieties resulting from the cross-breeding of Basmati rice cultivated in India and semi-dwarf rice cultivated in Texas filed by Rice Tech, a Texas-based company. Rice Tech was granted a patent titled 'Basmati rice lines and grains' in the United States in 1997 for these new varieties,[41] marketed under the trademarks 'Texmati' and 'Kasmati'. The 1–14 patent claims concern the characteristics of rice cultivated in the North, South and Central America under different forms: plants, seeds and progeny.[42] The 15–17 claims concern rice seeds without any cultivation limits or mention of territory.[43] The 18–20 claims concern the method used by Rice Tech

---

[40] Ibid., 179–180.
[41] Patent granted on 2 September 1997, no. 5, 663, 484 by the United States Patent and Trademark Office.
[42] Claim no. 1 was: 'A rice plant, which when cultivated in North, Central or South America, or Caribbean Islands (a) has a mature height of about 80 cm to about 140 cm; (b) is substantially photoperiod insensitive; and (c) produces rice grains having (i) an average starch index of about 27 to about 35, (ii) an average 2-acetyl-1-pyrroline content of about 150 ppb to about 2000 ppb, (iii) an average length of about 6.2 mm to about 8.0 mm, an average width of about 1.6 mm to about 1.9 mm, and an average length to width ratio of about 3.5 to about 4.5, (iv) an average of about 41% to about 67% whole grains and (v) an average lengthwise increase of about 75% to about 150% when cooked'.
[43] Claim no. 15 was: 'A rice grain, which has (i) a starch index of about 27 to about 35, (ii) a 2-acetyl-1-pyrroline content of about 150 ppb to about 2000 ppb, (iii) a length of about 6.2 mm to about 8.0 mm, a width of about 1.6 mm

to develop its rice varieties. The patent describes the detailed history of Basmati rice, traditionally cultivated in India and Pakistan, and the difficulty of cultivating these varieties elsewhere. Besides the question about how the genetic resources used for breeding were obtained,[44] and the problem of the inventive step of the patent, another question which arose, was that using the name Basmati for varieties which could be cultivated outside North India and Pakistan could lead to confusing them with the varieties cultivated in Pakistan and India, even more so because the new varieties of rice look very much like the traditional varieties. The possibility of this confusion could have seriously affected the export of Basmati rice from India and Pakistan to the United States. The American patent also rendered the hypothesis that the superior quality of Indian and Pakistani Basmati rice is due to a combination of cultivated varieties, climate and pedological conditions and local cultural practices of North India and Pakistan[45] doubtful.

The Indian government, via its government office Agricultural and Processed Food Products Export Development Authority (APEDA) filed an appeal in the United States Patent and Trademark Office (USPTO) in April 2000. The USPTO examiner asked Rice Tech to justify its patent in the light of the APEDA[46] documents. Rice Tech responded by reducing its wide claims covering the plant, method and seeds. The examiner asked Rice Tech to change the patent title to 'Bas 867, RT 1117 and RT 1121'.

At the same time, the Navdanya NGO and two American NGOs based in Washington, DC, the Center for Food Safety and the International Center for Technology Assessment, filed a complaint with the US Federal Trade Commission, based on the *New River* case, whereby when a geographical origin acquires a certain significance in the market, the indication of such origin cannot be used to designate a product not from this origin, even when the other product's quality is identical. However, in its reply of 9 May 2001, the Federal Trade Commission stated that its '...efforts are focused on

---

to about 1.9 mm, and a length to width ratio of about 3.5 to about 4.5, (iv) a whole grain index of about 41 to about 63, (v) a lengthwise increase of about 75% to about 150% when cooked and (v) a chalk index of less than about 20'.

[44] See http://www.grain.org/publications/mar983-en.cfm.
[45] See §2.3 of the patent.
[46] Latha R. Nair and Rajendra Kumar, *Geographical Indications: A Search for Identity* (Delhi: LexisNexis Butterworths, 2005), p. 182.

those areas which may affect the greatest number of consumers, may pose a risk to consumers' health or safety, or may cause significant economic harm to consumers. Based on our review of your petition and related U.S. regulations, we do not have reason to believe that significant consumer injury is likely to arise from current rice marketing'. The reply continues by qualifying Basmati as a generic name: 'Under U.S. Department of Agriculture regulations, Basmati and jasmine rice are included as examples of aromatic rough rice and are not limited to rice grown in any particular country. Thus, there is no specific statutory or regulatory limitation on references to U.S. grown rice as "Basmati" or "Jasmine"'.[47]

Rice Tech had applied for registration of the Texmati trademark in the United Kingdom for agricultural food products which also included rice. In 1999 and 2000, the Indian government opposed this trademark registration on the fact that it was deceptive, based on the similarity between the word *Basmati* and the mark, which was to designate rice cultivated in the United States rather than in India or Pakistan. Rice Tech, in its defence, argued that the word *Basmati* was not a GI for rice cultivated on the Indian subcontinent, but designated aromatic rice which could be cultivated anywhere in the world. The Indian government gathered a great volume of evidence, including declarations of culinary experts and ordinary consumers of rice in the United Kingdom in order to prove that in the United Kingdom, Basmati rice meant long-grained aromatic rice from the Indian subcontinent. Rice Tech then withdrew its trademark application.

Regarding Kasmati trademark used to designate rice cultivated in the United States, a fact which could not fail to trick consumers, as beside the trademark itself there was a graphic reproduction of the Taj Mahal accompanied by the phrase 'Indian style Basmati Rice'. The Indian government sought to annul the trademark as lacking in distinctive character and for appropriating Indian symbols. Here too, Rice Tech withdrew its registration for the Kasmati trademark.[48]

Considering Rice Tech's strategy, it is quite clear that the rice cultivated in the United States was marketed in such a manner as to make the consumers believe that this rice was from India, with the

---

[47] See http://www.ftc.gov/os/2001/05/riceletter.pdf quoted in Muriel Lightbourne, 'Of Rice and Men, an Attempt to Assess the Basmati Affair', *The Journal of World Intellectual Property* 6, no. 6 (2003): 878.
[48] Ibid., 875–893.

representation of the Taj Mahal and the expression 'Indian Style Basmati rice'. However, this type of expression is not forbidden by the standard protection provided to GIs by Article 22 of the TRIPS Agreement.

The repercussions of the Basmati case extended to many countries. In Greece, for example, following the APEDA lawsuit, the Greek Trademark Authority Administrative committee[49] cancelled the registration of Texmati and Kasmati trademarks. In this case, misuse of the name *Basmati* resulted from Indian exporters who registered several trademarks where the word *Basmati* was used for rice from different origins.[50] In 2013, 351 case in India and 211 cases in foreign jurisdiction were filed by APEDA to protect the denomination *Basmati*.[51] For example, the Tribunal de grande instance (TGI) of Paris, in an order dated 26 May 2011, rules against the Siam Grains Company Limited of Thailand who had filed a semi-figurative trademark, including the word *Basmali*.[52] Basmali Trademark was revoked on the ground of absence of serious use in France after the expiration of the five-year period from the publication of its registration. But the cost of an amount of ₹ 7.62 crores (₹ 7,620,000 = 108,000 euros) that has been paid to M/S K&S Partners as aggregate professional fee from 1995–1996 to 2011.[53] Yet this amount is little when looking at the total export of Basmati.[54]

To conclude, the Basmati case in the 1990s was a rare case where all the protagonists usually in opposing camps, such as India and Pakistan, researchers advocating for evolved varieties, farmers defending traditional seed stock, anti-globalization NGOs, exporters and the government, all joined ranks to defend Basmati as if they were defending the Indian flag against a

---

[49] *Business Line*, Chennai, 7 June 1997 cited in Prabuddha Ganguli, *Gearing up for Patents, the Indian Scenario* (Hyderabad: Universities Press (India), 1998), p. 9.

[50] For an overview of all the trademarks, see Harsh V. Chandola, 'Basmati Rice: Geographical Indication or Mis-Indication', *The Journal of World Intellectual Property* 9, no. 2 (2006): 166–188.

[51] http://spicyipindia.blogspot.com/2013/03/auditing-worldwide-litigation-involving.html, consulted 15 April 2013.

[52] Trademark no. 93496544, filed on 14 December 1993, renewed on 11 September 2003.

[53] http://spicyipindia.blogspot.com/2012/07/apeda-discloses-legal-expenses-on.html, consulted on 15 April 2013.

[54] India has exported 3,757,271.44 MT of Basmati rice to the world for the worth of ₹ 29,299.96 crores during the year 2013–14; see http://apeda.gov.in/aped-awebsite/SubHead_Products/Basmati_Rice.htm.

foreign invasion and neocolonialism. According to Vidal, the unexpected reaction to the Basmati case showed that 'the defence of tradition is utterly confused with the invention of new identities, of new natural species and of new definitions of places than agriculture'.[55] Yet Basmati is to be protected as a GI in India, in Pakistan and worldwide (see Chapters 4 and 8).

*Darjeeling Tea*

The tea industry's development is promoted by the government, and the geographic region where this tea is cultivated is controlled exclusively by the Tea Board of India, a statutory body founded in accordance with the 1953 Tea Act.

The protection of Darjeeling dates back to the creation of a logo in 1983. The logo was that of a woman holding a tea leaf in her hand and the word Darjeeling. The logo was registered by the Tea Board as a mark in 1986 in various countries such as the United Kingdom, the United States, Canada, Japan and certain European countries, based on certification mark no. 532 240 registered in India on 9 October 1986.

The tea industry has estimated the sales of Darjeeling tea in the world to be 40,000 tons, while its Indian production does not go beyond 10,000 tons.[56] The rest of this tea largely comes from Sri Lanka, Kenya and Nepal. The elevated level of fraud was used to justify the adoption of a more aggressive strategy on the part of the Tea Board, which, on 10 December 1998, applied for a certification mark (no. 831 599), for the name Darjeeling itself within India, in the United Kingdom (application 30 March 1998) and in the United States. At the same moment, the Tea Board hired the Compumark agency to watch any registration of trademarks comprising the word Darjeeling, all over the world. Consequently, the Tea Board filed 15 lawsuits in courts or in trademark offices against third parties misappropriating the mark in the countries of Bahrain, Belarus, Bangladesh, Canada, Estonia, France, Germany, Israel, Japan, Kuwait, Latvia, Libya, Lithuania, Norway, the Sultanate of Oman, Russia, Sri Lanka, Taiwan, Great Britain and the United States. Even

---

[55] Denis Vidal, 'In Search of Basmatisthan: Agro-Nationalism and Globalisation', in *Globalizing India, Perspectives from Below*, ed. Jackie Assayag and Chris Fuller (London: Anthem Press, 2005), p. 46.

[56] See Das, 'International Protection of India's Geographical Indications with Special Reference to "Darjeeling" Tea', 480.

in India, the Tea Board dispatched warning letters and filed lawsuits against the usurpation of the trademarks. The Tea Board's fight to assert its rights was an expensive affair and cost about US$200,000,[57] including only the lawsuits filed in foreign courts from 1998 to 2002.

Along with the protection of the Darjeeling logo and word via certification marks, the Tea Board also introduced a traceability system in 2000. Everyone in the industry, including producers, negotiators and exporters, had to sign a licence agreement with the Tea Board in order to use the Darjeeling logo and get a certificate of origin.[58]

It is during this period, confronted with the threat of dilution of the Darjeeling indication that the Tea Board decided that only tea made up of 100 per cent Darjeeling tea, excluding any blends, can be referred to as Darjeeling. Indeed blending is a tricky issue regarding the origin of teas, one of the grounds of objections from the European tea industry to the registration of the PGI Darjeeling in Europe, which ended with the acceptance of the European to the rules of 100 per cent of tea from Darjeeling.[59]

It was also the ground of the conflict with the Republic of Tea, an American company that had applied for registering a trademark 'Darjeeling Nouveau' in the United States in 2006,[60] after the certification trademark of the Tea Board comprising the logo and the word Darjeeling had been registered at the USPTO on 22 January 1991,[61] first used in 1987. The rules of the use of Tea Board's trademark certified that the tea blend contained at least 60 per cent tea from the Darjeeling region. The rules of use of the other trademark of the Tea Board, which comprised only the word Darjeeling and was registered in January 2002, stipulated

---

[57] The funds come from government sources and the Darjeeling Planters' Association which has set up a dedicated 'Promotion and Protection Fund'.
[58] Rules for the use of trademarks published by the Tea Board of India.
[59] See Commission Implementing Regulation (EU) No. 1050/2011 of 20 October 2011 entering a name in the register of protected designations of origin and protected geographical indications (Darjeeling [PGI]) and press article http://www.thehindu.com/business/Industry/tea-board-etc-join-hands-to-protect-darjeeling-tea/article4006308.ece.
[60] 12 January 2006 and 23 August 2006, United States Patent and Trademark Office, Trademark Trial and Appeal Board, Tea Board of India v. The Republic of Tea, Inc. Opposition No. 91118587.
[61] No. 1632726.

that Darjeeling shall be used henceforth for tea of 100 per cent Darjeeling origin and that the term 'blend' applied only for tea blends which individually had the right to the Darjeeling certification trademark.

The Republic of Tea, in order to prove that its trademark 'Darjeeling Nouveau' was valid, argued that 'Darjeeling' served to identify a type of tea or geographical origins other than Darjeeling as the only origin for tea, or even unauthentic tea, and not tea which was 100 per cent from Darjeeling. The USPTO's Court of Appeal did not condemn the first rules of the use of the Tea Board trademark comprising the logo, which provided for up to 40 per cent of tea of other origin than Darjeeling in the tea blend, as the indication Darjeeling could be rightfully used to identify only one component of the tea, on condition that the criterion of maximum 40 per cent tea from other sources is controlled rigorously by the Tea Board. On the other hand, the Court of Appeal decided that the current regulations of 100 per cent Darjeeling origin had to be respected.

To avoid the risk of Darjeeling becoming generic, the Tea Board on the one hand launched numerous actions of opposition and watch against similar or identical trademarks.

However, in the absence of GI registration in the countries of usurpation, only action against unfair competition is possible. Proof that is the name is well known should be provided as it is illustrated by a recent case about Darjeeling in France, where Jean-Luc Dusong was the holder of a semi-figurative trademark composed of the name 'Darjeeling' and the design of a teapot, filed on 14 November 2002 (no. 3.193.817), and registered for designated editing and communication-related products. The Tea Board sought for the cancellation of the trademark, rejected by the Court of First Instance, which considered that due to the difference between the two products, there would not be a risk of confusing the public. The Court of Appeal invalidated this decision, considering that it mattered little if the products in question were different, but rather, whether through the adoption of this denomination linked to the teapot design, Jean-Luc Dusong had sought to profit from the renown attached to this GI—which identifies, in the public imagination, the tea originating in this region—synonymous with excellence and refinement, and the savoir faire of the Tea Board in promoting this product, which was being exploited free of cost. The Court of Appeal declared that such type of use for designating products other than tea is harmful for this prestigious GI as it weakens and trivializes its distinctive character. The Court of Appeal first qualified Darjeeling as a GI according to Article 22 of the TRIPS Agreement, convinced by the product description and its link to its geographical origin, the quality of the tea depending on climate conditions and traditional methods of preparation. The court then considered the GI as equivalent to an appellation of origin for implementing the L.711-4 Article of the French intellectual property law which mentions appellations of origin as prior rights which cannot be prejudiced by a trademark even if there is no risk of misleading of the public. Then Darjeeling was qualified as notorious because of the documents provided by the Tea Board establishing that it was well known in France. Its reputation was proven with the help of some documents, particularly specialized books and articles of the daily press. This requirement of notoriety for the GI was necessary for the filing of a lawsuit against such parasitic behaviour weakening and confiscating its reputation, since Darjeeling was not at that time a PGI registered in Europe (PGI registered in 2011).[62] Since then, the indication Darjeeling in Europe benefits from the higher level of protection which prohibits any use of the GI, including for non-similar goods where such use exploits the reputation of the protected name. In conclusion, the powerful protection of the word Darjeeling as a PGI, combined with the protection of the logo as a trademark, recently enforced against two trademarks in France, registered by Teasources Europe, which were cancelled as they imitated the logo of the Tea Board (round form and an Asian lady holding tea leaves), even if the name Darjeeling was not copied,[63] qualifies Darjeeling as a super protected GI.

---

[62] Commission Implementing Regulation (EU) No 1050/2011 of 20 October 2011 entering a name in the register of protected designations of origin and protected geographical indications (Darjeeling [PGI]).

[63] Appeal Court of Paris, 30 March 2011 and TGI of Paris, 29 March 2013.

# 2
# An Analysis of the Diversity of Legal Concepts Underlying GIs

## The *Terroir* of the Appellation of Origin: A Strong Link

The protection of geographical origin in France emerged from a chaotic history, and it took a long time for a definition of the appellation of origin to be drafted.

### The Concise Definition of the First Appellation of Origin

*The Definition of the Area of Origin*
Contemporary history of the appellation of origin dates back to the *phylloxera* crisis which destroyed the vineyards in France in the late 19th century. Widespread fraud was recorded, including manipulations to obtain something that only resembled wine, and replanting plants beyond set traditional limit.[1]

---

[1] For a detailed study of the history of appellation of origin, see *Une Réussite Française: L'appellation D'origine Contrôlée*, 1–33.

The Law of 1 August 1905 fights against fraud in the sale of goods and adulteration of foodstuff and agricultural products, when the mention of the origin is the major reason for the sale.[2] The 1905 Law also provided the possibility to determine through administrative regulations the measures to be adopted regarding 'inscriptions and trademarks that indicate [...] either the origin of the goods, or regional appellations and specific places for growth'. The delimitation of areas that could exclusively claim appellations for their products was based on 'local, loyal and constant use'.[3] The uses mentioned were about the utilization of the appellation by producers, and served to determine the location where the term was used and then to define this place as the only area to benefit from the appellation. The nature of the link between the product and its origin was thus based only on the identification of the production area.

The production area will be defined under the 1905 Law for six appellations, including Champagne (decree of 17 December 1908), Cognac, Armagnac (decree of 25 May 1909), Banyuls (decree of 18 September 1909), Clairette de Die (decree of 21 April 1910).

Producers were not satisfied with the demarcation of regions, and violent riots followed, particularly with regard to the delimitation of the Champagne appellation. A new law was enacted in 6 May 1919 on the protection of appellations of origin[4] which stipulated that 'any person who saw that the application of an appellation would lead to a direct or indirect loss to him ...could initiate legal action to prohibit the use of the appellation'. Producers are free to use an appellation of origin for their products, and in the event a conflict arose regarding such use, the civil courts are competent to decide what is covered by the appellation of origin. This, consequently, could lead to the prohibition of any use against the product's origin, or its local, loyal and constant use. According to the Law of 1919, the uses covered only the use of the appellation by the producers to designate their products. They made no reference to the method of production, and geographical area is not described in a technical manner, what hardly matched up to the

---

[2] Law of 1 August 1905 on the fight against frauds in the sale of goods and adulteration of foodstuff and agricultural products, JO 5 August 1905, no. 210.

[3] Law of 5 August 1908 amending Art. 11 of the Law of 1905, JO 11 August 1908, pp. 5637–5638, called 'loi Cazeneuve'.

[4] Law of 6 May 1919 on the protection of appellations of origin, JO 8 May 1919, p. 4726.

expectations of professionals who wanted the essential qualities of the product to be defined in the appellation of origin.[5]

*The Premises of the Definition of Product Characteristics*

Although the Law of 1919 did not impose this requirement, some decisions of the court refer to product characteristics as for example, the order of the Court of Le Puy in 1935 ruling that[6] the appellation of origin Lentilles du Puy applied exclusively to lentils with the following characteristics:

1. Small grain with a diameter of 4–5 mm, thickness of 2–2.5 mm, dark blue-green marbling on a pale green background, rapid cooking, with a thin skin, a non-starchy kernel and a delicate taste.
2. Grown from seed harvested in the region.
3. Harvested from a well-defined limited area of production.

Eventually, some laws specific to a given product will incorporate technical characteristics of the area and conditions of production, such as the Law of 26 July 1925 on Roquefort.[7] However, the definition of Roquefort threw up a number of difficulties: whether to recognize the pre-eminence of the milk's origin or the location of refining cellars, of the raw material or the transformation process? Should the definition authorize mixtures of sheep's milk, cow milk and/or goat milk? In the end, the law chose to demarcate the area of milk production, and prohibited mixing anything but sheep's milk. The law would only be completed in 1961 by the jurisprudence for the localization of refining, and be restricted to the Combalou caves 'wafted by drafts of cool, moist air from the limestone formations in the mountain'.[8]

---

[5] 1er Congrès De L'origine, Tenu En Pays D'auge À Deauville Du 25 Au 27 Juin 1948. Marcel Plaisant and Fernand–Jacq, Traité Des Noms Et Appellations D'origine (Paris: Librairie Arthur Rousseau, 1921), p. 43.

[6] Tribunal civ. 1ère instance Puy, 17 January 1935, www.inao.gouv.fr.

[7] Law on the appellation of origin Roquefort, 26 July 1925, JO 30 July 1925, p. 7190.

[8] Claire Delfosse, 'La France *Fromagère*', *Thèse pour le nouveau Doctorat, sous la direction de M. GILBANK*, Université de Paris I Panthéon-Sorbonne (1992). 177, TGI Millau, 12 July 1961.

## Roquefort Cave

The appellation of origin Volaille de Bresse (poultry) is defined by a specific law of 1 August 1957, which completes the provisions of the judgement passed by the court on 22 December 1936: the appellation can only be applied to the white poultry breed reared in the defined area of the Bresse region and which adheres to all conditions that ensure their traditional qualities. However, these conditions are not specified in the law which points to the difficulty in determining the production conditions a priori.

The necessity to integrate the conditions of production and quality criteria became pressing for wines in 1927, and it was decided that wine could be entitled to an appellation of origin if issued from a wine grape variety and a production area according to local, loyal and constant use.[9] Local usage refers to rules that have developed spontaneously in a restricted geographical area.[10] The uses are loyal if they are free of typical fraud or deception and do not have any ambiguity, confusion or duplicity which may lead to an abuse of the appellation.[11] As far as constancy goes, a usage is constant if it is continuous, repetitive and ancient.[12] The 1927 Law thus denotes the combination of natural and human factors for the appellations of origin of wines.

The importance attached to methods of production that determine the quality of the wine increased with the need of controlling such processes, which led to the birth of the *appellation d'origine controlée* (AOC) for wines and spirits under the decree of 30 July 1935.[13] The National Committee for Appellations of Origin for Wines or Eau de vie, which was founded by this decree, would be transformed into the National Institute of Appellations of Origin (INAO) in 1947, and subsequently become the National Institute of Origin and Quality in 2006. Following consultations with producers' syndicates, the committee established

---

[9] Law of 22 July 1927 completing the Law of 6 May 1919, JO 27 July 1927, p. 7762, called 'Loi Capus', Art. 3.
[10] See Séverine Visse-Causse, *L'appellation D'origine: Valorisation Du Terroir* (Paris: ADEF-Association des Etudes Foncières, 2005), pp. 111–112.
[11] Nîmes, 22 May 1934, Gaz.Pal.19342.648, quoted in ibid., 113.
[12] Ibid., 114.
[13] Decree-Law of 30 July 1935 on the defence of the wine market and on the economic regime of alcohol, JO 31 July 1935, p. 8314.

production conditions for the products: production area, grape varieties, yield per hectare, minimum alcohol content of wine and methods for culture and winemaking or distillation.

The conditions for the protection of appellations of origin for cheeses were ruled by the Law of 28 November 1955.[14] To qualify for an appellation of origin, a cheese had to be made from milk that was produced, procured and processed in a traditional geographical area, under local, loyal and constant uses. The National Committee for Appellations of Origin of Cheeses delimited the geographical area of production and determined the conditions of manufacture and refining.

For products other than wines and cheese, there was no national-level committee to dictate production standards. Those production standards would be decided by courts on a case-by-case basis, which left a wide degree of latitude within the interpretation of product dossiers on the part of tribunals, both in relation to the areas of production as well as the methods.

## The Inclusion of Human Factors

### A Combination of Natural and Human Factors

The solution was found after decades of trial and error: it was imperative to add production conditions to simple geographical delimitation. These criteria would be expressed by notions of natural and human factors, the combination of which would guarantee the desired product.

Thus in 1966, French law benefited from a clear and lucid definition of the appellation of origin as: 'geographical name of a country, region, or locality, which serves to designate a product originating therein, the quality and characteristics of which are due exclusively or essentially to the geographical environment, including natural and human factors'.[15]

The inclusion of human factors, which was announced by the Law of 1927 on grape varieties, had been confirmed by various laws specific to certain products but was finally passed only in 1966, after France signed

---

[14] Law of 28 November 1955 on appellations of origin for cheeses, JO 30 November 1955, p. 11580.

[15] Art. 1 of the Law of 6 July 1966 amending and completing the Law of 6 May 1919, JO 7 July 1966, p. 5781, which is now art. L.115-1 C. Cons.

the Lisbon Agreement, which authored this clear definition. It had taken more than half a century of trial and error for the definition to arrive at this legal maturity. While human factors consist of the savoir faire and practices of producers, natural factors include environmental features like soil and climate. Although the place is physically predisposed, production can only take place due to human activities.[16] The localization of productions in a place comes from a past history and collective effort.[17]

For example, Comté is defined as a 'cheese originating in the Jura geographical environment, defined mainly by geological, climatic, topographical, botanical and agronomic criteria because of the character that such an origin gives to the product that is manufactured according to traditional practices and *savoir-faire*'.[18]

French and European courts introduced the concept of homogeneity to determine boundaries of production areas, which, in the case of vineyards, can be defined by recording similarities in natural characteristics of production areas and chemical and organoleptic characteristics of wines.[19]

The appellation of origin of cheese Valençay corresponds to the area formed by several communes where soil and climatic conditions have the same characteristics, where breeding goats is historically important and where a significant portion of the production is carried out by farmers.[20] The appellation Morbier is defined 'in terms of precise, objective criteria related mainly to the altitude of grassland used for production, to the flora and location the loyal and constant uses, while taking care to maintain the agreement of the municipalities' boundaries'.[21]

---

[16] Bérard and Marchenay, *Les Produits De Terroir, Entre Cultures Et Règlements*, 71.
[17] Ibid., 41.
[18] CE, 29 March 2000, no. 205253, société Fromagerie le Centurion, société des établissements Schoeffer et société Fromagerie Fromapac, www.legifrance.gouv.fr, 'Comté'.
[19] Anne F. Debrez, 'Les Tendances Jurisprudentielles "Des Délimitations" Des Appellations D'origine Contrôlées Viti-Vinicoles', *Recueil Dalloz* (2005), 281.
[20] CE, 21 June 2000, no. 212348 219211, Société Eurial Poitouraine, www.legifrance.gouv.fr, voir Simone Kieffer, 'Un Nouveau Statut Pour L'inao Qui Devient "L'institut National De L'origine Et De La Qualité"' *Revue de Droit Rural* 349 (2007).
[21] CE, 5 November 2003, no. 230438, Syndicat de défense et de promotion des fabricants et affineurs du Morbier, www.legifrance.gouv.fr.

Lyrical and romantic vocabulary is used for this relationship between man and nature, such as the one for Roquefort: the particular character of Roquefort is the culmination of an intimate relationship between man and nature. It relies, on the one hand, on the characteristics of milk from traditional breeds of sheep fed according to uses, and on the other, on the originality of the natural caves of Roquefort-sur-Soulzon, entirely dug in fallen rocks at the foot of Combalou's limestone cliffs, where a miracle of nature takes place that gives Roquefort its unique flavour.[22]

The procedure for legal recognition of appellations of origin by the courts set up in 1919 is maintained by the Law of 1966, and judges still can determine the qualities or characteristics of the product based on local, loyal and constant use.[23]

In 1968, the court recognized the appellations Olive de Nyons and Huile d'Olive de Nyons as designating olives from the Tanch variety of fruits, provided that the trees of this variety that give fruits are located within the defined geographical area, the olive trees are grown using methods described in the survey report and their fruits are processed using traditional methods that are also described.[24]

Finally, the Law of 1966 introduced an administrative procedure to grant national recognition to appellations of origin to facilitate their international registration under the Lisbon Agreement. An order in the Council of State can thus define the geographical area of production and determine the qualities or characteristics of a product that has an appellation of origin on the basis of local, loyal and constant uses.[25]

### An Identical Procedure for All Products

The appellation of origin, nevertheless, finds itself torn between the AOC for wines, whose production conditions are controlled, and the non-controlled appellation of origin for other products, between the wines and cheeses, each defined by a dedicated National Committee of experts

---

[22] Ibid.
[23] This article is still in force in the Code de la Consommation, C. cons. art. L.115-8, but it only applies to products that are not under the mandatory procedure of AOC.
[24] TGI Valence, 24 April 1968.
[25] C. Cons. Art. L.115-2 à L.115-4. As an example can be quoted the appellation of origin 'Monoï de Tahiti', 1 April 1992, JO 2 April 1992.

and other products defined by the courts. Given the accomplishment of the AOC, it was decided by the Law of 2 July 1990[26] to extend it to all raw and processed agricultural and forestry and food products. The nature of the link to the origin remains the same, as the AOC is primarily an appellation of origin whose production conditions are subject to scrutiny. The AOC specification describes the particular product characteristic, defines conditions of production, processing and possibly packaging, specifies, if required, the area and zones where different operations are carried out and the features that justify the link with the geographical environment or geographical origin.

The appellation of origin has evolved from a concept that describes a product's link to a simple geographical area to the concept of a link defined by a combination of natural and human factors which determine the quality of the product, in the sense of the overall quality or the quality of some of its features, which are such that it would be impossible to obtain an identical product in another place.[27]

## From the French AOC to the European PDO

Since 1990, French law has been enhanced by rules adopted at the initiative of France at the European level within the framework of the Common Agricultural Policy: the (CE) regulation No. 2081/92 of 14 July 1992[28] on the protection of GIs and designations of origin for agricultural products and foodstuffs, replaced by Regulation (EEC) No 510/2006 of 20 March 2006,[29] and recently replaced by Regulation (EU) No 1151/2012 of 21 November 2012 on quality schemes for agricultural products and foodstuffs. These regulations only apply to agricultural products and

---

[26] Law of 2 July1990 on the controlled appellations of origin of agricultural products and foodstuff, raw and processed, JO 6 July 1990, www.legifrance.gouv.fr.
[27] Denis Rochard, *La Protection Internationale Des Indications Géographiques* (Paris: Presses Universitaires de France, 2002). Ibid., 106.
[28] Council Regulation (EEC) No. 2081/92 of 14 July 1992 on the protection of geographical indications and designations of origin for agricultural products and foodstuffs, OJEU L 208, p. 1.
[29] Council Regulation (CE) No. 510/2006 of 20 March 2006 on the protection of geographical indications and designations of origin for agricultural products and foodstuffs, OJEU L 93, p. 12.

foodstuffs, with the exception of wines and spirits controlled by a set of specific texts, which, however, integrated the successful concepts of protected designation of origin (PDO) and protected geographical indication (PGI) into the European regulations on wines; this, though, is not covered in this book.[30]

EU Regulation No. 1151/2012 defines the designation of origin as being 'the name of a region, a defined place or, in exceptional cases, a country that designates an agricultural product or a foodstuff:

1. originating in that region, in this defined place or country and
2. the production steps of which all take place in the defined geographical area'.[31]

The previous definition in Regulation 510/2006, which was identical to Regulation No. 2081/92, was more detailed, with 'whose production, processing and preparation take place in the defined geographical area' but quite confusing,[32] yet based on the same principle that all operations take place in the same geographical area, including the sourcing of raw material, criterion which was not required by the Lisbon Agreement not the French AOC.

The EUCJ recognized, since the 1970s, that geographical designations constituted industrial property rights and were not a hurdle to the common market. However, the EUCJ held that geographical denominations

---

[30] Council Regulation (CE) No. 479/2008 of 29 April 2008 on the common organisation of the wine market, OJEU 2008, L 148.

[31] Art. 5.1(c).

For wines, the appellation of origin is defined in art. 34.1 of Regulation (CE) no. 479/2008 as 'the name of a region, a specific place or, in exceptional cases, a country used to describe a product referred to in Article 33(1) that complies with the following requirements:

(i) its quality and characteristics are essentially or exclusively due to a particular geographical environment with its inherent natural and human factors;
(ii) the grapes from which it is produced come exclusively from this geographical area;
(iii) its production takes place in this geographical area; and
(iv) it is obtained from vine varieties belonging to *Vitis vinifera*'.

[32] See Art. 3 of the Regulation 510/2006.

could only be protected if they were justified by 'the protection of rights that constitute the specific object of this industrial property',[33] the existence of a sufficiently strong link between the product and its origin. In the *Sekt* case where the European Commission opposed Germany in 1975, which had reserved the names Sekt and Weinbrand for indigenously produced wines, the court ruled that the names only satisfied 'their specific purpose if the products which they describe possess qualities and characteristics which are due to their specific geographical area'.

In the *Delhaize* case, bottling was not shown to be an operation that gave the wine special or indispensable characteristics to uphold specific characteristics.[34] However, later, this same operation was recognized as constituting a necessary and proportionate means to preserve the great reputation of Rioja wine by the court in the Belgium/Spain case known as *Rioja*.[35] In this case, the court considered that there were no alternative and less restrictive means that could help achieve the desired objective. This argument of 'necessary and proportionate means', in order to better safeguard the quality and authenticity as well as the existence or not of alternative measures, will be used to determine that the packaging operations, the slicing of ham in the *Prosiciutto di Parma* case or the grating of cheese in the *Grana Padano* case shall be localized in the defined area.[36]

The link between the quality or characteristics and the origin must be direct.[37] In the case of the PDO Feta, the European Court of Justice (ECJ) ruled that the natural factors are 'the duration of sunshine, temperature

---

[33] CJEU, 31 October 1974, aff. C-15/74, Centrafarm BV et Adriaan de Peijper c./ Sterling Drug Inc : Rec. CJEU 1974, p. 1147.
[34] CJEU, 9 June 1992, aff C-47/90, préc., point 19.
[35] CJEU, 16 May 2000, aff C-388/95, Belgium supported by Denmark, Finland, the Netherlands, United Kingdom c./ Spain supported by Italy, Portugal, Commission: Rec. CJEU 2000, I, p. 3123, point 58.
[36] 'Proscuitto di Parma', CJEU, 20 May 2003, aff. C-108/01, Consorzio del Prosciutto di Parma and Salumificio S. Rita c./ Asda Stores Ltd et Hygrade Foods Ltd: Rec. CJEU 2003, I, p. 5121; 'Grana Padano', CJEU, 20 May 2003, aff. C-469/00, Ravil SARL c./ Bellon Import SARL et Biraghi SpA: Rec. CJEU 2003, I, p. 5053. Following this jurisprudence, Regulation no. 2081/92 has been modified in 2003 by regulation no. 692/2003 of 8 April 2003 to include the packaging as one of the steps of the specification.
[37] 'Pistre', CJEU, 7 May 1997, aff. C-321/94 and 324/94, Haus Cramer, CJEU, 7 November 2000, aff. C-312/98.

differences, and the practice of transhumance, extensive grazing and the flora'. More specifically, the court held that 'the homogeneity of natural factors that distinguish it from adjoining areas, development of indigenous breeds of sheep and goats that are small, sober and resilient, sparse vegetation that is diverse, justify the existence of natural factors that confer specific qualities to cheese'. With regard to human factors, the court notes 'the interplay between the natural factors and the specific human factors, especially the traditional production method, imperatively requires straining without pressure'. In conclusion, the AOC, just as PDO, protects a strong link between the product and its geographical origin.

## The Concept of *Terroir* in Question

Products that benefit from an AOC/PDO are often known as *'terroir* products' as if it was obvious, whereas the truth is that the concept incorporates complex realities that have evolved over time. *Terroir* is not so much a legal term as it is literary word or a technical concept.[38] As such, the term does not exist in other European countries. The Italians refer to 'produtti tipici', while the Spanish speak of 'productos de la tierra'.[39]

Yet, this word is intimately related to the appellation of origin. Its significance is derived from the world of wines and has evolved over time, arising from, or rather preceding, legal definitions of the appellation of origin. The word *terroir* dates back to 1229, and is derived from old forms such as *Tioro*, *tieroir*, which trace their root to the Latin 'territorium'.[40] It denotes space, land or territory. Since the late 18th century, *terroir* has come to mean 'land seen from the point of view of its agricultural potential, specifically viticulture', which expresses the idea of a link between land and product. All analyses related to wine quality

---

[38] Jacques Audier, 'Réflexions Juridiques Sur La Notion De Terroir', *Bulletin de l'O.I.V.*, no. 747–748 (1993): 428.

[39] Laurence Bérard and Philippe Marchenay, *Produits De Terroir: Comprendre Et Agir* (Bourg-en-Bresse: CNRS, 2007): 18.

[40] A. Rey, 1998. Dictionnaire historique de la Langue française, Paris, Robert, cité dans François Casabianca et al., 'Terroir Et Typicité: Propositions De Définitions Pour Deux Notions Essentielles À L'appréhension Des Indications Et Du Développement Durable', *Terroirs viticoles* 2, no. Actes du VIème Congrès international des terroirs viticoles (2006), x.

published in the 19th century refer to wines having a *terroir* flavour as a wine for peasants and unfit for trade in cities. The concept of land use was introduced with the emergence of soil science in the 19th century. *Terroir* is then considered as immanent, and it pre-dates man who only highlights its potential. J. Capus, the French lawmaker behind the AOC (PDO), states that 'a *terroir* is the combination of soil and climatic factors that gives rise to the production area. An appellation of origin is thus the suitability of grapes varieties to a *terroir*'.[41]

For J. Audier, using the word *terroir* thus opens possibilities for substitution, acting as a synonym of the expression 'natural factors' that includes all physical characteristics of the area of growth.[42]

However, this connotation changed as a result of the growing importance of the human factors, the know-how of producers of the definition of appellation of origin in 1966, which recognizes that natural factors are not sufficient to confer the quality on the product. It could have been decided that the term *terroir* retained its original meaning and, the appellation of origin, on the other hand, was a combination between *terroir* and human factors. However, since the word *terroir* was often used singly, not to include the savoir faire of such practices in the definition of *terroir* risked marginalizing them, even as current regulatory developments were underlining their growing importance.

The American anthropologist E. Bahram highlighted the cultural aspect of *terroir* products and refers to the social composition of *terroirs* by revaluating them from a cultural point of view and the fact that soils are not fixed.[43]

L. Bérard also puts emphasis on the cultural dimension of *terroir* products. Such products have a history; they have been around for some time, are based on shared savoir faire and thereby distinguished from local products. 'Naturally they come from a particular place, but they are basically recorded in the local culture and society'.[44]

---

[41] Joseph Capus, *La Genèse Des Appellations D'origine Contrôlées* (Paris: INAO, 1947), x.

[42] Audier, 'Réflexions Juridiques Sur La Notion De Terroir', 431.

[43] E. Barham, 'Translating Terroir: The Global Challenge of French AOC Labeling', *Journal of Rural Studies* 19, no. 1 (2003): 132.

[44] Isabelle Téchoueyres and Virginie Amilien, 'Produits Locaux Entre Nature Et Culture: De La Ferme Voisine Au Terroir. Entretien Avec Laurence Bérard', *Anthropology of Food*, no. 4 (2005): 1–7.

However, the consideration of human factors, and consequently the cultural dimension, only adds to the firm basis of natural factors, which remain inherent to all talks of *terroir*. INAO's definition of *terroir* from 1992 will include these complex interactions that involve expertise in natural factors (soil scientists) and human factors (anthropologists) to carry out delimitation.

Finally, an authoritative definition of *terroir* was developed in France in 2006:

> *Terroir* is a delimited geographical area where a human community over the course of history generates and accumulates a collective body of production knowledge based on a system of interactions between biophysical and human factors. The sequence of socio-technical steps involved reveals originality, confers typicity and earns a reputation on a good originating in the geographical area in question.[45]

UNESCO has also developed a definition of *terroir* which is "geographical areas that are alive and innovative, rely on specific physical, biological and human environments, as well as on knowledge, skills and aptitude of people.[46]

In conclusion, the technical definition of *terroir* that combines natural and human factors matches the legal definition of appellation of origin. All products that benefit from an appellation of origin or PDO are *terroir* products. The concept of the product's typicity or distinctiveness matches with the concept of *terroir*.

## Geographical Origin of the PGI: A Weaker Link

Along with the creation of the PDO, it became necessary not to penalize products having a weaker link with their origin but still indicative of a specificity of the product, as do exist in Northern European countries.

---

[45] Casabianca et al., 'Terroir Et Typicité: Propositions De Définitions Pour Deux Notions Essentielles À L'appréhension Des Indications Et Du Développement Durable', 544–551.

[46] UNESCO, 10 November 2005, art. 4, quoted in Norbert Olszak, 'La Politique Communautaire Des Signes De Qualité Et D'origine', in *Congreso international sobre el desarrollo sostenible* (Burgos: 2008), 1–9.

Consequently, a second level of geographical reference was created, the PGI.⁴⁷

In order to encourage the policy on quality established by the EU within the common agricultural policy without discriminating between member states, it was decided that the same level of high protection be granted to PDO and PGI, which confers a very privileged place for PGI which is questionable.

## The Importance of Human Factors

Compared to the PDO, the strength of the link with the origin is both less stringent and less exclusive. This diminution is mainly due to natural factors moving to the background, which leads to products which are instead related to their origin through human factors, the savour faire.

The distinction between the PDO and PGI can be sourced in the EU and French jurisprudence. In the *Exportur* case, for example, the court rejects the position 'depriving of all protection geographical names used for products which cannot be shown to derive a particular flavour from the land ... and may nevertheless enjoy a high reputation amongst consumers and constitute for producers established in the places to which they refer an essential means of attracting custom. They are therefore entitled to protection, similar to the appellations of origin'.⁴⁸

Based upon a less robust level of protection than appellation of origin, but still justifying protection under law, PGI is defined as the name of a region, a specific place or, in exceptional cases, a country, used to describe an agricultural product or a foodstuff:

1. originating in that region, specific place or country, and
2. which possesses a specific quality, reputation or other characteristics attributable to that geographical origin, and
3. at least one of the production steps of which take place in the defined geographical area.⁴⁹

---

⁴⁷ Considering No. 9 of Regulation No. 510/2006.
⁴⁸ CJEU, Exportur C.3-/91, point 28.
⁴⁹ Art. 5.2 (c) of Regulation No. 1151/2012.
  Regarding wines, according to Art. 34.1 of Regulation (CE) No. 479/2008, GI means an indication referring to a region, a specific place or, in exceptional cases, a country, used to describe a product referred to in Article 33(1) which complies with the following requirements:

As for PDO definition, new regulation 1151/2012 has cancelled the details regarding the nature of productions steps to be localized which used to be production, preparation or elaboration, considered as confusing concepts. Yet, this provision of the possibility of only one step occurring in the defined geographical area distinguishes PGI definition from GI definition in the TRIPS Agreement which otherwise is similar, as a consequence of the concomitance of discussions on the 1992 EU Regulation and the TRIPS Agreement of 1994.

The link to the origin is less pronounced for PGI than it is for PDO; a product need only shows one specific quality or other characteristics and not the quality or the characteristic as in the case of PDO. The concept of reputation that follows has a similar uncertainty regarding its significance as for the definition of the TRIPS Agreement. The concept itself of reputation is not new, being in the 'Draft Treaty for the protection of Geographical Indications', prepared by WIPO in 1975,[50] and was already in the English version of the Lisbon Agreement, which translates the French word 'notoriété', whereas the French word 'reputation' is used for TRIPS and EU regulation. But in TRIPS and EU regulations, reputation is provided as an autonomous criteria of validity of GIs, whereas in the Lisbon Agreement, it was used to determine the country of origin 'whose name, constitutes the appellation of origin which has given the product its reputation',[51] the criteria of validity of an appellation of origin being the quality or characteristics.

(i) It possesses a specific quality, reputation or other characteristics attributable to that geographical origin.
(ii) At least 85% of the grapes used for its production come exclusively from this geographical area.
(iii) Its production takes place in this geographical area.
(iv) It is obtained from vine varieties belonging to *Vitis vinifera or* a cross between the *Vitis vinifera* species and other species of the genus *Vitis*.
Regarding spirits, according to Art. 15.1 of Regulation (CE) No. 110/2008, geographical indication shall be an indication which identifies a spirit drink as originating in the territory of a country, or a region or locality in that territory, where a given quality, reputation or other characteristic of that spirit drink is essentially attributable to its geographical origin.

[50] 'Project of Treaty on the protection of geographical indications' prepared by the WIPO experts committee on the international protection of appellations of origin and other indications of sources, TAO/II/2, see www.wipo.int.
[51] Art. 2.2 of the Lisbon Agreement.

There are no details regarding the vector of the link. Since natural or human factors are not mentioned, it could be assumed that only one of these two factors would be sufficient. Not considering the uncommon case where certain products are obtained without human intervention, that is, they are created solely by natural factors, a PGI would apply to products whose production has historically been located in a given area, independent of any specific condition related to the natural environment.

The manufacturing processes developed by producers from a particular production area may have contributed to the reputation of a product commonly known by the name of the area of manufacture. The location of the product can be explained by history. D. Rochard defends the merits of such protection as a support for producers who have given a specific significance to the geographical name against usurpations that take illegitimate advantage of its reputation.[52] The reputation of the PGI is fundamentally linked to the sole business activity of the region.[53]

This diminishing of interest of natural factors is defended by L. Bérard and P. Marchenay who believe that, with regard to PGI, the relationship with the place is associated to historical roots and shared practices. These latter are unequivocal criteria as compared to other more uncertain ones related to specific quality, reputation or other characteristics. According to them, natural factors must not officially be considered in the PGI, especially in France, as such products are mostly processed. The idea of a 'basin of skills' (*bassin de compétences*) can be introduced when they are developed over a large area.[54]

The definition of the PGI thus refers to a link between the product and its origin, implemented mainly through the help of local, ancient and shared cultural knowledge and savoir faire.

The given quality, a different characteristic or the reputation shall result from the geographical origin. The PGI Porc du Sud Ouest's exceptional characteristics, namely, a higher quantity of polyunsaturated fatty

---

[52] Rochard, *La Protection Internationale Des Indications Géographiques*, 108.
[53] Cortés Martin, 'La proteccion de las indicaciones geographicas en el comercio international y comunitario', Ministerio de Agricultura, Pesca y Alimentacion, Madrid, 2003, quoted in Luis Gonzales Vaqué, 'Indications Géographiques Et Appellations D'origine: Interprétation Et Mise En Oeuvre Du Nouveau Règlement no. 510/2006', *Revue du Droit de l'Union Européenne*, no. 4 (2006): 803.
[54] Bérard and Marchenay, *Produits De Terroir: Comprendre Et Agir*, 18.

acids than in other pigs, a high vitamin E content, a meat that is not dry but juicy when cooked and a strong taste as a result of its dent corn diet, were not enough to convince the European Commission to grant a PGI as they 'were a result of feeding of the animals and not the geographical origin or the farming system'.[55]

This case also illustrates the only requirement of human factors to justify the link to the origin. In fact, the European Commission decided there was no link to the origin because 'the farming system was not specific', which can be interpreted, *a contrario*, as if there was a farming system that was specific to the place, the PGI could have been granted. The farming system, a human factor, was later more specified and the PGI registered.[56]

However, according to certain experts of the Directorate General for Agriculture of the European Commission,[57] it is not so much the existence of natural factors that distinguish the PDO from the PGI, but the strength of the link with the origin. The quality of the product must be exclusively or essentially due to the geographical origin for the PDO, which is not the case for the PGI. In fact, the PGIs registered in France reveals that there is no systematic relevance between the product type and type of legal instrument. Miel de Provence is a PGI while Miel de Corse and Miel de sapin des Vosges are PDOs. Geographical area and history of the production and ancient notoriety are the grounds for the PGI Salt of Guérande delimitation of the geographical area, as confirmed by the French Conseil d'Etat (administrative Supreme Court) in an order against opponents to its registration, not included in the area.[58] But in this case, see the strong interaction between human and natural factors, PDO would seem more relevant.

---

[55] Commission Européenne, direction générale de l'agriculture et du développement rural, Direction H. Développement durable et qualité de l'agriculture et du développement rural, H.2. Politique de qualité des produits agricoles, 15 mai 2009.

[56] RÈGLEMENT D'EXÉCUTION (UE) No 421/2013 DE LA COMMISSION du 7 mai 2013 enregistrant une dénomination dans le registre des appellations d'origine protégées et des indications géographiques protégées [Porc du Sud-Ouest (IGP)].

[57] Interview with Cristina Rueda, European Commission, DG-AGRI, Unit F.4 Agricultural product quality policy, September 2007.

[58] Conseil d'Etat, 6 juin 2012, no. 348 084.

The requirement for origin of raw materials clearly differentiates PDO from PGI. In the case of PDO, all operations must take place in the same area and all raw materials, with some exceptions, must originate from the defined area. For PGI, on the other hand, it is enough that only one step in the production process takes place in the area giving its name to the product. The source of raw materials can be limited to a certain area only if it is shown that it influences the quality of the product. Any other reference to the origin of raw materials, which could include the commendable goal of rural development in the area, but which in fact has no impact on the specificity of the product, cannot be justified as it would violate the principle of free market competition. Thus, the PGI is a means to protect the place of production, whatever the origin of raw materials is, if the specialized knowledge used in this area confers a given quality, characteristics or reputation to the product.

Thus, in France, PGI is widely used for processed products, especially for cooked meats[59] for which the required raw materials do not originate in the concerned area.[60] Nevertheless France, where the importance of natural factors continues to predominate, insists on the geographically linked origin of raw materials for processed products as well.

In conclusion, the PGI category, although recent, is a definite achievement for European producers (see Table 2.1).

**Table 2.1**
*Data on PDO/PGI registered in the EU[61]*

|  | PDO | PGI |
|---|---|---|
| EU countries | 583 | 613 |
| Non-EU countries | 5 | 11 |
| Total | 588 | 624 |

---

[59] It seems that this practice is also prevalent in other European countries see Adriano Profeta et al., 'The Protection of Origins for Agricultural Products and Foods in Europe: Status Quo, Problems and Policy Recommendations for the Green Book', *The Journal of World Intellectual Property* 12, no. 6 (2009): 632.

[60] Commission's Green Paper of 15 October 2008 on agricultural product quality: product standards, farming requirements and quality schemes (COM[2008]0641), p. 17.

[61] http://ec.europa.eu/agriculture/quality/database/index_fr.htm, consulted on April 2015.

However, the PGI tradition in France remains weak,[62] reflected in the organization of the INAO, where there are National Committees which are split into various bodies, including a committee for wines, eau-de-vie and other alcoholic beverages, a committee for appellations for dairy products and food and forestry, a committee for PGI, red labels and guaranteed traditional specialties and a committee for organic agriculture.[63]

However, in a comparative approach, with legal frameworks directly emerging from the TRIPS Agreement, as in the case of India, PGI sheds new light on the nature of the link to the origin, too often seen only in the light of the appellation of origin which, notwithstanding its undeniable interest, cannot be exclusive in the era of the TRIPS Agreement.

## Rejecting the Concept of *Terroir* for PGIs

For the majority of PGIs, the step that is localized in the geographical area is the processing, involving practices that barely include, if at all, natural factors. The definition of *terroir* implies that local natural factors are an essential component and that no *terroir* can exist for products without natural factors. The author therefore put forward the hypothesis of *terroir* as inappropriate for PGI as it does not involve natural factors in a significant manner. This hypothesis does not come from a desire to keep the concept of *terroir* pristine, but rather an attempt to attach it to juridical reality and real practice around appellation of origin. The consequence of this restriction is not to signify that geographical indications are mere indications of source, that is to say, basic information on the place of manufacture, but rather to put the concept of *terroir* into perspective, which applies only to one category of geographical reference recognized in the EU, the PDO, and therefore does not cover the diverse realities of GIs.

This rejection of the concept of *terroir* for the PGI is in no way harmful. Quite on the contrary, it helps understanding GI in different innovative aspects of the link to the origin, such as those made by the Indian use of GI on handicrafts.

---

[62] The number of French PGIs registered on the 7 May 2013 is 184 against 425 PDOs, including wines and spirits, see Inao, www.inao.gouv.fr.

[63] See www.inao.gouv.fr and Kieffer, 'Un Nouveau Statut Pour L'inao Qui Devient "L'institut National De L'origine Et De La Qualité"'.

## The 'Uniqueness' of Indian GIs

### The Motivations of the GI Act

*The Protection for GIs Prior to the GI Act*
India has adopted a *sui generis* legal framework for GI protection which is considered responsive and more effective than legal measures that pre-dated the GI Act, such as the tort of 'passing off' or the registration of certification trademarks.

The tort of passing off, which is part of common law and comparable to an unfair competition action, allows the plaintiff to proceed against the actions of the defendant who attempts to dissimulate for commercial purposes, that his products are actually those of the plaintiff. This action had been extended to producers' groups to defend their collective rights in the use of geographical origin. The Scotch Whisky Association[64] succeeded in defending the GI Scotch whisky by highlighting the deception of the public regarding the perception it had of the Scottish origin of Scotch whisky, which has been marketed in India for a long time. The level of proof required for action in passing off would not allow protecting lesser known appellations or those that are recently introduced in the Indian market, regardless of the reputation they enjoy in their countries of origin, and even though the standard for transboundary reputation of a trademark in India is quite low.[65]

Prior to the entry into force of the GI Act, geographical names could also be protected through the registration of certification marks under the Trade and Merchandise Act of 1958,[66] which was subsequently

---

[64] L.R. Nair and R. Kumar, *Geographical Indications: A Search for Identity* (Delhi: LexisNexis Butterworths, 2005). p. 80. Delhi High Court, AIR 1980 Delhi 125; Bombay High Court, AIR 1992 Bombay 294. For an analysis of the cases, see S.C. Srivastava, 'Geographical Indications and Legal Framework in India', *Economic and Political Weekly*, 20 September 2003, and Nair and Kumar, *Geographical Indications: A Search for Identity*, p. 80–86. See also Michael Blakeney, *Geographical Indications and Trips* (Quaker United Nations Office, 2001), 5–7.
[65] See for example http://www.unitedipr.com/publicationlisting.php?id=16.
[66] Section 2(c) of the Trademark Act.

replaced by the Trademark Act of 1999.[67] Certification marks are trademarks capable of distinguishing goods and services according to their origin, materials used, method of production, quality and features certified by the trademark owner.

> The main problem with the certification mark system was in its lying within the domain of private regulation. The creation and adherence to certain criteria are left to the determination of private entities. Consequently, there arose the possibility of reduced compliance with regulations. An additional disadvantage was in the fact that actions for infringement were the sole domain of the proprietor, with authorised users merely entitled to use the mark upon certification. Further the reality that names would be protected only when they acquired intrinsic goodwill—too much was left to the vagaries of market dynamics. Consequently, there arose the need for a system of protection independent of market forces and one that could be administered publicly by a centralized authority.[68]

*From Parliamentary Debates to the GI Act*

India has benefited from the inclusion of GIs in the TRIPS Agreement which gave GIs a complete and specific protection. The preamble to the GI Act states that it will protect consumers from deception, add to the economic prosperity of the producer of such goods and also promote goods bearing Indian GIs in the export market.[69]

The 'GI Bill' was not subject to modification prior to its passage on 30 December 1999, the same day as the Trademark Act was also passed. The

---

[67] Section 2(e) of the Trademark Act.
[68] Balganesh, S. 'Systems of Protection for Geographical Indications of Origin: A Review of the India Regulatory Framework', *The Journal of World Intellectual Property* 6(1) (2003): 191–205.
[69] 'An Act to provide for the registration and the better protection of Geographical Indications relating to Goods.... In providing a statutory mechanism for the registration of GIs for the first time in India, it was felt that the "exclusion of unauthorised persons from misusing geographical indications would serve to protect consumers from deception, add to the economic prosperity of the producer of such goods and also to promote goods bearing Indian GIs in the export market". Unless a GI is protected in the country of its origin, there is no obligation under TRIPS for other countries to extend reciprocal protection. India would, on the other hand, be required to extend protection to goods imported from other countries which provide for such protection'.

debates highlighted the shift from the goal of international protection for export products to the objective of protecting and preserving Indian products that were in decline in the domestic market.

The 'statement and objects of reasons' of the Act directly refers to dangers of infringement related to international trade in Indian products, with the memory of the trauma caused by the case of Basmati when the United States declared that the name was generic. India did not want to be in a situation where its only obligation would be to protect foreign GIs on its territory, as occurred through action in passing off, but would also like to protect its own GIs abroad.[70] This risk of being genericized justifies India's desire to establish a framework for sui generis protection of GIs, a framework that was not mandated by the TRIPS Agreement. The Indian economist Srivastava thinks that the GI Act is a step forward to the minimum requirements of the TRIPS Agreement,[71] and considers the India GI Act can serve as a model for other countries.

The first subject that emerges from parliamentary debates is the concern of a specific law to protect India from the piracy of Western countries such as the United States, Japan and the United Kingdom. The patent on turmeric (*curcuma*) is cited as an example of bio-piracy.[72]

The Indian Minister of Commerce commented upon the historical law while referring to well-known agricultural and textiles products such as pashmina shawls of Kashmir and Kancheepuram saris.[73] The debates in the Lok Sabha provided the forum to present the best-known Indian indications, including export products like Darjeeling tea, Malabar pepper and green cardamom from Alleppey. Several GIs on textiles and food products were also listed: Shambalpuri sari, Nimmapara Chenna (dairy product), Baha rasgulla (dessert),[74] Tirunelveli halwa (dessert), Muscat halwa, Kadambur boli (fried bread), Kozhikode halwa.[75] Other products mentioned are Ayurvedic medicinal products.[76] The Chandrika

---

[70] Shri P.H. Pandiyan (Tirunelveli).
[71] Srivastava, 'Geographical Indications and Legal Framework in India', 4032.
[72] Shri Bikram Keshari Deo (Kalahandi), Shri Trilocan Kanungo (Jagatsinghpur).
[73] Minister of Commerce and Industry (Shri Murasoli Maran).
[74] Ibid.
[75] Shri P.H. Pandiyan (Tirunelveli).
[76] Shri Trilocan Kanungo (Jagatsinghpur).

Soap, claimed by a member of the Lok Sabha as a potential GI,[77] was challenged by another member of the parliament,[78] whose contention is that the name, which means 'blessed moonlight', a common name in India, is registered as a trademark. There thus seems to be some confusion between the trademark and the GI, which can be explained by the novelty of the GI concept.

This law was passed during the government of Bharatiya Janata Party (BJP), an ultra right-wing Hindu party which has built its entire political identity on a political history platform that promotes the Hindutva concept.[79] A section of the BJP MPs (members of Parliament) were delighted that this law allows India to be a global player with its own products in the market.[80] It was seen by these MPs as an awakening of India: 'Right from Ghori, Lodi, Moghuls to British, when they were taking away everything, of ours, we were sleeping. It was a sound slumber with loud snoring. We did not wake up. This is an enactment of awakening though it is a belated awakening'.[81]

While India viewed GIs with indifference during the Uruguay Round of the GATT negotiations, the GI Act transformed them into a symbol of national cultural identity. At the time the law was passed, there was a strong movement for the protection of GIs which can be explained by a desire to inventory Indian heritage. The number of GIs registered in India has witnessed a massive upswing. The GI Registry had received 527 applications for registration of GI as on 15 June 2015, of which 248 were registered.[82] Yet before applications for 130 GIs by the EU Commission on 28 November 2011, most of GI applications were from India, with only six foreign GIs registered.[83]

Presentations by officials at seminars organized by the GI Registry showcased not only the objective of legal and economic protection but

---

[77] Shri Varkala Radhakrishnan (Chirayinkil).
[78] Shri Bikram Keshari Deo (Kalahandi).
[79] Jean-Luc Racine, 'L'inde Et L'ordre Du Monde', *Hérodote* 108 (2003): 91–112.
[80] Shri Bikram Keshari Deo (Kalahandi).
[81] Ibid.
[82] See http://ipindiaservices.gov.in/GirPublic/index.aspx, last consulted 15 June 2015.
[83] Champagne, Pisco, Napa Valley, Prosciutto di Parma, Scotch whisky and Cognac.

also preservation, especially with regard to handicrafts. GIs help promote 'brand value with traditional flavour' and preserve cultural heritage.[84]

Murasoli Maran, the then minister of Trade and Industry, declared that India's rich heritage of products originating from specific regions were nurtured by knowledge and tradition built up by communities over the years.... These indications were vectors of 'national, regional and local cultural identities' providing value addition to the products. In a globalizing world, GIs represented more than a simple category of intellectual property rights (IPRs).[85]

GIs also play a role in preserving traditional products which do not face any risk of infringement as their markets are losing vigour. This corresponds mainly to a desire to inventory Indian heritage and revitalize products that are experiencing a decline.

The GI Registry conducted an India-wide survey and published a report in the latter half of 2008 that identified more than two million potential GIs that could be registered. Its policy has fuelled the desire to inventory the total heritage of India. The Indian economist K. Das stresses the importance of identifying products that are 'GI-able' with help from specialists. She stressed that the products that need protection are not necessarily those that boost national identity or are well known to the public. Even if the reputation of the place of origin is legally sufficient to obtain a GI, it is important, from a practical perspective, to assess the domestic and export markets of GI products.[86]

Finally, GIs are considered a means to protect disadvantaged producers: the poor against the shining India. The beneficiaries are clearly identified as the most vulnerable elements of society, craftsmen and producers of highly labour-intensive small businesses.

---

[84] V. Natarajan, GI Registry, July 2008.
[85] *The Hindu*, Sunday, 26 August 2001; Also available at the Indian Patent Office website: http://www.patentoffice.nic.in/ipr/photo_gallery/inaug_chennai.htm.
[86] K. Das, 'Selected Issues and Debates around Geographical Indications with Particular Reference to India', *Journal of World Trade* 42, no. 3 (2008): 502; Kasturi Das, 'Prospects and Challenges of Geographical Indications in India', *The Journal of World Intellectual Property* 13, no. 2 (2010): 148–201.

## The Concept of Uniqueness

*The Designation of all Products through GI*

'The Geographical Indications of Goods (Registration and Protection) Act, 1999' was passed on 30 December 1999, and entered into force on 15 September 2003, together with its regulations governing applications, 'The Geographical Indications of Goods (Registration and Protection) Rules, 2002'. GI's definition corresponds to that of the TRIPS Agreement, with, in addition, a definition of products that are eligible:

> Geographical indication, in relation to goods, means an indication which identifies such goods as agricultural goods, natural goods or manufactured goods as originating, or manufactured in the territory of a country, or a region or locality in that territory, where a given quality, reputation or other characteristic of such goods is essentially attributable to its geographical origin and in case where such goods are manufactured goods one of the activities of either the production or of processing or preparation of the goods concerned takes place in such territory, region or locality, as the case may be.

The following paragraph completes the definition of GI goods as any agricultural, natural or manufactured goods or any goods of handicraft or of industry and includes foodstuff. This list is, in most part, based on the list in the WIPO Model Law, with the exception of the manufactured products category which is originally found in the Indian law. The GI Act used the opportunity given by the TRIPS Agreement to protect all types of goods.

The definition of GIs in India is sufficiently broad to include both the definition of appellation of origin as defined by the Lisbon Agreement, the European PDO (and the French AOC) as well as the European PGI, with the clear exclusion of indications of source. Even though the definition of the Indian GI is close to that of the European PGI, it is a consequence of India's unique choice to use the term GI. The terms used to draft the criteria to localize operations are similar to those of the European PGI. They are, however, valid only for manufactured products. However, when registration for the famous Darjeeling tea, the earliest registered Indian GI, was applied at the European Commission, the application was made for a PGI and not for a PDO, notwithstanding that it is an agricultural product cultivated and processed in the same geographic area.[87] This fact demonstrates the ignorance surrounding the concept of appellation of origin in India. Another explanation given by the European legal counsel of the Tea Board is that 'at the time of filing application it was not clear the extent to which packaging of the tea took place in Darjeeling. The tea was often shipped in bulk and then packed in either Calcutta or in the EU. For this reason it was safer to go for PGI rather than PDO'.[88] Yet PDO definition does not provide for mandatory packaging in the area of production. On the contrary, such restriction is allowed only if it can be shown that packaging in the area is a necessary requirement to maintain the specificity of the product.[89]

Although the definition of GI appears to be clear, the text of Section 11 of the GI Act is confusing. In this section, which deals with the information to be provided along with the application for registration of GIs, the 'geographical origin' of Section 2 is replaced by the 'geographical environment, with its inherent natural and human factors',[90] more stringent. Clarifying on this apparent inconsistency, the GI Registry states that the definition to consider is the definition given in Section 2. Therefore, the presence of both human and natural factors is not requested which means that the Indian GI covers all levels of link to the source.

Indications cannot constitute a GI if they are any of the following: deceptive or likely to cause confusion, contrary to any law in force, comprising or containing scandalous elements that may offend religious feelings or a group of Indian citizens, if they would be disentitled to protection in a court, or if they are literally from a given place of production but mislead the public that they originate from another place.[91]

Registration of generic GIs 'which are determined to be generic names or indications of goods and are, therefore not, or ceased to be protected in

---

[87] PGI application for 'Darjeeling' filed at the European Commission on 26 November 2006, registered 21 October 2011 IN/PGI/0005/0659.
[88] Personal communication, April 2013.
[89] See Art 7.1(e) of the EU regulation 1151/2012.
[90] Section 11(2) of the Act and Section 32 of the Rules.
[91] Section 9(a), (b), (c), (d), (e), (g).

their country of origin, or which have fallen into disuse in that country'[92] is also prohibited. The generic character is evaluated in the country of origin and not in the country where protection is sought. This provision mirrors Section 25.6 of the TRIPS Agreement in an identical manner. Moreover, there is no obligation to protect a GI for products whose relevant indication is identical to the common term used in everyday language, for instance, the common name for such products or services in any part of India. However, this term should have become a common name before 1 January 1995.

Finally, there is the case of a GI which, although literally true as to the territory, region or locality in which the goods originate, falsely represents that the goods originate in another territory, region or locality, as the case may be.[93] This prohibition is combined with the provision on homonymous GIs, that is to say, identical indications that originate from two different geographical areas. A homonymous GI may be registered if the registrar is satisfied, after considering the practical conditions under which the homonymous indication in question shall be differentiated from other homonymous indications and the need to ensure equitable treatment of the producers of the goods concerned, that the consumers of such goods shall not be confused or misled in consequence of such registration.[94] The prohibition on homonymous GIs goes beyond the provisions of the TRIPS Agreement which only allows the coexistence of homonymous GIs that designate wines.[95]

*The Concept of Uniqueness*

The concept of 'uniqueness', an innovation of the GI Act, allows for the creation of a link to an origin through a more open conception of the meaning of GI, particularly due to its ability to protect artisan products and handicrafts, types of protection which are currently rare in France. Every application for the registration of a GI shall comprise the following:[96]

---

[92] Section 9(f).
[93] Many cities in the world bear the name Paris.
[94] Section 10.
[95] Art. 23.3 of the TRIPS Agreement.
[96] Section 11(2) of the Act and Section 32 of the Rules.

1. A statement as to how the GI serves to designate the goods as originating from the concerned territory of the country or region or locality in the country, as the case may be, in respect of specific quality, reputation or other characteristics which are due exclusively or essentially to the geographical environment, with its inherent natural and human factors, and the production, processing or preparation of which takes place in such territory, region or locality as the case may be.
2. The class of goods to which the GI relates shall apply.
3. The geographical map of the territory in which the goods are produced or originate or are being manufactured.
4. The particulars regarding the appearance of the GI as to whether it is composed of the words or figurative elements or both.
5. A statement containing such particulars of the producers of the concerned goods proposed to be initially registered. The statement may contain such other particulars of the producers, including a collective reference to all the producers of the goods.
6. The statement contained in the application shall also include the following:

   (i) an affidavit as to how the applicant claim to represent the interest of the association of persons or producers or any organization or authority established by or under any law;
   (ii) the benchmark standards for the use of the GI or the industry standard as regards the production, exploitation, making or manufacture of the goods with the detailed description of the human creativity involved, if any or other characteristic from the definite territory;
   (iii) the particulars of the mechanism to ensure that the standards, quality, integrity and consistency or other special characteristic in respect of the goods;
   (iv) three certified copies of the map;
   (v) the particulars of special human skills involved or the uniqueness of the geographical environment or other inherent characteristics associated with the GI to which the application relates;
   (vi) the full name and address of the association of persons or organization or authority representing the interest of the producers of the concerned goods;
   (vii) particulars of the inspection structure, if any; and

(viii) where the GI is a homonymous indication to an already registered GI, the material factors differentiating the application.

The part of the application dealing with the product's description is called the 'statement of case'.

The 'uniqueness' first seems to be the uniqueness of the geographical environment. However, it is an autonomous concept that can be described as a criterion in its own right. The GI-1 form of a GI application includes thirteen sections that must be filled out by the applicant, six of which serve to determine the link to the geographical origin: 'Specification', 'Description of the goods', 'Geographical area of production and map', 'Proof of origin [Historical records]', 'Method of Production' and, finally, 'Uniqueness'.

In practice, the data provided under 'Specification' and 'Description of the goods' is similar, relatively brief and mentions the main characteristics of products, whereas the 'Method of production' section is consistent and provides numerous details that can even, for instance, specify the position of weavers on either sides of the loom, in the case of the GI Kancheepuram silk. The section 'Proof of origin [Historical Records]' is entirely devoted to the history of the product and/or the place, without any systematic link being created between the product's history and the place's history.

Finally, the concise 'Uniqueness' section is presented as extracts chosen from the data given in the application for GIs that clearly identify the original characteristics of the product, production method or geographical area. These are the original features that are highlighted. The selected elements are somewhat suggestive of patent specifications, particularly the claims which are the part that determines the scope of the right conferred by the patent.[97] In fact, the GI Act is influenced by the laws that organize other IPRs. Thus, many of the experts involved in the process of drafting GI applications are patent attorneys used to drafting patent applications, and make sure to describe the production processes in great technical detail, as if they were describing a technical invention.

Uniqueness in this context may relate to natural or human factors or any characteristic of the product. However, the concept is mostly used

---

[97] For example, the application for GI Pochampally Ikat describes the tie-dye process.

to describe the product, and we speak of the uniqueness of the product as we speak of the specificity, the *typicité*, in France. The 'uniqueness' of handicrafts may be due solely to manual skills, an example being the GIs that designate saris woven by hand. In relation to agricultural products, the uniqueness may arise from the use of traditional varieties requiring specific cultivation practices.

The link between the product and its geographical origin may be unclear. The product and its manufacturing method will be described accurately under 'Description of the goods' and 'Method of production' to demonstrate the uniqueness of the product but without necessarily explaining the causal link with the geographical origin. It appears that the concept of uniqueness does not, in itself, contain any reference to a geographical origin. The product is unique, but this is not necessarily due to the localization. The term *uniqueness* carries the sense of value, or rather superiority. Thus the website of the office of GI employs the term 'Indian Treasures' to designate products that benefit from a GI.[98] There are numerous Indian Treasures and they all merit protection, but the term does not directly link this precious characteristic to a geographical origin. It seems still far from the purely French term *terroir* product. An initial explanation is related to the nature of the product. Broadening GIs' scope to include non-agricultural products opens new product ranges linked to the origin, mainly via specialized knowledge and savoir faire. Another explanation rests on the premise that the founder concept of GI in India is the protection of Indian heritage products, or products that constitute Indian cultural identity. GIs are also used to cover loopholes in international law for the protection of traditional knowledge, which is always in need of an adequate protection as an IPR.

This explains the lack of importance given to the boundaries of production areas such as the map required under Section 11 that is often not included in the file. Yet, according to the GI Act, the map shall be certified, giving the name of the publisher and date.[99] In practice, production area boundaries refer to administrative areas (generally at least the

---

[98] http://ipindiaservices.gov.in/GirPublic/index.aspx, consulted on 13 August 2008.
[99] Rule 32.6(d).

size of a district, which is approximately the size of a French department) identified through a map, without having to give additional details about the towns concerned. While accuracy is given by longitude and latitude, such information may seem excessive. The difference with the history of French appellation of origin, which for a long time was only defined by limits of production areas in accordance with the uses of the appellation, the inclusion of human factors being delayed and eventful, is remarkable. The Indian experience is based on the predominance of savoir faire and practices whose location is established by history. Consequently, delimitation is secondary, or simply serves as administrative support. The delimitation of the geographical area can also be very loose, the result of a compromise between numerous co-applicant as in the case of Banarasi silk, which has a location specified in up to six districts. Yet, there is a fundamental difference between the French approach to the appellation of origin and the Indian approach to GI.

# Rights Conferred to GIs in France, Europe and India

French and European laws provide complete legal protection to the appellation of origin that is superior to that of trademarks and affirms its importance in France and Europe.

## Strong Protection of the Appellation of Origin in France

### Inalienability and Imprescriptibility

French law affords public policy protection to PDO, which prohibits private ownership in PDO and institutes the principle of inalienability.[100]

[100] See, for example, the case of 'Fourme de Bresse', Cass., 26 octobre 1993, Union des coopératives agricoles anciennement dénommée Fromageries Bresse Bleu c./ Comité interprofessionnel et interdépartemental de Fourme d'Ambert et de Montbrison, no. 91-20472, BID no. 11/1994, 94-016; RIPIA 1993.289, www.legifrance.gouv.fr, and the case 'Bain de Champagne', Cass. com., 4 févr. 2004, no. 02-10576, Sté Parfums Caron c/ Comité interprofessionnel du vin de Champagne (CIVC); Juris-Data no. 2004-022543. www.legifrance.gouv.fr.

Unlike other IPRs that are granted for a limited period, the appellation of origin, following the Act of 6 May 1919 can never be regarded as being generic in nature and thus come into the public domain.[101] Similarly, at the international level, the Lisbon Agreement also holds that it is impossible for an appellation of origin to become generic from the moment it is protected in the country of origin.[102] This protection against the erosion of the denomination highlights the importance given to appellations of origin in France. In comparison, trademarks do not enjoy such support, and their registration must be renewed.

*The Protection of Production Areas*

Areas delimitated for an appellation of origin benefit, in a novel manner, from protection. As regards urban planning projects, the competent administrative authority can be required to intervene if (a) a landscaping or town planning project under development, (b) investment project, (c) construction, soil or subsoil exploitation and (d) implementation of economic activities are likely to affect the area or production conditions, quality or image of the appellation.[103] Similarly, INAO is consulted when a facility subject to authorization provided by Article L.512-1 of the Environmental Code is proposed in communes that include production areas of an appellation of origin and surrounding communities.[104] Finally, permission to quarry in some vineyards is subject to consultations under the fifth paragraph of Article L.515-1 of the Environmental Code.[105]

*Penalty for Fraud and Violation*

The following provisions of French law apply equally to the French appellation of origin, the European PDO and PGI. Henceforth, information will be presented for both geographical levels.

<u>Provisions for corrections regarding AO, PDO and PGI</u>

The Act of 6 May 1919 introduced the possibility to initiate corrective actions against incorrect uses of the appellations of origin that the

---

[101] Art. 10 of the Law of 6 May 1919 and C. rur. art. L.643-1.
[102] Art. 6 of the Lisbon Agreement.
[103] C. rur. art. L.643-4.
[104] C. rur. art. L.643-5.
[105] C. rur. art. L.643-6.

legislation terms as usurpations,[106] later introduced in the Consumer Code. Thus, Article L.115-16 of the Consumer Code punishes with a two-year imprisonment and a fine of 37,500 euros for:

1. producing a controlled appellation of origin without satisfying the requirements of Article L.642-3 of the Rural Law;
2. producing a controlled appellation of origin that was not subject to approval following Article L.641-7 of the Rural Law;
3. using or attempting to use an appellation of origin in a fraudulent manner;
4. including or displaying by addition, excision or by any alteration an appellation of origin on products that are natural or manufactured, sold or intended to be sold while being aware it is a misrepresentation;
5. making use of a presentation that leads to believe, or could lead to believe, that a product enjoys an appellation of origin; and
6. convincing, or attempting to convince, that a product with an appellation of origin is guaranteed by the State or by a public body.

Similar penalties apply for usurpation related to PDO and PGI.[107]

The purpose of these corrective actions is to penalize the bad faith usage of appellations of origin and misrepresented PDOs or PGIs for products that are similar to those covered by the appellation of origin, PDO or PGI but which do not have the right to use these. The qualification of use in bad faith can easily be determined by experienced professionals.[108] Under these terms, penalties were issued for the following: the sale of Comté cheese without mandatory labels,[109] the distribution of nuts that did not comply with the appellation of origin Noix de Grenoble,[110]

---

[106] Cass. Crim., 7 Dec. 1999, no. 98-82252, www.legifrance.gouv.fr, 'affaire Comté'.
[107] Art. L.115-22 of the Code de la consommation.
[108] See Cass, crim., 10 November 1998, no. 98-81257, www.legifrance.fr, 'Mont-d'Or' et 'Vacherin du Haut-Doubs'. Regarding the sale of products bearing false appellation of origin, see Cass., crim., 1 April 1998, no. 97-81260, Société coopérative union agricole comtoise, www.legifrance.fr.
[109] Cass., crim., 17 December 1969, no. 69-90938, Syndicat de défense du Comté, www.legifrance.fr.
[110] Cass., crim., 17 January 1974, no. 73-90094, Soc. CEDIS, www.legifrance.fr, 'Noix de Grenoble'.

the use of the appellation of origin Roquefort for mixing the original Roquefort cheese with another,[111] the use of the PDO Reblochon even though the company was suspended following a ban by the regulatory commission,[112] the use of non-compliant milk for Comté cheese,[113] the words 'Gruyère fabriqué en Franche-Comté' used on a label for cheese that had no right to the appellation Gruyère de Comté[114] and the use of the name Fleur des Vosges for honey that was not entitled to the appellation Miel de Sapin des Vosges.

Legal actions

The Act of 29 October 2007 on the fight against infringement includes provisions for legal actions in case of disputes regarding GIs which are identical to those for other industrial property rights.[115] Thus, 'any infringement of a GI involves its perpetrator's liability'.[116] As with other IPRs, precautionary measures are provided and include a process similar to that of seizure of counterfeited goods.

Rural code provisions for appellation of origin, PDO and PGI

Article L.643-2 of the Rural Code prohibits the use of indications of origin and source which may mislead the consumer regarding product characteristics, or dilute or weaken the reputation of a name recognized as an appellation of origin or registered as a PGI or, more generally, to infringe by wrongly using a GI in a sale description, specifically in terms of the protection reserved for appellation of origin and PGI.

---

[111] Cass., com., 5 July 1994, no. 92-17534, Confédération générale des producteurs de lait de brebis et des industriels de Roquefort c./ société Fromarsac, www.legifrance.gouv.fr.
[112] Cass., crim., 23 March 1999, no. 98-82721, www.legifrance.gouv.fr, aff. Reblochon.
[113] Case Comté.
[114] Cass., com., 23 Oct. 2007, no. 06-12022, Lidl c./ Comité interprofessionnel du gruyère, www.legifrance.gouv.fr.
[115] Law no. 2007-1544 against counterfeiting, JO 30 Oct. 2007, C. prop. Int. Art. L.722-1 à L.722-7.
[116] C. prop. Int. Art. L.722-1.

## Specific Protection of the Appellation of Origin's Reputation

The jurisprudence created a specific rule, established by the law of 2 July 1990, to reinforce the scope of the rights conferred by the appellation of origin: 'the name that constitutes the appellation of origin, or any other mention that suggests it, shall not be used by any establishment and for any other product or service, if such use is likely to dilute or weaken the notoriety of the appellation' (Article L.643-1 of the Rural Code). In a case related to the appellation 'Champagne', the trademark 'Bain de Champagne' used for cosmetics by the company Caron was considered by the court as a misuse of the reputation of the appellation Champagne, because the appellation Champagne had acquired, over several centuries, both in France and abroad, a particular reputation and glamour, well before the filing of disputed trademarks, and that the appellation was recognized by the decree of 17 December 1908.... Caron was considered to have misappropriated the image of prestige and sophistication that was attached to that name and had usurped the power of attraction this name held for its own benefit.[117] This decision is all the more remarkable in that the infringing trademarks pre-dated the former appellation.

The conditions required to benefit from the protection extended to products that are not similar appear simple to fulfil because it is sufficient that the misappropriation or impairment of reputation are likely to occur, and they need not be proven. This provision has allowed the Tea Board to fight successfully against the semi-figurative trademark Darjeeling filed by Jean-Luc Dusong for communication and paper products (see Chapter 1).

## Protection against Trademarks

The registration of an appellation of origin as a trademark is one of the uses that are prohibited by the Rural Code. Moreover, general

---

[117] Case 'Bain de Champagne', Cass., com., 18 February 2004. See the analysis of Georges Bonet, 'Des Cigarettes Aux Parfum, L'irrésistible Ascension De L'appellation D'origine Champagne Vers La Protection Absolue', *Propriétés Intellectuelles*, no. 13 (2004): 853–862. J. Schmidt-Szalewski, note ss CA Paris, 4e ch., sect. A, 12 September 2001, Parfums Caron c/ Comité interprofessionel des vins de Champagne: Juris Data no. 2001-180066; D. 2002, p. 1894, note N. Olszak; PIBD 2002, no. 735, III, p. 57; *Propriété industrielles*, 2002, 38.

intellectual property law stipulates that a trademark that infringes prior rights, mainly the appellation of origin,[118] cannot be registered. Thus, a trademark that consists of a simple appellation of origin or a GI as such (that is to say without being integrated in a composite trademark) may be turned down or invalidated simply because it has used an appellation of origin or GI, without trying to identify if there is a risk of confusing consumers. A trademark may be refused for non-similar products in the case of appellations of origin.

Concerning complex trademarks comprising an appellation of origin or a PGI associated with an arbitrary term, their use is allowed or not depending on whether the products can benefit from the GI or not. Such a complex trademark can be refused for registration or be invalidated if it is to designate products from outside the delimited area of the GI as it would be deceptive.[119] On the other hand, a complex trademark comprising a GI to designate products that are entitled to the GI is valid if it is sufficiently distinct, that is, if the terms of addition are sufficiently arbitrary with respect to the identified product.[120]

## Strong Protection of the PDO and PGI in Europe

The protection given by the European regulation is high and equivalent to that of the Lisbon Agreement, and it goes beyond the additional

---

[118] Article L.711-4.
[119] Cass., com., 26 Oct. 1993, no. 9120472, Comité interprofessionnel de la Fourme d'Ambert et de Montbrison C./ Société laitière coopérative agricole Les Fromageries Bresse-bleu, www.legifrance.gouv.fr. See analysis of Eric Agostini, 'Nullité De La Marque Utilisant Une Appellation D' Origine Pour Des Produits Ne Relevant Pas De L'aire Géographique Précise De Cette Appellation', *Recueil Dalloz* (1995), 58.
[120] The trademarks 'Russian Champagne' and 'Soviet Champagne' registered for wines benefiting of the appellation of origin Champagne have been cancelled because they were considered as deceptive according to Art. L.711-3.c of the CPI; see CA Paris, 4e ch. sect. A, 25 April 2007, RG 2006/03001: PIBD 2007, no. 855, Caroline Le_Goffic, 'Retour Sur Le Cas Du "Champagne Soviétique" (Commentaire De L'arrêt De La Cour D'appel De Paris Du 25 Avril 2007)', *Propriété industrielle*, no. 4 (2008): 18–22. On the contrary, the trademark Aoste Excellence has been only partially rejected, i.e. the trademark cannot be used for products which do not comply with the appellation of origin, Cass., com., 31 January 2006, no. 04-13676, Société Aoste c./ INPI, www.legifrance.gouv.fr.

protection given to wines and spirits in the TRIPS Agreement. The EU provisions complement French provisions, with the EU Regulation being directly enforceable in all member states, including France. The protection given is similar for PDO or PGI.

*Imprescriptibility of PDO and PGI*

Echoing French legislation and the Lisbon Agreement, it is natural that EU law conferred this 'immunity' to registered names, whether they are PGI or PDO, that they cannot become generic.[121] However, EU Regulation provides that where the commission considers that the specification of a product is no longer guaranteed, it shall cancel the registration.

*Prohibited Uses*

Uses that are prohibited in order to protect the PDO and PGI take inspiration from the provisions of the Lisbon Agreement and French laws. Thus, Article 13 of the EU Regulation prohibits

1. any direct or indirect commercial use of a registered name in respect of products not covered by the registration in so far as those products are comparable to the products registered under that name or in so far as using the name exploits the reputation of the protected name, including when those products are used as an ingredient;
2. any misuse, imitation or evocation, even if the true origin of the product is indicated or if the protected name is translated or accompanied by an expression such as 'style', 'type', 'method', 'as produced in', 'imitation' or similar;
3. any other false or misleading indication as to the provenance, origin, nature or essential qualities of the product, on the inner or outer packaging, advertising material or documents relating to the product concerned and the packing of the product in a container liable to convey a false impression as to its origin; and
4. any other practice liable to mislead the consumer as to the true origin of the product.

Compared to Regulation 510/2006, protection against the use of GI products as ingredients which exploits the reputation of said ingredient GI has been added. Indeed in France, many cases have

---

[121] Art. 13.2 of Regulation no. 1151/2012.

prohibited the mention of the GI when the ingredient was in very small quantity and not conferring any quality of the final product which itself could be of very bad quality and spoiling the reputation of the GI, whether the ingredient was Champagne or Roblochon, or Tomme de Savoie.[122]

The absolute protection given to French appellations of origin against use for non-similar goods is conferred by EU Regulation, for PDO and PGI, but with a difference: the EU Regulation requires that such use 'exploits the reputation of the protected name', while the use condemned by French law covers even what is 'likely to weaken reputation'.

A very powerful protection of GIs is achieved with the principle of evocation, which is broader that the concept of imitation as evocation does not require that the consumer might be misled. An example is the decision of the EUCJ[123] regarding the name Cambozola which is an evocation of the PDO Gorgonzola. The court holds that 'evocation' covers a situation where the term used to designate a product incorporates part of a protected designation, so that when the consumer is confronted with the name of the product, the image triggered in his mind is that of the product whose designation is protected. It is possible for a protected designation to be evoked where there is no likelihood of confusion between the products concerned and even where no community protection extends to the parts of that designation which are echoed in the term or terms at issue'. The same concept of evocation was used to prohibit the use of name considered as evocative of the PDO "Parmigiano-Reggiano'.[124]

---

[122] 'Foie gras de canard aux deux poivres et au Champagne' (TGI Paris, 15 mars 2012, no. 11/04203), sandwiches 'Mc Cheese' receipt with Beaufort, Reblochon sauce and Tomme de Savoie sold by McDonald's (Cass. crim., 30 juin 2009, no. 08-86919), whereas the sauce contained only 8% of Reblochon or Tomme de Savoie), 'Saint-Môret au Roquefort' (Cass. com., 5 juillet 1994, no. 92-17534).

[123] EUCJ 43/1999 (C-87/97), Cambozola vs Gorgonzola.

[124] CJEU, 26 February 2008, aff C-132/05, Commission c/ Allemagne, Rec. CJEU 2008, I, p. 957, see analysis 1–5. The OHMI has also applied the concept of evocation for OHIM (Community Trade Mark Office), RONCARIFORT evoked (PDO) ROQUEFORT, CAZORLIVA evoked (PDO) SIERRA DE CAZORLA.

## Protection against Trademarks

The protection of GIs against trademarks,[125] similarly for PDO and PGI, is extensively covered in EU Regulation. Thus, when a PDO or PGI is registered, the application for registration of a trademark corresponding to one of the situations referred to in Article 13 concerning the same type of product[126] is refused if the application for registration of the trademark is presented after the date of filing the application for PDO or PGI. The prohibition applies only to products from the same type, thus weakening the scope of protection of Article 13, which extends protection to non-similar products. This provision was applied in several decisions the EUCJ took, one being the cancellation of the EU word mark 'Grana Biraghi' on the grounds that the PDO 'Grana Padano' already existed.[127]

European regulation provides the opportunity to register a PDO or PGI even if an earlier trademark exists, introducing the principle of coexistence between the trademark and the GI. In fact, the use of a trademark which contravenes Article 13(1) which has been applied for, registered, or established by use if that possibility is provided for by the legislation concerned, in good faith within the territory of the union, before the date on which the PDO or PGI application is submitted to the commission, may continue notwithstanding the subsequent registration of a PDO or PGI.[128] This provision is combined with that of Article 6.4 which states that a PDO or PGI is not registered when, considering a trademark's reputation and the duration of its use, the registration is likely to mislead the consumer regarding the true identity of the product.

The date to consider is either before the date of protection given by the PDO or PGI in the country of origin or before 1 January 1996.

It is therefore possible to register a GI despite the existence of an earlier trademark (unless it is famous or well known). This provision was considered in line with the TRIPS Agreement according to a decision of the Dispute Settlement Body (DSB) of the WTO, following a complaint

---

[125] Article 14.
[126] The prohibition of registration of trademarks is only for the same kind of products.
[127] TCE, 2 September 2007, aff. T-291/03, Rec. 2007, II, 3081.
[128] On the condition that the trademark is valid according to under Council Regulation (EC) No. 207/2009 of 26 February 2009 on the Community trade mark (1) or under Directive 2008/95/EC.

by the United States and Australia against the EU.[129] The ground of the dispute was that the United States thought that the European Regulation No. 2081/92 did not allow trademark owners to prevent the registration of GIs that could lead to confusion with existing trademarks. The panel rejected the US argument on the grounds that Article 17 of the TRIPS Agreement concerning the protection afforded to trademarks allows limited exceptions to rights conferred by the trademark: 'Members may provide limited exceptions to the rights conferred by a trademark, such as fair use of descriptive terms, provided that such exceptions take account of the legitimate interests of the owner of the trademark and of third parties'.

This unique coexistence between a trademark and a GI was recently implemented in France by the Council of State which ruled that the earlier trademarks, the collective trademark 'Moules de bouchot', filed on 2 July 1994, and the trademark 'Moule de bouchot de la baie du Mont-Saint-Michel et Cancale', filed on 31 May 2000, were not well known and thus were not an obstacle to the registration of a PDO 'Moules de bouchot de la baie du Mont-Saint-Michel'.[130] This decision, however, makes us wonder how consumers can distinguish between three names that are so similar but do not refer to the same definition of the product. It primarily reflects how Europe favours the GI over the trademark.

*Coherence of Same Protection to PDO and PGI?*

The protection given at the EU level is the same for PDO and PGI despite the fact that the nature of the link to the origin is different for the two, with access being easier for PGI than for PDO. Thus, all the provisions set out in PDO apply equally to PGI. This is all the more remarkable as, by definition, PGI refers to the definition of GIs as given in the TRIPS Agreement. In other words, the standard protection given by the TRIPS Agreement to all products is well below the level of protection given to the European PGI.

It reveals policy choices made by the EU, which wants to vigorously promote a policy of legislation on origin within the EU agricultural

---

[129] *European Communities—Protection of trademarks and geographical indications for agricultural products and foodstuffs,* WT/DS174/R, p. 190.

[130] CE, 26 mai 2008, no. 297326, Syndicat des mytiliculteurs de la Baie du Mont Saint-Michel, de Cancale et d'Ille-et-Vilaine, www.legifrance.gouv.fr.

policy by encouraging products exhibiting a link with their origin without, however, complying with the strict definition of appellation of origin.[131]

The level of protection was debated following the publication of the Green Book by the European Commission, which suggested some simplification measures: 'perhaps a merger of two existing instruments, PDO and PGI, and the establishment of different levels of protection throughout the EU', while maintaining core principles: 'any new system should maintain the link with the area of production as well as the collective nature of geographical indication'.[132]

Rather than merge the two instruments, it seems necessary in the light of the diversity of the link between the product and its origin, as the next chapter will illustrate, to think of the introduction of different levels of protection. This, without questioning the legal nature of PDO and PGI, would allow consistency between the requirements to be complied with in order to benefit from one of the instruments, and the level of rights conferred. It appears useful to conserve the two levels of geographical references, namely, the PDO and PGI, in relation to the strength of the link to its origin, as the diversity of links to their origin is present not only in Europe but also in India where the innovative concept of 'uniqueness' helps protect GIs that designate both *terroir* products and products of origin for which the link is expressed through the know-how. Yet, the new European regulation for the protection of GIs of November 2012 maintained most of the previous system, with two signs, PDO and PGIs, associated with the same level of protection.

## Minimum Protection in India

The protection given to the Indian GI corresponds to the 'standard protection' of the TRIPS Agreement, and is not equal to that of French

[131] Joanna Schmidt-Szalewski, 'La Protection Des Noms Géographiques En Droit Communautaire', *La Semaine Juridique Entreprise et Affaires* 44, no. 703 (1997).
[132] 'Communication De La Commission Au Parlement Européen, Au Conseil, Au Comité Économique Et Social Européen Et Au Comité Des Régions Sur La Politique De Qualité Des Produits Agricoles', (Commission des Communautés Européennes). Ibid., 12, voir commentaire de Vincent Ruzek, 'La Stratégie Communautaire De Protection Des Indications Géographiques En Question', *Revue de Droit Rural*, no. 373 (2009): 1–9.

and European PDO/PGI, beginning with the principle of a term-ended and, therefore, prescriptible GI.

## The Duration of Protection

The validity of a registered GI is 10 years, unlike French AOCs which are imprescriptible. The case is similar for the registration of authorized users. Applications are renewable and are subject to the same procedure.

## The Unavailability of GI

The law prohibits the assignment, transmission, licensing, pledge, mortgage or any such other agreement of a GI.[133] This inalienability of the GI, a principle that is as valid under French law, will bring into question the relevance of the qualification of GI as a property right brought by the Indian law. The commentary on the article also states that this protection is justified by GI being a public property.

## Protection against Infringement

The registered owner and all registered authorized users have the right to initiate legal action in case of infringement.[134] A GI is misused if a person who is not authorized uses such a GI by any means in the designation or presentation of goods that indicate or suggest that such goods originate in a geographical area other than the true place of origin of such goods in a manner which misleads the persons as to the geographical origin of such goods,[135] or uses any GI in such manner which constitutes an act of unfair competition, including passing off.[136]

An additional protection can be granted to products notified in the official gazette by the central government. The rights that are granted help prevent the use of the GI for products that do not originate in the place indicated by the GI, even though the real origin of goods is mentioned or when even where the true origin of the goods is indicated or the GI is used in translation or accompanied by expressions such as 'kind', 'type', 'style' 'imitation' or the like.

Thus, India generally has the legal possibility of conferring additional protection on products it chooses, which suggests a space for

---

[133] Section 24 of the Act.
[134] Section 21(a).
[135] Ibid.
[136] Section 22(b).

political will.[137] In international negotiations on GIs at the WTO, India supports the extension of additional protection to all products, arguing that it would increase the well-being of farmers and artisans by allowing them to obtain better prices and access new markets for both agricultural products and handicrafts.[138] It is surprising that despite this clear stand in the negotiations, no notification has been made so far,[139] even for the GI Darjeeling, which despite requests from numerous stakeholders, with the notable inclusion of the Tea Board has not been notified yet.

The language of the Indian law is very similar to that of the TRIPS Agreement. Indian law thus uses the terminology of infringement normally used for patents and trademarks, whereas French regulations refer to usurpations and false indications. Indian law contains penal provisions to help curb fraud that are reminiscent of the provisions of the French Consumer Code. Indian law includes many provisions that punish fraudulent conduct, provided the ill will of the offender can be proven.[140] This mechanism that we can describe as control of fraud does not set conditions regarding the risk of consumer confusion.

Finally, contrary to French and European laws, Indian Act does not provide protection for non-similar goods, as was judged by the High Court of Calcutta in the case of a trademark Darjeeling Lounge, applied by ITC Limited for hospitality/hotel chain. The Tea Board of India lost its injunction against ITC Limited from using the word 'Darjeeling' in connection with its tea lounge. The Tea Board unsuccessfully argued that the use of 'Darjeeling' as name of a lounge constituted dilution of the geographical indication—as that particular lounge in ITC-owned Sonar Bangla served several beverages including Darjeeling tea.[141]

---

[137] Communication from Tea Board, anonymous. Other authors also advise India to grant the additional protection to other goods than wines and spirits; see Balganesh, 'Systems of Protection for Geographical Indications of Origin: A Review of the India Regulatory Framework', 203.
[138] Ministry of Commerce Press Release (Hong Kong: 18 December 2005) : http://commerce.nic.in/Dec05_release.htm.
[139] Section 22.2 of Act.
[140] Sections 38, 39, 40 de la loi.
[141] Calcutta High Court, *Tea Board, India vs. ITC Limited* on 24 August 2011.

*Protection against Trademarks*

A GI cannot be registered as a trademark if the trademark consists of or contains the GI for products similar to those registered in the application for the GI and does not originate in the place indicated by the GI, provided there is a risk of confusing or misleading the public. This prohibition is absolute for the GI that benefit from additional protection, regardless of the risk of confusing or misleading the public.[142] In the case where earlier trademarks were filed or registered in good faith or have acquired rights by use in good faith before the entry into force of the law on GIs, that is, 15 September 2003, nothing in the law can prejudge the admissibility or validity of the registration of a trademark or the right to use a trademark on the ground that it is identical or similar to a GI.[143] Actions against contentious trademarks must be initiated within either five years from the infringement coming to the notice of the owner or user of the GI by the trademark, or five years from the publication of the registration of the trademark, the earlier date being considered as correct and such GI is not used or registered in bad faith.[144] This provision is in accordance with the TRIPS Agreement, and member states are free to either apply or not. India, by choosing to apply it, has reduced the scope of protection granted to GIs.

Much like the infringement action, the relationship between GIs and trademarks does not favour GIs, since a later trademark is only prohibited if there is a risk of public confusion.

In conclusion, the weak legal protection of the Indian GI Act has not, however, adversely impacted the elevated rate of GI registrations in India. Indeed, the purpose of the law on GIs in India is to preserve Indian cultural identity and fight against infringements.

---

[142] Section 25.
[143] Section 26.1.
[144] Section 26.4.

# 3
# GIs on Handicraft Goods in India Compared to France/Europe

In India, the first GIs were essentially for non-agricultural and non-agri-food products which are qualified as handicraft products because they are mainly handmade (see Figures 3.1 and 3.2).

**Figure 3.1**
*Nature of GI products: 226 GIs for Indian products, March 2015*

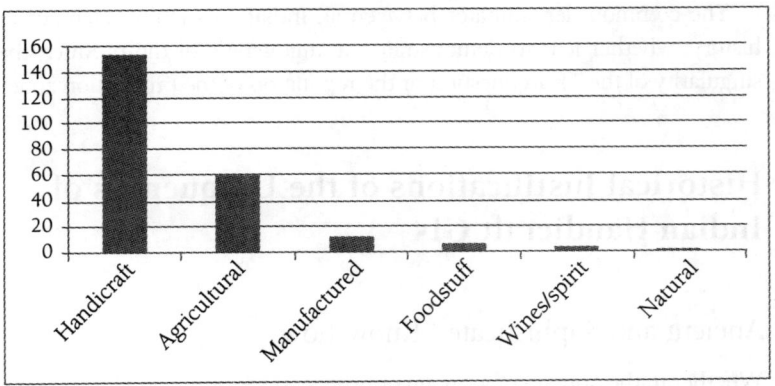

**Figure 3.2**
*Non-agricultural GIs: 151 registered GIs for Indian products, March 2015*

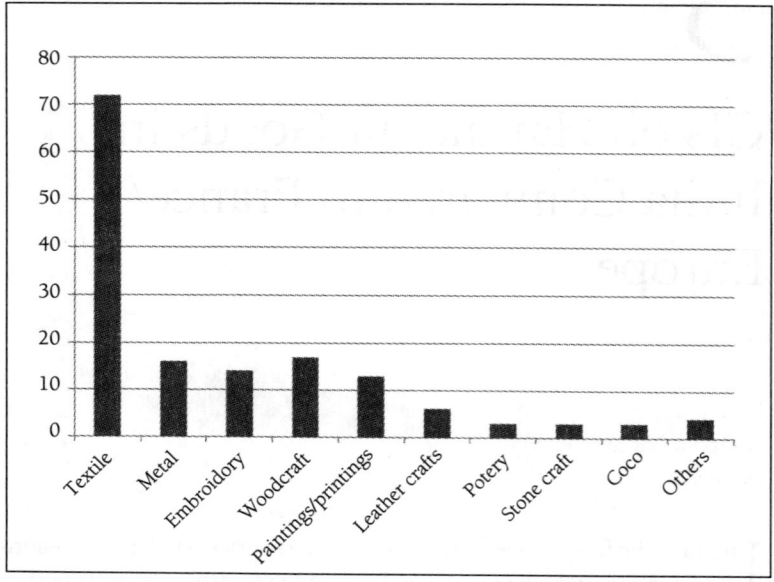

The ratio of registrations as of March 2015 was about two-thirds non-agricultural GIs to one-third agricultural GIs. In India, the fascination with GIs for non-agricultural products was quite unexpected, especially in the light of the parliamentary debates held on the subject.

The common denominator between all Indian GIs is the reference to history, whether it is to demonstrate the uniqueness of the product, the singularity of the TK in question or the reputation of the production zone.

## Historical Justifications of the Uniqueness of Indian Handicraft GIs

### Ancient and Sophisticated Know-how

Whether in the domain of weaving or bronze, stone and wood handicrafts, sculpture or painting, the requisite knowledge reflects the sophistication and expertise of craftsmen, inheritors of an ancient tradition. The savoir faire involved is sophisticated, and in the GI applications, the related reputation is declared as exceptional. Experts and researchers claim that the techniques described cannot be found 'in any other place'. Kani shawl (designating shawls from Kani valley) is described as a world-famous handicraft. Aranmula metal mirror abounds in superlatives, representing 'a phenomenon of extraordinary skill': 'no other similar mirror is available anywhere in the world'. The description continues with the statement that 'the world's renowned metallurgists and scientists have tried to produce similar mirrors with the same composition of metals but have failed in their attempts'. The GI application for Kovai Kora cotton saris proclaims that they are magnificent saris spun with silk and cotton threads by weavers using techniques 'unsurpassed in the annals of the textile industry'.

This reputation is justified because it is undeniable that the know-how involved in making these saris is truly ancient and still based in complex handmade techniques. These manual techniques are described as unchanged and used in one place, which guarantees that they are local.

Since the textiles which best reflect regional cultures are essentially in the domain of the handloom[1] and additionally benefit from favourable public policies, the GI Act should be viewed as applicable primarily to handle products.

*The Savoir Faire of Transformation*

One of the most reputed GIs in the domain of textiles, the only non-agricultural GI which was quoted during parliamentary debates, is for Kancheepuram silk. It designates silk woven in the ancient, royal town of Kancheepuram, famous for its temples, situated in south India, Tamil Nadu. Kancheepuram saris are in great demand for marriages. The GI application describes the production technique in 10 pages of densely written script, as characterized by the use of thick silk yarn which gives it its heavy weight and bright colours. One of the characteristics is the contrasting colours between the body of the sari and the approximately 10-cm top and bottom borders.

---

[1] P. Chandra, 'The Textile and Apparel Industry in India', Indian Institute of Management, Vastrapur, Ahmedabad, 2005, October 2005, p. 4. The article cites in saris of cotton or silk, particularly Pochampally or Varanasi, which are both subject to GI.

The specificity of the Kancheepuram sari also lies in the use of silver, gold and red silk threads called *zari* on which the cost of the sari depends. To get different colours for the body and the borders, a special technique is used which consists in using two extra shuttles on each side of the loom, besides the shuttle used for the main body. It is pointed out in the specifications that two people have to be there on either side of the loom to make it work. It is generally agreed that fake Kancheepuram saris are made of thinner silk yarn, have only one border instead of two and the sari does not contain gold.[2]

The manufacturing process is described in detail: the preparation of the yarn by twisting, degumming and dyeing, the loom and then the weaving itself. The specifications indicate that dressing the yarn is done by stretching it out in the open. Sizing is done before sunrise to ensure that the ends do not stick to one another. Degumming of the yarn is also described with many details, mentioning the number of times it is rinsed and the time required to do so. The dyeing process is described meticulously. Lemon juice, composed of the juice of five lemons diluted in two gallons of water, is applied to improve the lustre of the silk. The mark of dye manufacturers is also evident in the GI application, which includes directions regarding the dilution of powder. At least 15 days are required to make a Kancheepuram sari, with two weavers working on the loom for 10 hours.[3]

The quantity of details provided on the manufacturing process shows how sophisticated the know-how is. However, there are repeated inconsistencies all along the text. For example, under the heading 'method of production', the raw material is described as: 'gold lace and gold thread unit is a Marc weighing 245 gm containing eight skeins, the length of which is 2200 to 2400 yards. The total constituent of the lace is gold (1%), silver (78%), silk (21%)'. In the next description, the composition indicated is quite different: 'the contents of zari used by the Silk Weavers' Cooperative Societies are: gold (0.59%), silver (57%), silk (24%) and copper (18.41%)'.

---

[2] Interview with a *responsable* of the Weaving service centre of Kancheepuram, December 2006.

[3] Interview with the 'Kamakshiamman Cooperative', Kancheepuram, December 2006.

These sometimes contradictory details reveal the ambivalence of specifications, legal documents divided between anthropological, technical and historical aspects. It seems thus difficult to determine exactly what the object of GI is. Thus, what happens if certain details such as the position of the assistants for weaving the border are not respected to the letter? Similarly in the specifications, the precise length of the yarn for the loom is indicated, the warp has to be 18 yards long, while clearly it is not this that makes the sari unique. The description of a common base is more adapted to a legal instrument as a GI, conferring monopoly of use to users who have to respect the technical criteria indicated in the specifications.

Other areas of handicrafts are also protected by GIs, such as the case of specialty woodcrafts where the product is entirely chiselled manually and then painted. Take, for example, the GI Kondapalli Bommalu for painted wooden figurines. To make them, the craftsman has to know about the wood, its selection, cutting and seasoning, as well as to be skilled in woodcarving and painting on wood. The uniqueness arises out of the use of a special tool, called *Bahudara* in local language, as a means of chiselling the wood. This is a very unique feature in the production of Kondapalli Bommalu. The wooden figurines representing animals and birds, male and female figures depicting rural life and mythological figures are very expressive due to the particularities of their design and production.

In the domain of metal craft, the GI Thanjavur art plate designates bronze plates with side decoration figures which are embossed in silver and copper foil, depicting different motifs among which are Hindu divinities.

A GI application still not registered following oppositions proceedings regarding the nature of the applicant describes a Pavithra ring made in Payyanur. The ring is made of gold and is unique for its Pavithra knot at the centre of the ring. There are three lines on the rings which represent the three *nadis*: Ida, Pingala and Sushumna. The knot at the centre by joining the above three lines indicates the glands in the human body.[4] IPAB confirmed the uniqueness of the product as 'though there may be other Rings in the market called Pavithra Ring, this particular design and the manner in which the Ring is made is special to this area'.

---

[4] GI application no. 6.

The specialized knowledge involved is thus multifaceted, involving different skills. The GI Orissa[5] Pattachitra designates paintings done on unique canvas, a base called *patta astra* prepared by pasting layers of old and used cloth with the help of tamarind glue. The TK also involves making the tool out of plywood board on which silk fabric is pasted with the help of Fevicol which is used for painting, the preparation of pigments and the selection of motifs representing stories from the Bhagavata (Krishnalila portion), Ramayana and the Jagannatha.

The complexity of the different steps is also demonstrated by the GI Kashmir pashmina which designates shawls from Kashmir situated in the Himalayas. This shawl is made of the undergrowth of fleece from the mountain goat *Capra hircus* having a fineness of 12–16 microns.

Spinning the yarn is a very difficult process regarding the fineness of the wool. The specification describes the following steps: procurement of the raw material either by way of natural shedding, combing or sharing with a knife, cleaning and separation of the remaining coarse hairs and the second's wool which is fibres of shorter length; soaking in clean cold water usually for 24 hours, draining of the water and mixing with rice flour, storage of delicate pads of wool in deep stone pots and spinning of the yarn on the traditional 'chakra'; warping, dressing and reeling the yarn, weaving, clipping the loose threads, dyeing and, finally, washing and packing.

Each GI thus demonstrates that sophisticated and varied know-how can be found in all domains of handicraft.

*The Savoir Faire of Motif Creation*

Besides the specialized knowledge involved in making an object, assembling it and treating the raw material, GIs in the domain of handicrafts are also registered for products related to the creation of motifs and drawings. Contrary to the example of Kancheepuram silk saris, where the choice and creation of designs are not specific to the hands of the weaver,[6] the uniqueness of many GI products lies in the choice of motifs and drawings, since the manufacturing process is widespread. The motifs and drawings thus are specific to a region while the techniques related to making the objects, whether they are originally from India or elsewhere, have been widely disseminated. The uniqueness lies only in

---

[5] The name has been changed to Odisha in 2011.
[6] Interview with weavers, Kancheepuram, December 2006.

the motifs, which according to IPR laws normally fall under the protection of 'models and designs laws', but rights in designs and models are only granted for a limited time for new models and designs, which is not the case of motifs in traditional Indian products.

In addition, the type of motif may ensue from the technique used and vary according to the degree of sophistication of the technique, as demonstrated by the GIs Pochampally Ikat and Orissa Ikat. Pochampally Ikat was the first textile GI registered in the context of the support programme initiated by the Government of Andhra Pradesh. *Ikat*, a Malaysian–Indonesian word which means tie-dye, involves tying and dyeing the threads in a visualized design prior to the weaving of the fabric. Ikat, or resist dyeing, involves the sequence of tying (or wrapping) and dyeing sections of bundled yarn to a predetermined colour scheme (pattern) prior to weaving. Thus, the dye penetrates into the exposed sections, while the tied sections remain undyed. The patterns formed by this process on the yarn are then woven into fabric. A minimum of 15 days are required to make a sari, and it can even extend up to 40 days.

The headings 'Specification', 'Uniqueness' and 'Method of production' of the GI application deal entirely with a very detailed description of the Ikat technique. Only the brief section 'Description of goods' refers to the diamond-shaped motifs, *chowka*. However, it is quickly apparent, and it was confirmed during the registration of the GI application Orissa Ikat, that the Ikat technique is not specific to Pochampally. The textiles made in Pochampally are unique, thanks to the motifs, which, because of the recent history of Ikat production in Pochampally, are simpler than Ikat made in other regions of India.[7]

Thus, during an examination of the GI application Orissa Ikat, which was submitted after the GI Pochampally Ikat was published, the consultative group asked the applicant to demonstrate the specific characteristics of Orissa Ikat which differentiate it from Pochampally Ikat.[8] The applicant replied that the uniqueness lay in the floral motifs with sophisticated shaded effects. These motifs can be very complex such as

---

[7] These simplified designs, modern, are paradoxically more popular with new generations.

[8] Applicant's reply, dated 3 November 2005 to the letter from the GI Registry dated 21 October 2005, accessed in the file available at the GI Registry, Chennai.

calligraphic motifs. It is thus clearly stated in the GI application Orissa Ikat that its specificity lies in the type of design.

The case of Pochampally Ikat and Orissa Ikat GIs are especially interesting because the know-how involved in the creation of motifs specific to the region is enmeshed with the know-how of the Ikat technique, which is generic. The creation of designs cannot be disassociated from a mastery of the technique. Imitations can be distinguished from the originals on the basis of two elements: they are machine-woven, and above all, the motifs are printed after weaving and not created during the weaving process with pre-dyed yarn.[9] The uniqueness thus lies in the particular way the technique is applied in a specific place. And this is what makes the registration of a GI feasible. It is also a more desirable tool of protection than the mere protection of designs and models according to Subodh Kumar from Confederation of Indian Industry (CII) who acknowledges that GIs being protected for an indefinite period on condition that the registration is renewed every 10 years are more attractive.[10] The GI is also much sought after because it protects the name Pochampally which is reputed. And it seems very unlikely in the present, that even if the weavers of Pochampally decide to learn other motifs which are typical of Orissa they will abandon their own motifs, and above all their name, as well known as the appellation Orissa.

The registration of a GI for generic techniques raises the question of adding a geographical location to the name of the technique in the appellation. For example, the GI Kalamkari designates an ancient craft of painting on fabric characterized by the use of a *kalam* (pen) to draw the outlines and fill in areas with dyes. This is known and practised in various regions of India using either a pen or hand blocks.

Following legal proceedings against the Kalamkari GI on the grounds that it was generic,[11] the parties agreed to add the name of the village

---

[9] A case between the owner of the Pochampally Ikat GI and an infringer who manufactures saris with machine-printed pattern. Complaint to the High Court of Delhi, 887/2005.

[10] Personal interview, April 2010.

[11] Opposition filed by Shri Mohan Dewan, Room 38, Podar Chambers, SA Brevli Road, Mumbai 400001, 5 January 2006. File available at the Office of GIs. The opposition mentions that such registration would cause harm to other artisans of Kalamkari.

'Srikalahasti' to the name, thus localizing it. The GI registered is henceforth Srikalahasti Kalamkari. It is thus not a coincidence if a few months later another GI with the name Kalamkari along with the name of another locality, Machilipatnam, was registered. The two GIs can be distinguished from each other on the basis of the different ways the technique of Kalamkari is used. In the case of Machilipatnam Kalamkari, pencil and blocks are used to create the motifs, while in the case of the Srikalahasti Kalamkari, they are drawn only with pencil which enables the artisan to draw freely, generally mythological scenes.

Patchwork or appliqué is another generic technique for making textiles. Thus, the GI 'Appliqué work of Bihar' or 'Khatwa work of Bihar' in the local language designates fabric which has been made with this technique, to decorate walls or used as tents to provide shelter from the sun. According to the specifications, the uniqueness resides in the motifs inspired by the natural environment. This is recounted very romantically as being a unique glimpse of contemporary accomplishment of ordinary women with extraordinary vision of the world.

This simplicity of description contrasts with the patchwork method described in the Pipli appliqué work GI specification, which lists various ways of cutting appliqués depending on the motifs decided beforehand, describes the large range of stitches used and gives a repertory of the designs created. The uniqueness of the product lies on the one hand in the appliqué motifs and on the other in the sophisticated stitches used to sew the appliqués. It reminds one of embroidery and is described in a more logical manner than what we find in the GI appliqué work of Bihar. The reason behind this contrast can perhaps be explained by the fact that the GI applicants are different, but above all, it reveals the great divergence in the manner of describing traditional forms of knowledge, reflected in all the GIs registered in India.

The sophisticated knowledge related to designs is especially remarkable in the domain of embroidery. Many GIs have been registered in this field, sometimes directly for embroidery techniques. Thus, the Chamba Rumal GI specification, which designates handkerchiefs from the Chamba valley, states that the uniqueness is due to the technique of double satin stitch carried forward and backwards alternately, done simultaneously on the two sides of the cloth, known as *dorukha-tanka*, as well as the outline in black thread and the colour combination.

Historians quoted in the column 'historical proof' compare Chamba Rumal to miniature paintings embroidered on cloth. The motifs chosen are inspired from Hindu mythological stories and embellished by drawings of flowers and birds.

A remarkable aspect is the professionalism of the designers who create these designs. Originally exclusively done by artisans who made the product, this activity is henceforth entrusted to professional designers, trained in prestigious Indian design schools. The aim is to attract a rapidly changing clientele with designs which are supposed to be innovative, modern and of superior quality. Thus, the GI Chamba Rumal describes two styles: the one of the painter well versed in Pahari painting, elegant and fine in draughtsmanship, and the other one of the artisans, which are rough and bold in treatment. Such an assessment in the specifications is indeed astounding, given the fact that the motifs which lend uniqueness to the product are no more the prerogative of artisans. The link to the origin is thus weakened unless the technique independent of the motif is so famous that it merits being registered as a GI.

*Secret Savoir Faire, Surrounded by Rituals*

Secret savoir faire

Some Indian GIs have been registered for objects whose production methods are kept secret and surrounded by religious rituals. The reputation of the product is based on the 'magical' quality of the know-how, and only producers who have been initiated have access to this know-how. Thus, the GI Aranmula Kannadi has been registered for metal mirrors (*kannadi* in the local language) made in a little village in Aranmula, situated in Kerala, in south India, by about 30 producers. The 'method of production' comprises the preparation of the alloy of copper and tin, preparation of the mould with the local clay made in the shape of the mirror to be cast, heating of the mould before the wax inside is drained out completely and pouring of the alloy. The mould is then left undisturbed for two to three days to allow it to cool. It is then taken out and the layers of burnt clay removed from the new metal mirror plate. The plate is then polished. The composition of the alloy and the mysterious plant which is added during the preparation is kept secret. At each step of the production process, there is a religious ritual. A legend about the mirror is noted in the specification. The bronze artisans were asked by the temple priest of the Aranmula temple to make bells, and they succeeded in making a metal alloy which when polished reflected objects like a real mirror, thanks to 'divine grace'.

Similarly, the exact composition of the blend of perfumes for the GI Mysore Agarbathi (Mysore incense) is a secret. The secretiveness surrounding such knowledge raises the issue of whether new producers would be able to join the association and manufacture the mirror. Indeed, it seems that they are excluded from using the GI for cultural reasons.

### 'Sacred' savoir faire

A rather unusual GI's reputation is based on its use during religious pilgrimages. The GI Tirupati laddu designates sweets made exclusively in the renowned temple of south India, the Srivari Temple in Tirumala, near Tirupati in Andhra Pradesh. These 'laddus' are eaten by pilgrims and offered to the divinity Venkateswara, which makes them sacred. Only pilgrims who visit the temple can have the laddus. The specifications highlights the holiness of the laddus in order to justify their reputation and also indicates their size, the method of preparation, their appetizing taste and the quality proceedings followed in the temple kitchens, the only place where they are made.

The laddus are made in a vessel called Srivari *pottu*, by about a 130 cooks. Around 20,000 laddus are made every day for approximately 70,000 pilgrims who throng the temple each day. Some laddus are offered to the deity so that they can be blessed and then mixed with the remaining laddus. All the laddus are then placed in front of Vakula Devi, the mother goddess, and distributed to devotees.

The raw materials, milk and sugar, are of very good quality, but their geographical origin is not mentioned. Recommendations regarding the preparation of the sugar syrup have been issued by the Mysore Central Food Technological Research Institute. They are scrupulously followed by the cooks in Tirupati temple. The sacred nature of the laddu has given rise to a deep controversy: The singularity of the applicant gave rise to another controversy (see Chapter 8).

*Some GIs for 'Non-traditional' Products*

Some GIs have been registered for 'modernized' products, with the production techniques becominge mechanized or the traditional raw material not being used any more. GIs are not against innovation per se, but if traditional production methods are the reason for the product's reputation, the legitimacy of such a GI is questionable.

For example, Mysore rosewood inlay GI, a craft where the flat surface of the rosewood is scooped out in the desired designs and natural wood of different colours, is inlaid in the hollow spaces to form pictures. Other raw material is yellow wood, ebony, *pathangadamara* and other varieties of wood. White plastic is used nowadays instead of ivory for inlay. The specialized knowledge involved thus consists only of wood chiselling, since ivory inlay work is not required any more by the Indian government. The reputation of the product partly based on ivory quality becomes questionable.

For financial reasons, gold and gems have been replaced by silver and artificial stones to make Temple Jewellery of Nagercoil used for temples. Even though this affects the quality of the product as for the GI Mysore rosewood inlay, the consumer is not fooled because the replacement of the original material by cheaper material is quite easily discernible and widely known.

This replacement of the original raw material by artificial material can be considered as fraud if the consumer is liable to be misleading about product features. Kullu shawl from the Kullu valley, situated in the mountains of north India, is derived from natural raw material, sheep wool according to the statement of case which later describes a list of different types of wool: 'local wool, angora, merino, pashmina, synthetic, cotton and yak wool'. The odd man out in this list, contradicting the natural raw material claim, is 'synthetic wool', today the real production situation. Such gap between the reasons for which the product has become reputed and production reality casts doubt upon GI registration.

The GI Mysore Agarbathi (for scented joss sticks) is made of a variety of sandalwood tree, *Santalum album*, which according to the GI application grows only in Karnataka, the ancient kingdom of Mysore, which, however, does not correspond to the present reality as today the perfumes are often synthetic, with the uniqueness of the product lying in the knowledge of blending perfumes.

Similarly, various dyes used for textiles and leather, which were traditionally natural, have been replaced by artificial dyes. Madurai Sungudi sari, characterized by the selection of vegetable-based dyes from which colours were extracted in the past, is now made of industrial dyes.

Few GIs designate products always machine made, with a more recent history linked to the industrialization of India. The geographical area is where factories were set up, under the facilitation of the British crown, as for example the soap factory producing GI Mysore sandal soap, launched in 1916 on the three sites of the ancient kingdom of Mysore, unique at that time. Soap's uniqueness lies in the entirely natural raw material used, especially sandalwood, which in the past was abundant in Mysore region.

GI Mysore silk weaving is entirely mechanized in the factory built by the Maharaja what was the ground for opposition, other weavers wishing to include the manual processes.

Last, an extremely marginal case, against which numerous lawsuits have been filed, demonstrates the attraction of the GI legal tool for the most unlikely products, such as petrol by-products. Four GI applications, Jamnagar petrol, Jamnagar fuel, Jamnagar LPG (liquefied petroleum gas) and Jamnagar diesel, were filed for products from the ultra-modern refinery in Jamnagar, situated in Gujarat. If it meets the high ISO (International Organization for Standardization) standards, it is very doubtful there is a link between the quality of the product and the place where the refining is done.

## Savoir Faire Safeguarded by Specific Communities

In the domain of handicraft, the knowledge and skills involved are specific to certain communities, which they keep to themselves. M.C. Mahias considers that the word *community* associated to a domain of production which is socially recognized refers to the caste system. This notion, deliberately left out in debates for political reasons,[12] highlights the link between a specific group which grows bigger from generation to generation and a type of production. This link seems to exist in GIs if we believe in what is noted in the specifications.

[12] Mahias, 'Les Sciences Et Les Techniques Traditionnelles En Inde', 108.

The Pipli appliqué work GI mentions 54 families constituting a total of 270 producers from the caste of Darjis, belonging to communities Mahapatra and Maharana, given by various rajas since the 11th century and who work for temples, also called *sevaks*. They hand down their title from generation to generation.

Kancheepuram silk weavers were originally from another state, Andhra Pradesh, and they migrated 400 years ago when their village was swept away by the sea according to the GI application. They thus still speak their original language, Telugu. The weavers form a sizeable part of the population, and we can truly talk about a 'reservoir of expertise' as field research done by N.S. Gopalakrishnan[13] shows that 75 per cent of the population is involved directly or indirectly in the silk industry. Kancheepuram silk was originally woven only by the Salia community, but now all the communities found within 8 km around Kancheepuram weave silk.

Though the Kashmir pashmina GI application is found wanting in historical data, it mentions the name of the community of artisans who exercised this craft in ancient times, the Tantuvayas. Thanjavur paintings were made by artisans who belonged to the community of Rajus and Naidus and migrated to Tamil Nadu in the 17th century. GI Kondapalli Bommalu artisans, skilled in sculpture and painting, pass on their knowledge from generation to generation. The craftsmanship of the Payyanur Pavithra ring has been handed down from generation to generation.[14]

These communities are guardians of TK and savoir faire handed down a hereditary manner. The hypothesis is that individuals isolated from the community or even small groups cut off from the main community might not be able to utilize this knowledge and savoir faire with equal proficiency. The uniqueness linked to the collective nature of GIs is thus respected, but are the communities rooted to a place? Do they move away easily?

According to the history recounted in certain GI applications, to a great extent the communities are local and other communities in the same area benefit from the dissemination of the relevant skills and

[13] Gopalakrishnan, Nair, and Babu, *Exploring the Relationship between Geographical Indications and Traditional Knowledge: An Analysis of the Legal Tools for the Protection of Geographical Indications in Asia*, 36.
[14] See IPAB Order regarding Payyanur Pavithra ring, 14 November 2012.

knowledge, as in the case of Kancheepuram silk, reinforcing the link to the place. Other GI applications describe population migration following natural catastrophes, but these migrating communities create new products in the new place which are then specific to it.

## Written Proof on the Ancient History

*Historicity*

The majority of GI applications demonstrate the link to the origin through a precise history of the product, in a section specially meant for this purpose: 'Proof of origin (Historical Records)'. The title of the section itself, combining proof of origin with historical data, suggests that it is through history that the link to the origin can be proved. Generally historical dates are provided, with GIs ranging in antiquity from the 3rd century AD up to the 20th century.

Colonial history does not seem to be at the origin of any specific skills, practices, know-how or innovations in the domain of handicraft, contrary to the case of agricultural products, where the British developed cash crops such as coffee, tea and spices.

The historical section generally begins with a description of the geographical place, which is famous independently of the handicraft produced there. This is followed by the story of the artisans settling down in the region, and it ends with the history of the product itself. Artisanal objects are often linked to the history of the kingdom's elites, for whom many of these products were made, whether such products be religious (often linked to temples) or civil. For many GIs, it is the town's fame which attracts reputed products and not the other way around.[15]

Thus, the handicrafts of Pipli, an important place for the rice and textile trade, are linked to the Jagannath temple of Puri in Orissa, which dates back to the 12th century. It was later influenced by Islam, the motifs became more sophisticated, and only elite artisans continued to exercise this craft. The GI application quotes the name of skilled textile artisans nominated by the Maharaja during the 11th century and refers to certificates from the 18th century containing lists of weavers (*sebaks*).

---

[15] The many GIs in the city of Thanjavur (Tanjore) are an example.

Exactly in the same manner, the historical data in the Kondapalli Bommalu GI refers to the famous Kondapalli fort, built in the 14th century. The history of the town, named after the shepherd Kondadu who advised the king to build his kingdom there is narrated in details, together with the history of the production of toys, which began in the 16th century.

The historical section of the Kovai Kora cotton GI (designating saris which are a blend of cotton and silk yarns) relates in detail the arrival of the Devangar community, pioneers in making this fabric, who were said to hail from Ahmednagar in Gujarat and migrated to south India as a result of the annihilation of Vijayanagara Empire in the Talikota War in 1565. The Devangar community's name refers to the object designated by the GI, with the term being used to mean the weavers of dresses used for clothing the celestial bodies (*deva*—god, *anga*—body).

These silk and cotton saris were woven for members of the royal family during the Vijayanagara Empire. But the GI description continues by quoting from an article written in 1999 in the first Indian English daily, *The Hindu*, according to which '[f]ifteen years ago, weavers in Coimbatore were using only cotton to manufacture saris. When the competition became stiff because of similar saris produced by modern mills, a new method was devised by the handloom sector in weaving. Thus was born the Kora Silk'. It is thus above all the history of the community which is narrated, which has been living in this region for a long time, but has only recently started implementing the special knowledge embedded in the GI product, after the invention of the extra-thin cotton thread. It does not matter that the reputed product is recent. What is highlighted is the artisans' long presence in the region, dating back to hundreds of years.

The Kancheepuram silk GI's history also relates to the relocation of such a community. The weaving of silk was developed in order to meet the needs of royal dynasties who succeeded one another in Kancheepuram, described in the GI application from the 2nd century BC till the colonial period: the Pallavas, the Cholas, the Vijayanagara Empire and, finally, the Mughals. The link between the history of these dynasties and the sari is not specified, however.

Certain handicraft goods began to be produced when local kings set up art schools to train artisans in different techniques, particularly painting and inlay work. The history of the Thanjavur traditional paintings GI is linked to the painting school of Thanjavur which flourished between the 17th and the 19th century. The GIs for Mysore traditional paintings is linked to the painting school of Mysore which was created in 1578 and reached its peak between 1799 and 1868 under royal patronage. The Mysore rosewood inlay GI is linked to the Chamaraja Technical Institute, founded in 1892.

More recently, rural development policies have given rise to specific productions. For example, Pochampally Ikat is produced by weavers originating in a seaside village in Andhra Pradesh making small pieces of fabric (scarves) with diamond-shaped patterns for fisher folk and trained to weave saris in 1960, under the All India Handicrafts Board development scheme implemented in Pochampally.[16]

*Written Sources for Historical Data*

The GI Registry is increasingly strict regarding the sources quoted as reference to substantiate the claims for the link to the origin. The 'Proof of Origin (Historical Data)' section is the only section which requires 'proof'. The other sections are merely descriptive.

Information provided by oral sources often tends to be undependable. In certain GI applications, it is seasoned artisans, chosen from the older generation, who testify, as for example, the testimony of Mr Hatta Maharana, an 84-year-old native of Pipli making appliqué.

The history of the creation of the Aranmula metal mirror is entirely based on legend.

The priority is given to written sources, ancient or recent, in vernacular languages or in English. The first category is composed of ancient poems, Hindu mythological stories and memoirs of temple priests such as a poem from the 2nd century for Kancheepuram silk, an *Arthashastra* ascribed to the author Kautilya in 321 BC describes Muga silk of Assam, red as sun (*batarkaprabhan*), soft as the surface of gem and being woven while the threads were very wet. Temple documents are also used such as the 'Record of Rights—Shri Jagannath Temple, Puri, by the Temple Administration under the Orissa Act 14 of 1952 for the GI Pipli appliqué work'.

---

[16] Information gathered during interviews in Pochampally.

A particularly interesting case is that of the Kani shawl GI where we find a remarkable source amidst written sources: references to pieces of shawls from the 17th century, preserved in museums.

Other sources are history books on the concerned region. Among such texts are Western traveller's accounts such as *Travels in India* by Jean-Baptiste Tavernier, 1662, where the special red silk of Assam is mentioned.

Finally, frequent reference is also made to official documents published by the administration, whether it is the *Gazetteer of India*, or *Census of India*, both of which provide the results of periodical censuses taken of administered regions or on a thematic basis.

These sources are relatively recent and date back to the time of British rule, but they serve to vouch for productions which existed much before these gazettes were published. GI applicants have to follow a legal process for registering an IPR in a country with a bureaucratic tradition, and thus find them valuable as proofs, thanks to their official character.

## Lack of Precision in the Delimitation of Geographical Areas

*Lack of Maps*

Traditional knowledge constituting the primary link between non-agricultural products and the geographical area, the description of the geographical region is of secondary importance, or even unessential. The GI Act, however, requires that a map of the area covered by the GI be provided. The towns and villages are rarely mentioned individually; instead, it is the administrative region's map which delineates the contours of the production zone. Moreover, maps are often absent in GI applications, revealing the novelty of a territory-based concept. The GIs Kashmir pashmina, Kancheepuram silk and Pochampally Ikat refer to a reputed products, and it is acknowledged that these have been created in specific places and always been made in these places, but these origins are not necessarily regarded as exclusive.

The information provided on the Internet site of the GI office corroborates the lack of awareness regarding the importance of the production zone. In the section 'Geographical area', the area described in the application is not provided; instead, the information is linked to the name of states in the case of Indian GIs and the names of countries in the case of foreign GIs.

*The Demarcation of Limited Administrative Zones*
The zones for handicraft products are relatively small compared to the geographical areas specified in GIs for agricultural products, the size of a small town, sometimes including the surroundings, or the size of a district. The handicraft in question is thus extremely localized.

When there is a map along with the application, it seems that the targeted area consists of an entire administrative zone, an easier task in a bureaucratic country rather than defining boundaries according to environmental criteria, and/or human practices. Therefore, the administrative zoning does not necessarily correspond to real production zones with details regarding the relevant villages and towns lacking. Even if the GI is based only on human factors, such practices can be mapped to delimitate the zone.

This demarcation of boundaries contrasts with the GI office's insistence regarding the precision of official maps, indicating the latitude and longitude.

Definition of geographical area of production based on historical criteria may lead to a risk of exclusion of producers. For example, Kancheepuram silk area of production has evolved through time with silk weavers settling down in the outskirts of the town, while previously they were all found in the town centre around temples.[17] The geographical area in the GI application, however, refers only to the historical town centre and thus excludes artisans who have settled further afield.

# Absence of Natural Factors in Indian GIs in Comparison with the French Concept

The emphasis placed on savoir faire is even greater when natural factors are less or even non-existent. This situation is thus truly unlike the French tradition of appellation of origin or even that of the more flexible PGI.

---

[17] Interview with A. Mohamed Jamaluddin, Director of the Department of Handloom, Government of Tamil Nadu.

## Indian Handicraft GIs Indifferent to Natural Factors

*The Importance of High-quality Raw Material*

The raw material used for non-agricultural GI products meets quality standards, which are not linked with their origin. Good-quality raw material implies traditional raw material with a few exceptions of artificial material. When the consultative group examines GI applications for textiles, one of the six key points they evaluate is the use of natural dyes.[18] Counterfeits can be recognized because of the 'fake' raw material used, often in the guise of artificial or synthetic thread. Similarly, woodcraft is examined according to five critera: timber quality, age of wood, seasoning, use of natural dyes, protection against pests and fungi. The 'generic quality' and not the 'specific quality' of raw material is prevalent.

Either the geographical origin of raw material is not described, or this origin is far away from the product's manufacturing zone and quoted on a purely documentary basis without being mandatory. For example, Kancheepuram silk GI specification indicates that the silk yarn is bought from Gujarat, situated in north India. The Chanderi sari GI specifications mention that raw silk yarn comes from China or Korea and cotton yarn from Coimbatore, south Indian town, or Jaipur in Rajasthan. Other GIs do not describe the geographical origin of raw material but specify generic quality criteria. The Sankheda furniture GI insists on the use of 100 per cent teak wood, Machilipatnam Kalamkari GI specifications on the use of natural colours and teak wood for woodblocks.

The Konark stone carving GI, registered for sculptures of traditional dancers from Orissa, is made from snake stone, which derives its name from the colour and the stone's snake-like patterns, which are sculpted exclusively by artisans from Konark. The mineral composition of the stone is described, but its geographical origin is omitted, demonstrating the extent to which this aspect is considered superfluous.

---

[18] PowerPoint presentation of the Assistant Registrar of the GI Registry, Mr Natarajan, 17–18 September 2008, Delhi. The six criteria are 'quality of raw fibre, natural dye, quality of water, colour fastness, durability and professional skill'.

*Origin of Raw Material Explains the Localization of the GI Product but Is Not Mandatory*

Numerous GI products still owe their creation to a specific place because this is the place from where the raw material is sourced but in many cases it is not a condition to be fulfilled in order to reinforce the 'uniqueness' of the product, since it is not mentioned anywhere that the raw material must come from this specific area.

Kashmir pashmina is one exception to this rule: wool is obtained solely from the Ladakh region, in the mountains of Jammu and Kashmir. The specification retraces the geographical route of the different phases of production and identifies three sub-regions: Ladakh (the grazing ground of the goats where wool is collected), the outskirts of Srinagar and the capital of Jammu and Kashmir (where wool is spun) and the entire region of Jammu and Kashmir (where wool is woven). The link to the territory is characterized by the existence of traditional spinning and weaving knowledge and by the existence of local raw material. The Ladakh zone, however, is not delimited with as much precision, being given lesser importance combined with a certain disregard for those who collect the wool.

In contrast, many GIs mention the places of origin of the raw material without demarcating them accurately. The GI Kondapalli Bommalu indicates that the white sander wood used for the figurines comes from the surrounding region of Kondapalli, but the delimited geographical area corresponds only to the area where the figurines are sculpted, a village of 1.5 km$^2$ which does not include the surrounding forests. The Nirmal furniture GI for toys is distinctiveness thanks to the wood they are made of, called Poniki wood (Jiuotia Rotteri Fromis), which is found around Nirmal. The Channapatna toys and dolls are made out of light and flexible wood collected around Channapatna.

This lack of description of the zone from where the raw material is obtained, which should have some influence on the uniqueness of the GI, is not rectified by the GI Registry.

The case of the GI Mysore silk is particularly interesting. This crêpe de Chine silk is woven on machine loom. According to the specifications, its 'uniqueness' derives from the superior quality of the silk yarn used, a zari consisting of 65 per cent silver and 0.65 per cent gold and a special process of twisting the yarn which gives the fabric its wavy effect. However, the reputation of Mysore silk is based mainly on the silk yarn produced in the ancient kingdom of Mysore where there is a tradition of silkworm farming, and which produces silk of better quality than imported silk.[19] It is truly astonishing that there is no mention of this crucial element in the specification.

Other local products also depend on local raw material such as clay or stone. The Molela clay work GI, which designates terracotta objects, very succinctly describes the place where clay is collected, the ponds around Molela, in the 'Method of production' section. This element is not mentioned later in the specifications to justify the uniqueness of the product.

The reason behind the lack of clarity regarding the description of the raw material's origin, in spite of it being a decisive factor, can be explained by the fragmentation of the industry. Thus, the GI Alleppey coir (which designates carpets, doormats and other objects manufactured out of coir yarn spun from coir fibre extracted from coconut husk) does not demarcate the origin of coconuts, though their provenance does constitute a determining factor. Alleppey refers to the place where professional weavers are settled, along the large network of canals in the interiors of the tropical state of Kerala, in south India. The GI application briefly indicates that the raw material, coconut, comes from the coastal belt of Kerala. The coconuts cultivated in Karnataka, the neighbouring state, were not suitable for making coir and only coconuts from Kerala could be used to produce the finished product.[20] This exclusivity of origin is not indicated in the specification, one possible reason being that coconut production falls under the umbrella the Coconut Board, which is separate from the Coir Board.

Since there are no restrictions regarding the origin of the raw material, it is highly probable that the supply base of the raw material changes. For example, for the Mysore sandal soap GI, the sandalwood no longer comes from the region of the ancient kingdom of Mysore but from other places.

To conclude, even though locally available raw material was at the origin of handicraft creations and therefore their uniqueness, this specificity

---

[19] Interview with Mr Vijayan, the General Director of KSIC (Karnataka Silk Industries Corporation).
[20] Interview with Mr Govadrij, assistant director of the Coir Board.

is not highlighted in GI applications. It seems then that the concept of dichotomy between natural factors and human factors has not been adopted by India. This human factors/natural factors qualification, a legal concept serving to characterize the link between the product and the geographical origin, is replaced by other autonomous assessment criteria of generic quality standard, adapted to each product type, textile or wood, for example.

*Minor Influence of Soil and Climate*

Numerous GIs provide climatic data about the zone they cover, in terms of 'facts' elements along with population data, surface area of the district and the languages spoken. For example, the GI Kancheepuram silk indicates the average temperatures and the quantity of annual rainfall but there is no mention of their influence on the 'uniqueness' of the product. The GI Shantiniketan leather goods (designating leather products made in Shantiniketan district, West Bengal, north India) mentions that Shantiniketan leather is a creation of a unique geographical area of origin which has an extremely hot and dry climate, and a unique composition of earth and water but there is no link with the quality of the product.

*Influence of River Water*

River water is used in the domain of textiles for dyeing as well as for degumming yarn before weaving as an example for Kancheepuram silk. The GI application specifies that Kancheepuram water has unique properties and enhances the shine of the silk and the luminosity of colours, backed with documentary proofs: *Census of India of 1961* (published by the 'Indian Administrative Service'), *Gazetteers of India* 2000 on the district of Kancheepuram and an article from *The Hindu*. Strangely, the 'Uniqueness' section of the application does not contain any details about water quality but only about weaving characteristics. The 'Proof of origin' section contains only the description of the town's royal history and indicates that silk was required to clothe the princes. Thus, it seems that the natural element—the presence of rivers—was probably added to satisfy the GI Act criteria.

The GI applicant for Kancheepuram silk, the Department of Handloom of Tamil Nadu, also refers to local rivers for three other GIs: Kovai kora cotton, carpet yarn of Bhavani Jamakkalam and Salem silk. The quality of water used has thus become one of the GI Registry's examination criteria in the domain of textiles for the registration of a GI.

*The Influence of Clay*

An original link to the origin is put forward for local clay used to mould objects made in cast metal. Clay is not one of the final elements constituting the product and therefore is not a raw material but is rather similar to an environmental factor. The quality of the Aranmula metal mirrors, according to Mr Gopakumar, an artisan, apparently depends on the quality of clay gathered from the sacred river which flows beside the temple.

In conclusion, in spite of these few examples, in most handicraft GIs, natural factors are lacking, whether they are the source of the raw material or environmental factors. This is shocking when compared to the tradition of French appellation of origin and its *terroir*. However, theoretically, PGIs allow for goods not linked to the origin through natural factors, but this aspect is rarely implemented in France.

## The Predominance of Nature Factors for French GIs in Question

Are there GIs in France and Europe whose link to the origin are based on local knowledge in the same way as in India? A comparative analysis can be done with European and French PGIs of processed products.

The history of appellation of origin in France requires a constant attention to the importance of natural factors. This French vision of *terroir* and appellation of origin can skew the ways in which the European concept of PGI applies to France, with the issue of the localisation of raw material, one of the main natural factors, being seriously debated.

*Localization of Raw Material Necessary for AOC*

The definition of French AOC establishes the principle of an alliance between natural factors and human factors, but it is silent on the subject of the different operations to be conducted within the delimited geographical area. Yet according to the European PDO definition, the area of origin of the raw material shall be the same as the geographical area of the processing or elaboration. A special exemption applying only to PDOs registered before 1 May 2004 allows for using raw material coming from outside the delimited geographical area in order to avoid penalizing PDOs well known in their country of origin before the European regulation came into effect (Article 5.3).

Consequently to EU regulation, French cheese AOC specifications were rewritten, and thanks to higher yield and revitalization of local cow breeds, it was possible to relocalize the milk sources. For example, 'Roquefort' was initially made out of milk obtained from non-specific breeds of sheep and came from regions far removed from the production zone. Since then the milk supplying region has been limited to the mid-mountain ranges south of the Massif Central, where there has been a long tradition of farming sheep in a specific manner.[21]

The relocalization of raw material was not free of impediments. For the AOC 'Comté',[22] for example, the Conseil d'Etat confirmed that the clause obliging the processing unit to use milk obtained from within a radius of 25 km allowed was on the one hand to reduce the time between milking and the arrival of milk to the processing units because of the biological fragility of the raw material, and to identify the milk's source.

Contrary to Indian, localization of raw material in France is not equivalent to natural raw material as in the domain of cheese, among the 42 French cheese appellations (2004), only a dozen use only raw milk, in keeping with the traditional method, rather than pasteurized milk.

### Raw Material Source Not Mandatory for PGIs

In France, PGIs are mostly used by manufacturers of processed meat products, especially in the domain of pork-based charcuterie. In the 1980s, pork production had decreased to such an extent that the production zones of charcuterie, along with local pig breeds, such as the pigs of Ardèche, were on the point of disappearing. PGIs were therefore implemented to boost rural development by slowly relocating the production of raw material. Therefore, the supply zones of raw material in France noted in the specifications were initially far removed from the processing zones, with the intention of gradually narrowing down the distance between the two. Consequently, this external delimitation was

---

[21] Regulation (CE) no. 938/2008 of 24 September 2008, JOUE 25 September 2008, L 257/10.
[22] CE, 29 March 2000, no. 205253, société Fromagerie le Centurion, société des établissements Schoeffer et société Fromagerie Fromapac, www.legifrance.gouv.fr, 'Comté'.

regarded only as a transitory phase. The idea was also to stop producers from using pigs from Northern Europe and China.

For PGIs, the link to the origin can be either based on local raw material or on local knowledge. If the link is based on local raw material then it has to be proved that this factor influences product quality or reputation, something which can be difficult to demonstrate in the case of common pig breeds which are more or less similar all over France.[23] The inability to demonstrate this link is not very problematic in France which favours rural development through such means, but has been pointed out by the European Commission. Since 2006, this tendency has been even more pronounced with the Commission playing an increasingly important role in the examination of PDO and PGI applications, especially in regard to the origin of the raw material.[24]

For example, in France, the Conseil d'Etat cancelled the Saucisse de Morteau PGI delimitation because 'not a single specific quality of the raw material or the method of production used can be attributed to the production of the good in the sole zone consisting of villages situated at minimum 600 meters of altitude'.

The European Commission similarly asked questions and sought more precise information about the zone supplying raw material for Saucisse de Morteau and decided that 'since the zones supplying pork are different from the Saucisse de Morteau production zones, a PGI registration seems unjustified.... Indeed based on the arguments of the application it is not possible to establish a link between Bresse, the source of the raw material and Saucisse de Morteau's quality or reputation'.[25] Finally, the

---

[23] Beyond the ordinary pig breeds, there are still specific breeds such as the Blanc de l'Ouest, the Gascon and the Basque.

[24] See the new art. 6.1 of Regulation No. 510/2006, which increases the powers of the commission in examining GI applications. Yet since 2006, the examination is based on the single document, which is shorter than the specification that was the basis of the examination under Regulation No. 2081/1992.

[25] INAO, Comité National des IGP, Labels rouges et STG. PGI application 'Saucisse de Morteau ou Jésus de Morteau', request for additional information from the European Commission. Answer from the ODG, File No. 2008-414, 27 November 2008. The first letter of the commission is dated 24 August 2007, the response of the applicant group is of 13 August 2008 and the response of the commission is dated 3 October 2008.

PGI Saucisse de Morteau was registered in 2010[26] without any obligation regarding the source of raw material, the pork, only justified by the localization of the processing step.

The PGI applications for Rillettes du Mans were judged in the same manner by the French Conseil d'Etat.[27]

In 2010, a new PGI application for Rillettes du Mans removed any provision regarding the source of raw material was recognized by INAO, but such PGI has been again challenged on the ground of the delimitation of the area.[28]

The Géranium d'Alsace PGI application also demonstrates how the concept of *terroir* with its natural factors has influenced the French vision of PGIs. Horticulturists wanted to preserve a traditional geranium from Alsace which flourished in the 1950s: a resistant geranium variety flowering quickly and abundantly. Planting cuttings (with or without roots) in pots and monitoring their growth until they are ready to be sold: root development, potting, treatment, pinching, thinning, staking, finishing, final sorting and conditioning is localized in Alsace. The cuttings which previously came from Alsace now come from Kenya, which is not a concern according to horticuluralists providing that plants are obtained from 'cuttings which are raw material', but to grow Alsace geraniums, the know-how of horticulturalists is essential. That is why the applicants have noted down the qualities of the cuttings which must be healthy (free of virus and bacteriosis), without lignifications and identifiable by varieties. The application was rejected on the grounds that the raw material was from Kenya and revealed the INAO PGI Committee members' attachment to the French tradition of AOC products extending to PGI applications.[29]

The PGI application Calisson d'Aix presents the same eventful history of a product based on localized traditional knowledge since, to quote Marcel Pagnol: 'Aix candy is a blend of three fourths: one third almonds, one third candied fruits, one third sugar and above all one third savoirfaire

[26] RÈGLEMENT (UE) No 751/2010 DE LA COMMISSIONdu 20 août 2010.
[27] CE 15 October 1999, no. 196318, www.legifrance.gouv.fr, 'Rillettes du Mans'.
[28] CE 16 juin 2010, no. 311504, www.legifrance.gouv.fr, 'Rillettes du Mans'.
[29] Inao, Comité National des IGP, Labels Rouges et STG, 11 février 2009, PGI application 'Géranium d'Alsace' *Demande de reconnaissance en IGP Rapport final* 2009–113, Compte rendu Comité IGP 4 juin 2009.

and pride in work well done.'[30] According to the PGI specifications, 70–80 per cent of calissons (lozenge-shaped sweets made out of ground almonds) made in Aix are produced by eight calisson makers. There are only 21 calisson makers in France altogether. The local public authorities wanted to boost almond production in the Aix region by introducing in the PGI application a large almond supplying zone which corresponded to the zone around Aix, while calisson makers used almonds coming from California. The EC objected and the producers had to abandon the idea of localizing raw material in France, which was not their idea in the first place.[31] The final specification sent to Brussels thus does not contain any elements on the origin of raw material and the link to the origin is founded entirely on the special knowledge of the calisson makers.[32]

In conclusion, the origin of raw material is still a subject of debate in the EU as it contributes to rural development and provides consumers with accurate information. During the consultation organized by the Commission's last Green Paper in 2008, the Commission remarks that

> for many PGIs (and some PDOs) of processed products, the raw materials are sourced from outside the area concerned. Some consumers may expect the raw materials to come from the area while others may expect the specialist producers inside the geographical area to choose the best quality raw material from whatever origin.[33]

To avoid any risk of confusion of consumers who might expect the raw material to come from the delimited area of the PGI, the European Parliament asked the raw material's origin to be systematically noted on the label proposal rejected. France supported this proposal 'so that consumers can have access to more concrete information on the products proposed to them it seems highly important to mention the source of the

---

[30] Draft specifications for the PGI 'Calissons Aix', Union of Manufacturers of Calissons Aix en Provence, version 4 of the 4 January 2006, p. 3, underapplication for registration then not yet been accepted at the Community level, consulted http://www.inao.gouv.fr/repository/editeur/pdf/CDC-IGP/calissons-d-aix.pdf.

[31] Interview with E. Monticelli.

[32] Ibid.

[33] Green Paper on Agricultural Product Quality (Brussels, European Commission, 2008), p. 15.

raw material covered by GIs'. France has interpreted the PGI concept in its own manner, as influenced by its experience with AOC as if France had not understood the concept of PGIs or does not wish to do so. In effect, if the submitted application presents a localization of raw material based outside the zone of production but without influence on the final product, it will be rejected by Brussels, but alternatively, if there is no localization of such materials, as seen in the Géranium d'Alsace case, the application will not be accepted by INAO. AOC which historically arose out of the necessity to protect the link to the origin was especially adapted to wines, but cannot be the only vision of the link to the origin for products which are expressions of ancient, local knowledge. This interpretation does not seem to be shared by other European countries.[34] Yet France has just started in 2013 a legislative process to open PGI to non-agricultural products where natural factors are not mandatory, a real change of paradigm.

Interpreting the European Commission decisions on French PGI application, it can be deduced that PGIs registered solely for human factors are valid on the condition that human factors are localized in a particular zone of origin and confer a quality, characteristic or reputation to a product.

## Indian GIs' Link to the Origin Based on Local Knowledge: A Wake-up Call for PGI?

*French GIs Based Solely on Human Factors?*
The beginning of the history of origin appellations in France shows that prior to the Law of 1905, names of places were protected by the law of 28 July 1824 on misuse of names for manufactured products. Only 'manufactured' products were protected by this law, which did not

---

[34] The report of the National Council of Food calls for 'a review of procedures for recognition of PGI, to address differences of interpretation that may exist between France and the European Union, for example about the origin of raw material when the PGI is a processed product'. National Council of Food Recommendation No. 61 on the implementation of the reform of the identification of quality and origin signs for agricultural products and food, 12 June 2008, p. 32.

extend to natural products.[35] Therefore, a major issue at that time was to create a framework which took into account and protected names of places of natural products.

Yet the 1919 law applies to all kinds of products and some appellations of origin for handicraft were recognized by the courts, as for example the Dentelle du Puy appellation which was affirmed through a judgement of the Court of Le Puy on 19 February 1931, the Emaux de Limoges appellation (through a judgement of the Court of Appeals of Limoges on 18 February 1946), the Poterie de Vallauris appellation (through a judgement of the Court of Cassation on 18 November 1930) and the Cholet appellation (through a judgement of ruling of the Angers Court of Appeals on 17 November 1936).[36] That case confirmed the Court of Cholet's 8 January 1936 verdict,[37] according to which textile industries' employers' union of Cholet was given the right to use the appellation of origin Cholet. The Court of Cholet noted that the reputation of Cholet's sheets and textiles was due to the bleaching techniques used, an indispensable step in cloth and fabric manufacturing and which consist of stretching the textiles out on green, wet and clayey meadows. They are bleached with water pumped directly from the ground, qualified as exceptional and of best quality for bleaching, not available anywhere else in the region. Their special weight and strength depend also on natural elements of the soil and specific climate conditions of the area.[38]

*Dentelle du Puy*

The 1919 law which recognized this appellation is still effective because the same Angers Court of Appeal decided in 1992 that the trademark 'Création Maret Cholet France' used to designate woven textile is a misleading trademark since it could be confused with the Cholet

---

[35] Plaisant and Fernand-Jacq, *Traité Des Noms Et Appellations D'origine*, 18.

[36] C.A. Angers, 17 November 1936, Etablissements Béra c./ Syndicat patronal des industries textiles de la région de Cholet, archives départementales, Conseil général, Département Maine et Loire, côte 2U 1/538.

[37] Tribunal de Commerce de Cholet, 8 janv. 1936, Etablissements Béra c./ Syndicat patronal des industries textiles de la région de Cholet, archives départementales, Conseil général, Département Maine et Loire, côte 143a63.

[38] *La Blanchisserie De La Rivière Sauvagean Et Le Blanchiment Des Toiles À Cholet* (Cahors: Association des Amis du Musée du Textile Choleralis, REMPART, 1992).

appellation of origin, if the methods of manufacturing do not meet the appellation criteria.[39] In all these examples of appellation of origin in the domain of handicraft, the link to the origin is established via a combination of natural factors and specialized knowledge or only via human factors as the Dentelle du Puy.

Yet, since 1966, the definition of appellations of origin provides for the mandatory combination of human factors and natural factors, following the definition of the Lisbon Agreement. Therefore, even if the scope of the Lisbon Agreement extends beyond agricultural and agro-food products, the link to the origin for registered appellations such as Marbre Lepenica for natural products or Emaux de Limoges and Trojanska Keramika for processed products is based on a combination of natural and human factors.

In 1991, the AOC Faïence de Moustiers producers' association, which unites the earthenware producers of Moustiers, drafted an AOC application regarding the revival of earthenware production in Moustier. Yet Moustiers earthenware did not meet the criteria of appellation of origin specified in the 6 May 1919 Law, since the raw material (fuller's earth, enamel, etc.) no longer comes from Moustiers, as it used to in the 18th century. It was advised to register a collective trademark 'Faïence de Moustiers' with a distinctive logo[40] instead. For the same reasons, Porcelaine de Limoges and Porcelaine de Nevers appellations of origin applications were rejected. Hence, it remains the category of PGIs to consider if the link to the origin can be established solely on the basis of human factors: the savoir faire.

There are a few rare examples in France of products which have benefited from the protection conferred by PGIs which are linked to their origin solely on the basis of skills and knowledge practices. One can quote the PGI Bergamote de Nancy (for sweets made in the traditional manner with sugar, glucose syrup and natural bergamot essence), for an example. Bergamot essence started being used in Lorraine gastronomy since the 18th century. The link to the geographical origin lies in the reputation of this candy which principally developed at the regional

---

[39] C.A. Angers, Chambre 1B, 17 fév. 1992.
[40] See PIBD regarding "faïences de Moustiers", 1992, n° 509.I.85, Réponse ministérielle n° 15479 du 6 juin 1991 et JO Sénat débats du 26 septembre 1991, p. 2088, Frédéric *Pollaud-Dulian, Droit De La Propriété* Industrielle (Paris: Montchrestien, 1999). 734.

level'.[41] However, it is difficult to assess the validity of this PGI registered at the European level under Article 17 of the no. 2081/92 (CE) regulation which provided for the automatic acceptance of GI lists presented by the countries of the EU without any scrutiny by the Commission.

The PGI Pâtes d'Alsace represents another example which is rather more controversial due to a mechanization of the processing, something that is not compensated for by local sourcing of the raw material. Even if the specification explains that 'since ancient times, "pâte d'Alsace"[42] has been produced from flour and eggs ... with recipes and knowledge being handed down from mother to daughter', according to N. Olszak, only two producers are concerned by the PGI on factory-made pasta with raw materials from outside of Alsace. The PGI application was justified largely by an imitation from a small Italian producer of pasta. However, according to N. Olszak, a certification mark indicating the production process would have sufficed.

Finally, an example of the United Kingdom is given by the PGI Melton Mowbray pork pie whose manufacture dates from the ancient tradition of hunting in the region. This pie is made from pork from any source without any other natural factors occurring during manufacture. The pie has an accurate shape characteristic. The dough is golden brown with a rich texture. The filling is raw, so grey (the colour of roast pork), wet. The meat content of the whole product must be at least 30 per cent. In terms of flavour, the dough has a rich taste and cooked, while the meat and stuffing is peppermint. Pies must be free of artificial colours, flavours and preservatives.[43] The source link is here, justified by the mere existence of ancient know-how of producers.

*The Validity of Links to the Origin Solely through Savoir Faire*

The French approach towards appellation of origin and *terroir*, that impregnates the entire concept of PGI, can be explained by the nature of the product it was meant to designate, first wine and then foodstuffs.

---

[41] Regulation (EC) No. 1107/96 amended, 12 June 1996 on the registration of geographical indications and designations of origin under the procedure laid down in art. 17 of Regulation (EEC) No. 2081/92. PGI based on the specifications LA/19/90 Red Label.
[42] Book of requirement, 2 July 2003, www.europa.eu.
[43] See PGI specification, *Official Journal of the European Union* C 85/17, 4.4. 2008.

This is why this IP right is still strongly connected to agricultural policies, managed by the Directorate General for Agriculture of the EU. But neither the Lisbon Agreement nor the TRIPS Agreement limit their respective definitions for AO and GI to certain categories of goods. The issue of the origin of raw materials could pose greater problems for foodstuffs, as Bayonne ham is expected to be made from pigs from the region, whereas Kancheepuram sari is expected to be made of genuine silk and gold, but not necessarily local silk.

It is possible that we are witnessing a change in French traditions in the wake of a widening of the scope of French and European regulations on non-agricultural products. This opening is encouraged by France, as shown in response to the European Commission's Green Paper.[44] This extension is not only a legal constraint under the TRIPS Agreement but also a cultural issue as ancient localized knowledge of handicraft needs to be protected in India, and in Europe! In that sense the new French Law on Consumption of 17 March 2014 creates the GI for non-agricultural goods, defined in the same way as the PGI for agricultural goods, but to be registered at the French National Institute of Industrial Property.

The Indian experience inspires a new vision of the origin of products historically rooted in a territory without natural factors, a new vision that would also apply to foodstuffs. Indeed, practices show that the link with the geographical origin for both handicrafts and agricultural products can be assessed according to identical criteria: natural factors and human factors, whether individually or combined. There is a need therefore to remove the principle of categorization of products.

Then the questions are: Is a link to the place of origin through know-how alone, whatever the product is, legally valid with respect to the definition of GI? Can know-how be rooted in an area, and can it confer a quality or reputation linked to the origin to the product?

The link that TK and savoir faire has to its origin can certainly be justified historically, by considering the method as being developed in a specific area. In contrast, the link is fragile without other connections, as nothing is more easily passed on than a method. Not to mention the migration of artisan communities also suggests how feebly a group can be connected to a given area.[45] The GI Act provides for transferring the rights of use to

---

[44] Response of France, 6 January 2009.
[45] See GIs 'Orissa pattachitra', 'Nirmal paintings', 'Kota doria'.

descendants of authorized users in the event of death of the latter,[46] without specifying if the conditions that must be met in order to become an authorized user should be fulfilled by the descendants, for example, being located in the area and complying with the specifications. This fact becomes less problematic when it is considered that in India, succeeding generations continue in the same occupation and continue to live and work in the same area as their predecessors. Alternately, we can consider that the idea of transferring such rights to descendants is an incursion from other IPRs, and not desirable for GIs that confers a collective right to use a geographical name to producers who comply with the specifications, and is therefore not based on the principle of transmission of personal rights.

Beyond this provision of the GI Act, the question arises whether GI can be based only on human factors and does not grant a monopoly that excludes legitimate producers such as artisans who have migrated. In the event that artisans migrate outside the area of origin, would a reservation of the name only to goods produced in the demarcated area be a restriction?

First, artisans using their know-how to create products are influenced by their surrounding that includes natural factors and human interactions. A mapping of GIs demonstrates that climate influences the type of production, with light cotton saris being produced in south India, while shawls come from the mountainous regions of the Himalayas and Géranium need to be grown according to specific methods in Alsace. The natural environment is directly responsible for the development of the knowledge, a factor that can thus be considered specific to a place.

Second, French anthropologists L. Bérard and P. Marchenay consider that: 'the origin refers to a place having a certain meaning, to history, to shared know-how. Whereas the source indicates that a product comes from here rather than from elsewhere, without there being a specific cultural root'.[47]

Those two criteria of historical depth and shared knowledge seem relevant as a community located for a long time, and sharing the same techniques seems more linked to a territory than isolated producers.

---

[46] Section 24 of the Act.
[47] Laurence Bérard and Philippe Marchenay, 'Produits De Terroir Et Enjeux Européens: Une Approche Anthropologique,' in *Les Produits Agroalimentaires Régionaux: Approches Théoriques Et Résultats D'études*, ed. Lucie Sirieix, Fatiha Fort and Hervé Remaud (Montpellier: Cahiers de Recherche MOISA no. 1, 2001), 22–23.

The collective nature of knowledge ensures its continued existence in a certain place.

The two criteria of historical depth and shared TK put forward by anthropologists are undeniably fulfilled in India; the knowledge involved is very ancient and is practised by specific communities that pass them on from generation to generation. The rules of the Chanderi Foundation, owner of the GI Chanderi sari, stipulate that individual members who want to use the GI must have resided in Chanderi for at least 15 years. In France too, proof of human factors is throughout history (anteriority of savoir faire),[48] as for example in the section 'Proof of origin' in the PGI Brioche Vendéenne.[49]

The condition of sophistication could be added to the specialized knowledge of production to impart real uniqueness to the product and compensate for the absence of natural factors. Besides, the link to the origin of products characterized by specific designs and resulting in the creation of savoir faire seems rather fragile, due to the risk of changing fashion.[50] If the knowledge involved is not sophisticated and the uniqueness implicated is solely in the creation of renewed patterns, the GI is not a suitable category but that of designs and models.

In addition to the criterion of sophistication for the TK used, the delimitation of the production area should be determined in a more defined manner, based on a mapping of practices. As in France, the delimitation of the geographical area of production is probably the most challenging task during the process of recognizing an appellation of origin or a PGI. Thus, in France, although the delimitation of the production area of an appellation of origin is linked to a *terroir*, it does not necessarily follow from natural contours. Natural contours do not always match the geographical area of production. Usage and practices, by their adaptability, allow a precise delineation.[51] In India, the demarcation of non-agricultural products should certainly be implemented based on the homogeneity of practices and local knowledge, and not according to administrative boundaries.

---

[48] Bérard and Marchenay, *Les Produits De Terroir, Entre Cultures Et Règlements*, 74.
[49] Publication of an application according to art. 6, paragraphe 2, of the regulation (CEE) n°2081/92, C-187/02, JOUE 7 August 2003.
[50] Statement of A. Mohamed Jamaluddin regarding Kancheepuram silk GI.
[51] Visse-Causse, *L'appellation D'origine: Valorisation Du Terroir*, 117.

Removing the categorization of products criteria means that PGIs in France and Europe for agro-food products could also be essentially based on human factors with the same criteria of sophistication of ancient and shared knowledge, since PGIs, as we have seen earlier, are suitable instruments for designating products made with local savoir faire even without natural factors.

It also means that PGIs and PDOs shall be opened to any kind of goods. In France, following the misappropriation of the name of the city Laguiole, famous for its knives, the French authorities wish to extend GIs to cover processed products originating in a specific territory.[52] A French bill on consumers' rights has been presented on 2 May 2013 providing for the creation of PGIs for non-agricultural products,[53] and entrusting the National Institute of Industrial Property with their registration. But this bill maintains a product-based approach, as non-agricultural goods can only apply for a PGI and not for a PDO, even in the presence of natural factors. In Europe, separate regulations are still maintained for wines/spirits and agricultural goods/foodstuff despite the fact that new regulations are passed with the last one in 2012. The EU report on GIs for non-agricultural goods recommends a third legal instrument for handicraft goods, which would place the registration of GIs under the authority of the Office for the Harmonization in the Internal Market (OHIM) in charge of EC trademarks. This resilience of product categorization might prevent a necessary dissemination of the GI concept towards producers and consumers. A change of paradigm is therefore urgently required, as is the implementation of a global system for protecting the link to the geographical origin, based on the concepts of natural *and/or* human factors, replacing an approach based merely on product categorization.[54]

---

[52] Answer from France to question No. 5 to the European Commission's Green Paper regarding the scope of application of Regulation (EC) No. 510/2006, p. 3, 6 January 2009.

[53] A new article would be added to the Consumer Code: Art. L.115-1-1. 'Constitutes a geographical indication, the name of a region or a specific place used to describe a product, other than agriculture, forestry, food or the sea products, which is native and has a specific quality, reputation or other features that can be attributed to its geographical origin and whose production or processing, preparation, manufacture or assembly takes place in the defined geographical area.'

[54] Marie-Vivien, D. 'The Protection of Geographical Indications for Handicrafts: Or How to Apply the Concepts of Natural and Human Factors to All Products'. *The WIPO Journal*, 4(2) (2013): 191–203.

On the other hand, two levels of geographical reference continue to make sense if they are distinguished according to the strength of the link with the origin. Hence, the proposal to extend the principle of two geographical reference signs, such as PDOs and PGIs, by distinguishing them according to the criteria of human factors and natural factors: the equivalent of the PDO would be granted when natural and human factors are combined; and the equivalent of the PGI when only human factors are involved.

The actual revitalization of the Lisbon Agreement,[55] which for the first time introduced these criteria of human and natural factors to define appellation of origin, could consider the argument of employing the same criteria in an alternative manner for GIs whose definition is proposed to be introduced in an amended version of the Agreement.[56]

At WTO level, the distinction provided by the TRIPS Agreement between wines and spirit and other goods[57] should clearly be abandoned and replaced by a distinction based on the strength of the link. Such a distinction for wines and spirits reflects a history that has been largely modified with the implementation of GI laws in non-wine-producing countries and is no longer justified—a fact that should accelerate the current WTO negotiations on the extension of additional protection to all products.[58]

Ultimately, the question is whether it makes sense to maintain two legal categories if they are not associated with two distinct levels of

---

[55] Ibid. and Gervais, D. (2009a) The Lisbon Agreement's Misunderstood Potential. Ibid., 87–102.

[56] Draft revised Lisbon Agreement on Appellations of Origin and Geographical Indications LI/WG/DEV/7/2, 22 March 2013.

[57] Addor, F. and A. Grazzioli. 'Geographical Indications beyond Wines and Spirits, a Roadmap for a Better Protection for Geographical Indications in WTO/TRIPS Agreement', *The Journal of World Intellectual Property*, 5 (2002): 865–897.

[58] Evans, G.E. and M. Blakeney. 'The Protection of Geographical Indications after Doha: Quo Vadis? *Journal of International Economic Law*, 9 (2006): 575–614. Kongolo, T. 'Any New Developments with Regard to GIs Issues Debated under WTO? *E.I.P.R.*, 33 (2011): 83–90. Thevenod-Mottet, E. 'Avenir des indications géographiques dans le contexte international', *Revue suisse Agric.*, 41 (2009): 331–335.

protection, which is not currently the case in the European Union. Logic would suggest granting a different scope of protection, as it is proposed in the draft revised Lisbon Agreement.[59]

## Issues Not Yet Answered

GIs were introduced in India at the time the issue of protecting the TK and savoir faire of local communities was being deliberated, particularly in the countries of the South. The fact that GIs were seen as an ideal instrument to protect knowledge and know-how is open to discussion.

### Are GIs the Ideal Instrument to Protect Traditional Knowledge and Savoir Faire?

Since GIs take into account the shared knowledge of producer communities, settled for a long time in a specific place, knowledge not transferable, available to all producers who meet the specifications, and can be retained indefinitely, the idea that GIs, among all IPRs, are the most suited to protect TK was introduced. Indeed, the debate on the protection of TK is animated in the South and is the subject of discussions directed towards adopting a new ad hoc instrument in WIPO, in the Intergovernmental Committee on Intellectual Property and Genetic Resources, Traditional Knowledge and Folklore.

N.S. Gopalakrishnan[60] who focused on case studies from Asia to study the relationship between GIs and TK concludes that TK will only be protected if it remains secret, as is the case for the GI Aranmula metal mirror. However, TK is protected more by virtue of its non-disclosure than the registration of a name as a GI. The study cites the contrary case

---

[59] Ibid. note 104.
[60] Gopalakrishnan, Nair and Babu, *Exploring the Relationship between Geographical Indications and Traditional Knowledge: An Analysis of the Legal Tools for the Protection of Geographical Indications in Asia*. 1–65; Anselm Kamperman Sanders, 'Incentives for and Protection of Cultural Expression: Art, Trade and Geographical Indications', *The Journal of World Intellectual Property*, 13, no. 2 (2010): 81–93; and Raguvaran Gopalan and Sindhu Sivakumar, 'Keeping Cashmere in Kashmir—The Interface between GI and TK', *Journal of Intellectual Property Rights* 12, no. November (2007): 581–588.

of the GI Pochampally Ikat where the traditional technique of tie-dye is not protected as it is open to everyone in the local industry and known to many.

Are GIs then suitable to protect TK? First, GIs only protect the name and never the knowledge itself. If in order to protect the relevant knowledge and skills they must be kept secret, then it is hard to imagine how the condition of shared knowledge accessible to all producers in the area can be fulfilled. In fact, in order to obtain a GI, a description of the production method must be submitted that justifies, on the one hand, the link to the origin and, on the other hand, the collective nature of the GI.

The name attached to a product obtained, thanks to TK and savoir faire, can be protected by registering it as a GI. In this sense, the law on GIs is a crucial support to maintain, and even develop TK localized in an area. Nevertheless, and this may be even more alarming for products whose uniqueness is due to their design, the techniques and skills described in the GI are not protected against misuse by others as long as they do not use the name itself.

Thus, the law of GIs cannot replace a legal instrument that protects TK as such, which can conduct to the situation where a traditional product can be the subject of several intellectual property laws, for example, the protection of new designs by the law on designs and models, protection of a known geographical name by law on GIs and protection of TK with a suitable law that is yet to be formulated.

## The Designation of Services by GIs?

Some Indian stakeholders wish to protect GIs for services such as Ayurveda and yoga. The TRIPS Agreement is limited to products or goods while excluding services, despite the fact that the Swiss proposal, which was not considered in the Brussels document, included services.[61] D. Rochard is unhappy that services have not been included as was originally planned in the WIPO Treaty.[62] EU Community and Indian rules do not provide any further protection for GIs for services.

---

[61] Sachin Chaturvedi, 'India, the European Union and Geographical Indications (GI): Convergence of Interests and Challenges Ahead' (2002), 7–42.
[62] Rochard, *La Protection Internationale Des Indications Géographiques*, 120.

It is nonetheless useful to see how far GIs can be applied to services: to what end, for what type of service and with what link to the origin? If the GI concept is applied to services, it would mean that the service has a given quality, characteristic or reputation when the service is offered in a certain place to a person who is also in the same place. It seems simple to demonstrate this for a type of service offered in a distinct area, but it is hard to find an example in this age of globalization. It remains to be seen if non-endemic services can be 'typical' of a region.

Take the example of Ayurvedic treatment characterized by a holistic relationship between the doctor and the patient. The knowledge involved and the provision of the treatment include both the diagnosis and treatment. A GI on Ayurvedic treatment would suggest that such practices carried out in a given location would imply a quality or characteristic, or that a reputation is associated with a practice carried out in this place. This would result in preventing the use of the name 'Ayurveda' for the same practice carried out elsewhere. The parallel drawn with GIs of products whose link to the origin is only based on localized knowledge and practices is striking. However, the terms *Ayurveda* and *yoga* are not geographical names. In fact, they refer to practices that are used widely outside India. Ayurveda is widespread in the United States and is being applied on Western patients, a fact that has encouraged new interpretations for it.[63] It is therefore unclear, under the circumstances, how a claim on practices located only in India could be justified. We must therefore think about a hypothesis of the names 'Ayurveda' and 'yoga' as being associated with a localizing term.

Ayurveda was developed in the Himalayas using Himalayan herbs in Vedic times. It gradually spread across India. British colonization led to a decline in the practice of Ayurveda throughout India except in the state of Kerala.[64] It was at this time that a special treatment called 'Panchakarma' was established in Kerala, largely to meet the needs of Kathakali dancers, associated with a traditional theatre form. This treatment was mostly carried out during the monsoon when the body is actively recreating its cells. In this particular case, there is a combination of natural factors, such as climate, and human factors, which seems to justify the GI Kerala Ayurveda.

---

[63] Jean Langford, *Fluent Bodies: Ayurvedic Remedies for Postcolonial Imbalance* (Durham: Duke University Press, 2002), 1–312.
[64] Interview with Matt India Ayurvedic Hospital, Kerala, 10 April 2007.

Yoga has similar connection to natural factors. Bikram Choudhury developed a practice he called 'hot yoga' in the United States which attempted to recreate the climate of Kolkata deemed necessary to practice yoga. Hot yoga consists of 26 yoga postures (*asanas*) and two breathing exercises (*pranayama*) that are done over 90 minutes at an ambient temperature of 40°C. The creator of this technique registered a copyright in the United States for this method which was published in the book titled *Bikram's Beginning Yoga Class*. He asserts that the sequence of postures is protected under copyright due to its similarity with dance. Several trademarks, including 'Bikram Yoga', were registered in the United States.[65] Claiming to be protected under IPRs, Bikram launched a relentless attack against counterfeiting, and sent threatening letters to those using the Bikram Yoga 'style' without his consent. He even sued one of his former students, Kim Schreiber-Morrison, a conflict that was finally resolved amicably. A number of yoga enthusiasts and professionals got together to form an NGO called Open Source Yoga Unity (OSYU) to counter Bikram Choudhury's threats. In July 2003, OSYU brought an action against Bikram asking him not to threaten followers of yoga with infringement actions. The dispute was settled in May 2005 with a mutual agreement.

What are the advantages of protection under the GI law? GIs like Kerala Ayurveda or Indian yoga would find it useful to bar the use of such names elsewhere, which could contradict stated aims, namely, to ensure that a category of practices has originated in India. In fact, apart from the particular point of climate having an influence on treatment, we may well wonder whether Ayurveda depends more on the place it is practised in, or on the place of learning. The worth of the practice would then be linked more to the place where the therapeutic training was got than to the place where it is provided to consumers. Ayurveda and yoga would then correspond to a set of rules that can vary according to the schools. Indian yoga would correspond to a type of practice taught and practised in India, but without any exclusive link with the origin, in the sense of the GI. A certification mark therefore seems more appropriate.

[65] 2 March 2002, No. 76,378,915.

# 4
# Indian GIs for Agricultural Goods? Uniqueness Justified by Natural and Historical Factors

One-third of Indian GIs are registered in the domain of agriculture (see Figure 4.1), for cereals, horticultural products and spices for the local market or for export markets. For many of these products, the link with the origin is based on a combination of natural and human factors, just like the French appellation of origin and *terroir* concept.

However, as in the case of GIs in the handicrafts domain, history becomes the glue linking the product to its origin. This historical data which constitute the 'proof of origin' are as primordial for agricultural goods as for handicraft goods. For example, according to the GI application Alleppey green cardamom, cardamom crops have existed in south India since the 4th century BC. Its history is described in length and embellished with many details. Similarly, the cultivation of jasmine is a very old practice in India, dating back to 4th century. This predominance of history will lead to registering GIs which are also names of traditional plant varieties, conducting to confusion. Finally, history is conflicting with present time's production reality as illustrated by the case of Basmati, 'modernized'.

**Figure 4.1**
*Agricultural GIs: 60 registered GIs for Indian products, March 2015*

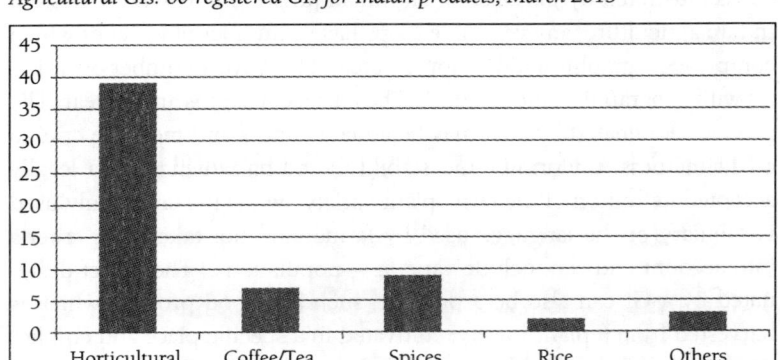

## Reputation of GIs Based on Plant Varieties

### The Relationship between GIs and Plant Varieties

In India, GIs are regarded as a legal tool to protect an ancient heritage which may be threatened by innovations and the introduction of evolved varieties. Thus, a large number of GIs in the domain of agriculture are for local, traditional varieties. Following the Basmati case, all the authorities concerned with the protection of genetic resources received a letter from the Ministry of Commerce asking them to identify and protect all traditional plant varieties, so that they are not pirated. Was there a misunderstanding regarding the aim of the GI Act, which does not protect genetic heritage per se? The difference of finality between the protection of plant varieties which confers a temporal exclusivity on new seeds and the sine die protection of the name, as a GI is clearly demonstrated by S. Nagarajan, the former president of the Indian office for the protection of plant varieties.[1] However, it is unclear that GI applicants are aware that the protection conferred by a GI covers only the name and not the genetic resources, which can be used by a third party if it is identified by

---

[1] S. Nagarajan, 'Geographical Indications and Agriculture-Related Intellectual Property Rights Issues', *Current Science* 92, no. 2 (2007): 170.

another name. The confusion between the concept of plant varieties and GIs is illustrated by J.P. Mishra, an Indian jurist on IPRs who writes: 'In Indian agriculture, any vegetable crops have a number of varieties which comprise geographical indications. Cereals also have a number of varieties with geographical indications'.[2] The GI specifications are unclear. The product designated by a GI may be a plant variety and meet the criteria of distinctness, uniformity and stability,[3] criteria which gives a legally accepted definition of the term 'plant variety', while the commonly used vocabulary or the language used by farmers do not take these criteria into account and can include varieties—populations.[4] The object designated by a GI can also be a product, such as a food product which is harvested from a plant variety, cultivated in a specific place and edible.

In Indian GIs, when the names of plant varieties include a geographical name, eponymous to the geographical name embedded in the GI, those plant varieties can be qualified as local plant varieties, guaranteeing a strong link with the geographic origin. But what is a local variety? According to P. Marchenay, the varieties, including local ones which have travelled widely: 'most of the varieties have become local because they have been adopted at some time, in a zone where they suited the climatic conditions, the soil, the cultural techniques and above all local needs'. It is not rare to come across varieties which are foreign to a region or even to a country, which have been 'assimilated' locally. They have left traces of their culture, due to their role in the collective memory and ability to bear witness to the role they played in the regional economy. This tends to prove that the local or traditional status depends less on the origin of a cultivar than the importance it has acquired in a region through the years.[5]

---

[2] Jai Prakash Mishra, 'Intellectual Property Rights and Food Security', *The Journal of World Intellectual Property* 4, no. 1 (2001): 8.

[3] DHS criteria are imperative for the registration of varieties on the Official Catalogue of Varieties. For more details, see the website of the national intergroup seeds and plants: www.gnis.fr.

[4] Variety population for pollinated plants means a variety consisting of a broad-based population and resulting in a generally unsophisticated selection from ecotypes, source INRA: http://www.inra.fr/internet/Directions/DIC/ACTUALITES/SIA1999/FiSIA62a63glossaire.pdf.

[5] Philippe Marchenay and Marie-France Lagarde, *A La Recherche Des Variétés Locales De Plantes Cultivées* (Paris: BRG et Page PACA, 1987), p. 41.

The habit of naming a variety after its geographical origin is not exclusive to India and can be accounted for in Europe as well, according to F. Roncin, as evidenced by the long debates held between botanists at the end of the 17th century, before the acceptance of genetic theory. The upholders of 'transformism' and 'acclimatation' of the plant to its milieu have long prevailed over upholders of the existence of a 'vital specificity' as an integral part of the plant, independent of its milieu.⁶ The Comte d'Odart describes his experiences in his book published in 1845. He cultivated plants from Champagne in different regions and demonstrated that all these plants brought together in identical conditions immediately regained the same characteristics. Thus, the concept of grape variety came into being. The experiment having convinced him, in 1843 he established the idea that grape varieties should not be designated by the name of the region where they were identified.⁷ This measure, however, was not adopted in other fields where the conflict between the name of the variety and the appellation constituting the GI continues to exist.

## Indigenous Plant Varieties versus Widespread Plant Varieties

The recourse to ancient local varieties proves that there is a strong link between the product and its origin which justifies the registration of a GI, but the risk of confusion caused by the homonymy between the variety name and the GI name has yet to be solved.

In numerous GI registrations, the specification does not include the precise name of the plant variety, which makes it difficult to ascertain whether the appellation designates a plant variety or a food product. Even when the word *variety* is used, it is not always easy to know in which sense it is used. Does it refer to seeds/plants or to the food product?

What happens when a variety spreads beyond its region of origin and the geographical name of its cradle of origin is used even though it

---

⁶ J. Magnin-Gonze, *Histoire de la botanique* (Paris: Ed Delachaux et Niestlé, 2004), pp. 133–186, cité dans François Roncin and François Boulineau, 'Valorisation Des "Légumes De Terroir" Par Les Signes Officiels D'identification De La Qualité Et De L'origine (Aop-Igp), Comment Est-Ce Réalisable?' (Angers 7–9 September 2005), 4.
⁷ Ibid., 4.

is grown elsewhere? According to this hypothesis, reserving the name of the variety for the sole benefit of producers of the region of origin can be detrimental for producers of other zones. Moreover, the public can be confused when the same geographical name is used for a variety cultivated in different zones.

The Indian GI Act does not authorize the registration of GIs which can confuse the public.[8] The Indian law on the protection of plant varieties, the PPVFRA, stipulates that a new variety shall not be registered if the denomination given to such variety comprises solely or partly of geographical name, provided that the registrar may register a variety, the denomination of which comprises solely or partly of a geographical name, except if the use of such a denomination is an honest use under the circumstances of the case.[9] However, this article deals only with new plant varieties, and does not seem to apply to extant varieties. For other varieties, that is, those which are not new, the provisions of the GI law come into effect and the GI can be identical to the name of the variety, if it is not confusing. There is possibly no risk for confusion when the variety is not cultivated outside the geographical area whose name designates the variety, that is, when it is a local endemic variety. If the variety has spread elsewhere, carrying with it its original name, the product obtained from its cultivation in its place of origin can certainly have a quality, characteristics or a reputation which merit a GI, while a conflict would remain due to the fact that the variety which has travelled beyond its region of origin cannot use the name protected as a GI anymore. There remains the intermediary situation of local varieties which are not explicitly endemic.

*Explicitly Endemic Local Varieties*

Certain agricultural and horticultural products are clearly described in the GI specifications as a product obtained from the cultivation of a variety endemic to the region. A GI having the same name as the local variety which is cultivated exclusively in its region of origin seems to be in conformity with the GI law since the risk of confusion between the name and the variety is ruled out.

---

[8] Section 9: Prohibition of registration of certain geographical indications. A geographical indication (a) the use of which would be likely to deceive or cause confusion; shall not be registered as a geographical indication.

[9] Section 15.4.

A particularly interesting example is that of Navara rice, which designates rice resulting from the cross-breeding of two indigenous varieties of Kerala in south India, called Navara, the 'black colour glum' and the 'golden colour glum'. Both of them are violet in colour. This rice is also known by the name 'Shashtika rice', which means 'red rice cultivated in 60 days' in Sanskrit. 'Navara' is the translation of 'Shashtika' in Malayalam, the language spoken in Kerala.[10] 'Navara' is not a geographical name but instead corresponds to the name of a rice variety, named after its cultivation cycle. Historical sources from 2500 BC testify to the medicinal properties of this rice for Ayurvedic medicine, which is widely practised in Kerala.[11] This rice is used in mixtures for Ayurvedic message and especially for specific treatments such as the Panchakarma, or for diets during the monsoon for treating problems of blood circulation, digestion and rheumatism, and finally, the rice is also used in religious ceremonies. The producers of Navara rice call it 'Golden rice with fragrance' in keeping with the high price at which it is sold or 'the grain of Kerala', as a symbol of cereals of this region of south India.

This rice is slowly becoming extinct being difficult to cultivate with low yield.[12] It should be cultivated under irrigation because it is delicate and cannot withstand the rains. Certain traders propose 'false' Navara rice, which is rice grown in the same geographical zone but from other varieties.

The cultivation process described in the GI application is exclusively organic since it is used for medicinal purposes. This implies a certain type of specialized knowledge and a specific manner of proceeding. Less water is required, organic fertilizers are used and tree species which repel pathogenic plants are planted. It also demands intensive manual care to ward off rats and other predators. However, until recently Navara rice was not produced using organic methodsexcept at only one farm

---

[10] George Thomas, Sreejayan and Dinesh Raj, 2nd International Rice Congress, New Delhi, 9–13 October 2006.
[11] *Sushruta Samhita*, Sushrutacharya, 2500 BC.
[12] See http://njavara.org, consulted 15 April 2008; and 'Njavara facing extinction', *The Hindu* dated, Monday, 7 June 2004 by G. Prabhakaran.

'Navara Eco Farm', belonging to P. Narayanan Unny,[13] who first applied for the GI.[14]

The GI application mentions that Navara rice is originally from Kerala and has not spread elsewhere. One can thus suppose that it is endemic Kerala rice. The production zone mentioned in the application is quite large, covering nine districts, but it appears that the zone where the rice is currently cultivated is smaller, spread over only Malappuram, Palakkad and Calicut districts.

P. Narayanan Unny's project is to protect Navara rice under the Plant Variety Act, which demonstrates by itself the ambivalence of a GI bearing the same name as the variety name, but he was deviated from it by government bodies who advised him to apply for a GI. As it is not a new variety, this will probably be possible only under the category 'extant varieties', which allows it to be designated with geographical names. Because these applicants are similar, there should not be any conflicts between GI users and those of the variety. The double protection would make it necessary to differentiate between the plant variety and the product obtained from the plant variety cultivated in the zone defined by the GI. This could seem a trifle sophisticated given the current state of knowledge.

Another example is that of jasmine, one of the most ancient flowers grown in the gardens of India, strung into garlands for marriages and festivities.

There are many GIs for jasmines, such as Mysore jasmine, Udupi jasmine and Hadagali jasmine from Karnataka and Madurai jasmine from the state of Tamil Nadu, which are constituted by the name of the product, the jasmine (or *malli* in vernacular language), and the geographical

---

[13] Farmer very active in promoting organic farming and preservation of old varieties. Its action is described in several Indian journals: Innovate, value add and succeed, Handbook for farm entrepreneurs, Harvesting money, the Indus entrepreneurs, Kerala.

[14] View website www.navara.in of the Navara Eco Farm, which initiated the GI application, interview with P. Narayanan Unny, Navara Eco Farm. The farm is certified organic INDOCERT, a certification body of India. This certification is in accordance with the National Programme for Organic Production (NPOP) and complies with community rules on organic farming EEC 2092/91 et 1788/2001.

name of the region. It also serves to designate the eponymous varieties cultivated in each region. The three jasmines of Karnataka have been chosen for GIs from among eight varieties of jasmines cultivated in the state of Karnataka in south India. The specifications contain the description of the specific traits of each flower in terms of their phenotypical characteristics and perfume. The Mysore jasmine has the headiest perfume. The pedoclimatic conditions and the cultivation methods are also indicated for each flower. The soil in Mysore is sandy loam with comparatively high pH and the climate is hot and dry, whereas Udupi has laterite soil conditions, heavy rainfall from south-west monsoon and warm, humid weather with high humidity. In Hadagali, which means 'flower' in Kannada, the language spoken in Karnataka, the soil is sandy and red and the climate is hot and dry. Thus, a good irrigation system is required to cultivate the plants. The three GI applications indicate that the uniqueness of the products lies in the combination of natural factors and the chosen plant variety. According to an expert,[15] the designation registered as GIs are names of plant varieties and also the names of horticultural products obtained from harvesting. Thus according to the same expert, even when the name Mysore jasmine corresponds to a variety, as suggested by the phrase 'Mysore jasmine is an important variety of jasmine', the horticultural product is different depending on the place of cultivation of the variety. The difference lies especially in the scent of the flower. We have thus a *terroir* effect, which is a strong link between the qualities of the flower and the geographical environment. The specification of the Mysore jasmine GI claims that the variety is only cultivated in the region of Mysore, which confers upon it a local, endemic variety status. Consequently, the homonymy between the name of the variety and the product does not lead to any confusion of the public. The GI registration thus seems to comply with the law.

*Non-explicitly Endemic Local Varieties*

Whether the variety is endemic or not cannot be ascertained by going through the GI specification and the examination report which do not indicate if the variety is cultivated elsewhere.

The GI Coorg orange was primarily to reanimate production of a traditional crop threatened by the cultivation of coffee and the outbreak

---

[15] Dr Nirmala K.G., Indian Institute of Horticulture Research.

of a disease. The region of Coorg, which is a part of the Western Ghats and has been identified as one of the 25 points of richest biodiversity in the world, is reputed for the uniqueness of its forests' ecosystem. It is situated at an average altitude, is densely forested and agro-forest crops such as coffee are cultivated there. Previously in coffee plantations, there were orchards of tangerines, which were known as Coorg oranges. However, this particular detail has not been mentioned in the GI.[16] This production has now been virtually wiped out, and the Karnataka government, which applied for the GI, is aware of the need to preserve it. Yet, Coorg coffee producers argued that Coorg oranges were also cultivated in Tamil Nadu, the neighbouring state of Karnataka where Coorg district is situated. Then even if the orange cultivated in Coorg has unique characteristics, registering a GI stops the producers of Tamil Nadu from using the name.

The GIs Virupakshi Hill banana and Sirumalai Hill banana are for ecotypes, varieties of 'Vannan'. These varieties are cultivated in Madurai district in Tamil Nadu, south India, between 1200 m and 1500 m of altitude. They yield bananas with a special perfume when it is cultivated in higher altitudes. The GI seems to be for a food product which has the characteristics of its geographical origin. However, it cannot be asserted with certainty that the eponymous variety is endemic.

The GIs for Malda Laxman Bhog mangoes and Malda Fazli mangoes (designating mangoes cultivated in Malda district in West Bengal, in north India) were modified following the request of the consultative group to add Malda to the denomination Laxman Bhog mango and Fazli mango, names which designate the varieties but did not include geographical names, probably to avoid the appropriation of the name of the variety. The name of the variety not being a geographical name, it is easy to distinguish the GI from the variety by adding the geographical name to the name of the variety.

The same rule applies to the Allahabad Surkha guava (a guava initially selected and cultivated in Allahabad, a town situated at the confluence of two rivers with specific pedoclimatic conditions). The specialty

---

[16] C. Garcia et al., 'Biodiversity Conservation in Agricultural Landscapes: Challenges and Opportunities of Coffee Agroforestry in the Western Ghats, India', *Conservation Biology*, 24, no. 2 (2010): 479–488.

of this guava is that it is red in colour, a fact which gives it its name 'apple-coloured guava'. The GI application mentions that there are about a 150 varieties of guava, about most of which we know little, with the most well known among them is the *Psidium guajava*. The GI application also presents a list of the most promising cultivars of each state.[17] During the examination procedures carried out by the GI office, following the consultative group's request, the geographical name 'Allahabad' was added to the name of the variety 'Surkha guava', implying that this variety could be grown elsewhere and have other qualities. There is thus no restriction on using the appellation Surkha in other production zones. On the other hand, the specification does not describe natural factors and does not assert that this variety yields a unique fruit when it is cultivated in the Allahabad region. Is this because the applicant is not the same as for other horticultural products (here it is an association of producers)? Whatever it may be, it clearly demonstrates the difficulty in distinguishing between variety and product.

*Local Varieties That Have Become Widespread*

A particularly striking example of an escaped variety is that of the GI Eathamozhi tall coconut which designates a variety of tall coconut trees initially cultivated in the Eathamozhi region. The GI application indicates that this variety (cultivar) manifests its genetic potential when it is grown not only in the Kanyakumari (KK) district of Tamil Nadu (which corresponds to the region delimited by the GI) but also in other regions of Tamil Nadu where its seeds have been widely distributed for years. The GI application specifies that about 80 per cent of crops cultivated around Eathamozhi consist of this variety, which implies that the production of this crop is deeply implanted in the local culture, but the application indicates further that the government coconut nursery, Puthalam, located in KK district, produces quality seedlings of Eathamozhi tall coconut variety with a target of 30,000 seedlings every year to be distributed to other parts of India and other Asian countries, where it may perform better compared to the local varieties and hybrids, as it is a hardy cultivar. The registration of a GI in this case appears to be

---

[17] Anonymous, *Raw Materials: Wealth of India, Vol. I* (New Delhi: CSIR, 1960), cité dans *Advances in Horticulture, Vol. 1. Fruit Crops, Part 1*. Eds K.L. Chadha and O.P. Pareek (New Delhi: Malhotra Publishing House, 1993).

detrimental to other producers using the same variety, if they wish to use the name of the variety for their product.

## Traditional Variety or Evolved Variety: The Case of Basmati Rice

The eventful case of Basmati rice, which has been described previously,[18] illustrates three issues. The first issue is that how to define a list of varieties which can be qualified as Basmati, at least from the legal point of view. The second issue regards the delimitation of the geographical area and the third issue concerns the nature of the applicant.

### The First Legal Definitions of Basmati Rice as a Variety

Basmati rice has been subject to intensive plant breeding programmes since the beginning of the 20th century, in order to increase the rather low yield of traditional varieties. The different varieties which have been obtained, qualified as traditional or evolved, were registered in accordance with the 'Seed Act' of 1966, a law for regulating the marketing of seeds. Eleven varieties have been notified at the present time.[19]

Since 1990, the 'Export (Quality Control and Inspection) Act' has been monitoring the export of Basmati rice. Since 1996, because of the exceptional quality of Basmati rice, the EU has set up a policy of exempting duty on Basmati from India and Pakistan. The peak in Basmati rice export since 2000, combined with the Rice Tech case (see *supra*), has led the government to come up with a more precise definition of Basmati rice to avoid further cases of fraud. Traditional varieties fetch a better price in the international market and thus were distinguished from the evolved varieties by India. Thus, the Export Act was modified to arrive at a more precise definition of Basmati rice:

> Basmati Rice is grown in the Indo Gangetic plains and has the following characteristics: exceptional length of grain, which increases substantially

[18] For more details, see Delphine Marie-Vivien, 'From Plant Variety Definition to Geographical Indication Protection: A Search for the Link between Basmati Rice and India/Pakistan', *The Journal of World Intellectual Property* 11, no. 4 (2008): 321–344.
[19] Basmati 217, Basmati 370, Type 3, Punjab Basmati 1, Pusa Basmati 1, Kasturi Haryana, HKR 228, Mahi Sugunda, Taraori HB 19, Ranbir, Basmati 386. Voir http://seednet.gov.in/SeedVariety, consulté nov. 2007.

on cooking; the cooked grain has high integrity and high discreteness and distinctive aroma, taste and mouth feel; it is a traditional variety or is an evolved variety.... Traditional variety shall mean land races or varieties of rice of uniform shape, size and colour traditionally recognized as Basmati and evolved variety shall mean a variety whose one of two parents is a traditional variety and which has been recognized as a Basmati variety.[20]

Next, the notification stipulates that the 11 varieties of Basmati rice which have been notified in accordance with the Seed Act have been qualified as Basmati rice, six varieties among them are traditional and five are evolved varieties.[21]

Consequently, the EU adapted its exemption of duty policy for promoting only the six traditional varieties, which in Europe are considered to be of better quality.[22] Pakistan and India objected violently to this restriction however, and succeeded in adding the evolved varieties Super Basmati and Pusa Basmati[23] to the list of rice exempted of duty.

## Increasing Openness to Evolved Varieties

In the current decade, the demand for Basmati rice continues to rise exponentially even though the Indian Agricultural Research Institute has come out with new varieties. This gave rise to the question as to whether the list of varieties qualified as Basmati could be enlarged to include the new varieties. In 2006, the Ministry of Commerce notified approved Super Basmati as an evolved variety in accordance with the Export Act,[24]

---

[20] The parent selected from a traditional Basmati variety shall be any parent and not a direct parent of the genealogy.

[21] See notification 68. 'The Export of Basmati Rice (Quality Control and Inspection) Rules, 2003', 23 January 2003, Export Act.

[22] Règlement (CE) no. 2294/2003, 24 déc. 2003 modifiant le règlement (CE) no. 1503/96.

[23] UE signed in 2004 an agreement with India and Pakistan, implemented through regulation (CE) no. 1549/2004 of 30 August 2004 which provides that "With respect to the import regime of husked rice of the varieties Basmati 370, Basmati 386, Type-3 (Dehradun), Taraori Basmati (HBC-19), Basmati 217, Ranbir Basmati, Pusa Basmati and Super Basmati, the EC's specific bound rate of duty shall be zero'. Same agreement with Pakistan for the following varieties: Kernel (Basmati), Basmati 370, Pusa Basmati and Super Basmati.

[24] Basmati Rice (Quality Control and Inspection) (Amendment) Rules 2006, 24 May 2006.

but the Ministry of Agriculture was offended that such an authorization was granted because the parent varieties were not Indian land race varieties and thus not notified under the Seed Act.[25] Pakistan, the only country to cultivate Super Basmati rice, was also unhappy with this initiative. Basmati Grower Association in Pakistan filed a Petition No. 957/2008 titled Trading Corporation of Pakistan in the Delhi High Court for cancellation of such notification.[26] After many controversies, the decision was taken to remove the one traditional parent clause in the definition of Basmati rice. The principle is to qualify all varieties as Basmati, referring to the criteria that the family history (genealogy) includes a Basmati variety (traditional or evolved) notified under the Seed Act, 1966, to pass the 'Basmati quality genes' into the newly evolved varieties. The aim is to be able to notify more evolved varieties with much higher yield that the varieties initially notified according to the Seed Act. Thus, following a meeting between the Ministry of Commerce and the Ministry of Agriculture, an office memorandum was issued by the Ministry of Agriculture on 29 May 2008, which defines Basmati according to characteristics, that is, certain pre-determined standards, tested and evaluated through National Basmati Trials and notified under the Seed Act 1966; the varieties should be suitable to be grown in the Indo-Gangetic Plains of India of GI of Basmati growing areas, the variety should be proposed for notification with the term *Basmati* in the body of denomination, along with its initial evaluation trial (IET) number; the Ministry of Agriculture will decide if varieties are traditional or evolved, and the only authority for notification of Basmati varieties.

The issue here is the risk of delocalization because evolved, high-yielding varieties are adapted to different milieu which thus do not necessarily preserve the qualities or characteristics of traditional varieties cultivated only in its milieu of origin.[27] The Indian Council for Agricultural

---

[25] Parent varieties are Basmati 320 and l'IRRI 662.
[26] 24 May 2006.
[27] See studies of F. Thomas about consequences of plant breeding on the strength of the link with the origin, Frédéric Thomas and Dao The Anh, 'Qualités Et Origine Au Vietnam: L'épineuse Question De L'administration De La Preuve Entre Qualité Et Origine' (Paris: Conférence 'Localiser les produits: une voie durable au service de la diversité naturelle et culturelle des Suds?' UNESCO, 2009), 1–17.

Research has even implemented programmes to plant Basmati in Goa and south India.[28] There is thus a great risk that traditional varieties and traditional cultivation zones will be abandoned.

*Basmati GI Application*

The Ministry of Trade and Industry applied for a GI in November 2008 through APEDA, object of nine oppositions while the first GI application made in August 2004 by an NGO was refused in 2010. Some oppositions deal with the nature of the applicant (see Chapter 8), whereas some deal with the definition of the GI Basmati. The application from APEDA as submitted on 22 April 2010 (after the meeting of the consultative meeting on 28 January 2010) refers to the list of 11 Basmati varieties agreed in the office memorandum. Regarding controls, the Ministry of Commerce, vide a circular dated 31 March 2010, has decided to designate the Basmati Export Development Foundation (BEDF) laboratory, Modipuram, as an authorized centre for the testing of samples of Basmati rice for variety identification, in addition to AGMARK testing centres. BEDF, founded by APEDA in 2003, is directed by Arvind Gupta, adviser for APEDA. BEDF is testing random samples, around 1000 in a year, from millers, retailers, markets. The tractability is checked on documents from millers.

GI application Basmati is under many oppositions. In particular, there are six oppositions from MP claiming to include the state of MP in the geographical area which was limited to the states of Punjab, Haryana, Delhi, Himachal Pradesh, Uttarakhand and part of Uttar Pradesh and Jammu and Kashmir. All are filed by same legal counsel. One is from the state itself (opposition no. 19); one from the Madhya Kshetra Basmati Growers Association Samiti (opp. no. 13); one from the Madhya Kshetra Basmati Rice Exporters Association (no. 17); and three from private companies, SSA International Limited (no. 16), Daawat Food (no. 16) and Narmada Cereals Private Limited (no. 14). Twenty-three documents have been annexed on 13 February 2013 by the opponents, comprising many scientific documents of early 20th century showing that Mushkin is a recognized variety of Basmati, called red Basmati, cultivated in the Malwa region of MP, that the same quality of soil in MP as in UP, that

---

[28] See http://icargoa.res.in/basumati_rice.htm.

temperature in MP are adequate for Basmati cultivation, that farmers have been cultivating Basmati for decades, with the help of certification of seed agencies. It is thus a question of both varieties eligible to be called Basmati and geographical area.

Endly, there is as expected an opposition from Pakistan, more precisely from the Basmati Growers Association, BGA (opp. no. 18). Indeed, there is no doubt that Basmati comes from both Pakistan and India, same country before the Partition. There was an intent to register a common GI with the setup of a joint working group which has met until 2008, with the objective of disclosing the content of the GI application in India to Pakistan. But the joint discussion did not work, so Basmati underwent a registration process in each country. BGA applied for a trademark in Pakistan, which was registered[29] in spite of the opposition filed by APEDA claiming that it was an exclusive trademark and not a certification trademark, opposition rejected due to procedural requirements. Appeal has been formed in front of the Sindh High Court of Karachi. Moreover, APEDA considers that BGA are only producers, not exporters, but still qualify the legal suit as an improvement and not a cancellation process.[30] As a reciprocity reaction, BGA opposed GI application in India. BGA's opposition is based on the assertion that the geographical region, that is, the Indo-Gangetic Plain, is not exclusive to India alone. It is submitted that the areas of Punjab in Pakistan, inter alia, consisting of Sheikhpura, Nankana Sahib, Gujranwala, Hafizabad, Sialkot, Narowal, Gujrat, Mandi Bahauddin, Lahore, Faisalabad, Chiniot, Jhang, Toba Tek Singh, Sargodha and Khushab are the areas known for cultivation of Basmati rice as these areas are in the Indo-Gangetic Plains falling in Pakistan. BGA relies on the agreement in the form of exchange of letter entered into by EC separately with India and Pakistan with respect to the import of Basmati rice by EC, which says that Pakistan and India will protect Basmati rice as a GI. Moreover, BGA considers that photoperiod sensitivity is a defining characteristic of all Basmati varieties, while APEDA, inter alia, recognizes PUSA-1 and PUSA-1121 as Basmati varieties, two photoperiods insensitive lacking the typical Basmati aroma.

---

[29] TM Application No. 216742 in class 30 filed by BGA, registered on 10 May 2008.
[30] Mr A.K. Gupta, APEDA.

Here also, the question of evolved varieties is central. Yet first, the share of the geographical area between India and Pakistan remains the major issue to be solved for Basmati to be protected as a transborder GI.[31]

# The Reputation of GIs Created by Colonial History

## The Emphasis on the Impact of the Natural Environment

As many of the varieties used are commonplace, the quality of agricultural products here is strongly linked with natural factors, such as the soil, the climate and the altitude. Natural factors can have an influence during cultivation or during processing. They can also be absent, as in the case of non-agricultural products.

*Common Varieties but Importance of Natural Factors Environment*

The GI is the geographical name of the region of cultivation and not the name of the species or the plant variety. These products can definitely be referred to as *terroir* products, strongly linked to their origin via the soil, the altitude and the climate.

For example, the GI Darjeeling refers to a tea whose qualities spring from the exceptional natural environment, the soil, but above all, the altitude and the climate. The tea is cultivated on a surface of 19,000 ha with an annual rainfall of 320 cm, between 600 and 2000 m of altitude, on steep slopes, in very specific weather conditions: wet and cool in summer and dry and cold in winter. It is called 'Champagne of teas'.[32] The species *Camellia sinensis* is used for cultivating all Indian tea. It is a hardy, multi-stemmed, slow-growing evergreen shrub which if allowed

---

[31] Rangnekar, D. and S. Kumar. 'Another Look at Basmati: Genericity and the Problems of a Transborder Geographical Indication', *The Journal of World Intellectual Property*, 13, no. 2 (2010): 202–230.

[32] See Das, 'International Protection of India's Geographical Indications with Special Reference to "Darjeeling" Tea', 459–495 and C. Niranjan Rao, 'Geographical Indications in Indian Context: A Case Study of Darjeeling Tea', *Economic and Political Weekly*, no. 15, October 15 (2005): 4545–4550.

to can grow up to 2.5 m in height. It takes four to six years to mature and is able to withstand severe winters, extended drought and the high altitude of Darjeeling. The leaves are small, leathery, dark, glossy green in colour often covered with a downy silvery pubescence, and yields are much lower than in non-Darjeeling districts. Processing is done in the area of production, and manual plucking begins in March and closes by late November. The GI application also mentions a set of agricultural practices that has been developed to sustain growth of shoots, while maintaining bush heights suitable for manual plucking.

Darjeeling tea leaves are processed in the production area, in the traditional 'orthodox' way invented by the British, who adapted in India the processes used for tea growing in China. Once the leaves reach the factory, they are 'withered'. The object is to evaporate moisture from the leaves. The leaves become limp so as to withstand twisting and rolling under pressure without crumbling. The withered leaves are then removed from the trough and loaded into rolling machines, which, by subjecting the withered leaves to a rolling movement under pressure, twist the leaves, rupture the cells and release the natural juices, promoting oxidation and accelerating the pigmentation. Next, the leaves are thinly spread in a cool, well-ventilated room to slowly oxidize (ferment). This is the stage in which the flavanols combine with oxygen in the air and develop the unique flavour of Darjeeling tea. Experts regularly evaluate the tea quality and its perfume while it is being processed. In order to stop the fermentation process, the leaves are dried at 90°C for 20 or 30 minutes. Then they are sifted. This separates the tea leaves according to their size, each 'grade' having a different appellation: Fine Tippy Golden Flowery Orange Pekoe, Tippy Golden Broken Orange Pekoe, and Golden Orange Fannings.

When compared to another GI on tea, Kangra tea, it is truly surprising that the defined production method for Kangra tea consists only of the processing techniques and not the cultivation methods. One hypothesis, as presented by the applicant, is that the uniqueness is the result of a combination of natural factors such as the soil, the climate, the altitude and the knowledge involved in the processing of the raw material.

Kangra tea is known for its distinctive aroma, taste, lightness of colour and liquor. In comparison, Darjeeling tea is described as having less 'body liquor'. It is available in different forms: green tea and black tea; the black tea category consists of different leaf sizes: Pekoe, Pekoe Souchong, Coarse and Fannings. To obtain these various categories, a different processing technique is used for each of them, described in detail in the specifications. The production method presented in the specification, justifying the uniqueness.

To conclude, the uniqueness of Kangra tea and Darjeeling tea reflects the combination between a variety, the natural environment and processing techniques. They are thus truly *terroir* products.

*The Importance of Natural Factors for Processing*
The GI Monsooned Malabar coffee (arabica and robusta) is registered for a coffee which is processed following a technique directly linked to the climatic conditions, discovered while shipping coffee in the past, which took a considerable amount of time. On one occasion, before being shipped, the coffee stayed in the storage area for a long period than was customary, ultimately undergoing an unexpected transformation because of the hot and wet weather of the Malabar Coast during monsoon. This process was called 'monsooning'. Natural factors thus play a role in processing the product, like Roquefort in France.

The geographical origin of coffee processed in such a manner is not exclusive and includes coffee cultivated in a number of places in India, including Karnataka, Tamil Nadu, Andhra Pradesh and Orissa. The varieties are commonplace and their description does not mention that they have any influence on the final quality of the product. The geographical origin of coffee thus processed is not exclusive. even though the climatic conditions and the natural environment have been described for all the cultivation zones as well as for the place where the processing takes place. The 'monsooning' process, with its physical changes, as well as the chemical and biological changes, is described thoroughly, being the main reason for the coffee's uniqueness, by a highly qualified[33] scientist of the Coffee Board Research Institute.

The consultative group which examined the GI application asked that it be separated into two, one for robusta coffee and another for arabica coffee, because they are two different species. Thus according to them, even though the processing techniques were the same, arabica and robusta coffees were two different products.

[33] Dr Ragu.

Finally, it is the first example of a GI registered for an intermediate product, a raw material, a green coffee which has not yet been roasted and which is not directly offered to consumption. It raises the issue of the use of the GI to designate the final product and thus the role of professional buyers in the value chain.

## The Emphasis on Human Factors

*The Importance of Processing Know-how in the Absence of Natural Factors*

The first Indian GI registered for a liqueur, Feni, illustrates a longstanding traditional processing method regarding the fermentation and distillation of juice of cashew apples. The word *Feni* from froth, which in the local Konkani language is known as *Fen*, formed when the liquor is shaken in a bottle or poured in a glass.

The cashew tree was introduced in Goa by the Portuguese in the 16th century. According to the specification, Goa is the only place where cashew apples are used for the production of Feni, cashew trees being usually cultivated for nuts. The apples, which have fully ripened and fallen on the ground, are collected, crushed for the extraction of juice and the extracted juice is fermented and distilled without the addition of any foreign ingredient to obtain Feni. Distillation is characterized by the use of a bamboo pipe and an earthen pot to collect the distillate which is cooled down by a water circuit, requiring constant attention.

Yet, according to D. Rangnekar, who led a research project concerning the implementation of the GI Feni,[34] the distillation process described in the GI is seldom used today. Instead, the receptacle is often made in aluminium and immersed in a big cement tank full of water.

What is most striking is that the GI does not highlight the natural factors, even as it specifies that the quality of apples vary depending on the soil characteristics and the place of cultivation. The cultivation zone is also not delimited, although the distillation zone is restricted to Goa.

---

[34] Project funded by British research. His study focuses on socio-economic issues and therefore focuses on the product, its markets, industry players and organization. Dwijen Rangnekar, 'Geographical Indications and Localisation: A Case Study of Feni' (CSGR Report, 2009), 1–64.

Even though Feni undoubtedly is a farm product, its link to origin is only through human factors, the distillation techniques. It reminds us of the European PGI category.

*The Use of the Product Determining the GI Name*

The GI name Palakkadan Matta Rice expresses an interesting combination between cultivation methods, a variety, natural environment and above all habits of consumption. Pallakad is the geographical name, and Matta refers to the areca leaf name traditionally used for keeping rice. A number of extant and popular varieties are used: Chenkazhama, Chettadi, Aruvakkari, Aryan, Vatton, Illupappoochampan, Chitteni and Thavalakkannan. More recent varieties such as Kunjukunju and Jyothi have been added to this list.

The methods used to cultivate these varieties are rather special and they yield nourishing, coarse grain rice with a red husk. This rice is widely cultivated and is the staple diet of Kerela. The GI application describes that the uniqueness springs from natural factors such as the soil and the climate. The production method is described in great detail, using words from the local language, as well as all the religious rituals followed while harvesting this rice. Thus, according to the specification, in the farm (*kalam*), there is a house built with a courtyard to dry the husked rice (*kalappura*) 'aynkolpura', 'kattakkalam', a tank for irrigation (*aeri*) and a reservoir situated in the highest part of the farm (*thalakkulam*) to collect rain water. The seeds are left out in the sun for three days and then in the moon during a full moon night. This step is called *mampookkattal*. After the second harvest in January–February (*mundakan*), the soil is ploughed intensively and then planting is done without any watering, accompanied by Hindu religious rituals. The plants are replanted under the auspices of a religious festival. Special plows are used to cover the seedbed. The sowing period is very important because the germination of seeds depends on it. This time is called *pattu*. The harvesting method is also original. It is done with bamboo rods called *Kattaparambu*. The rice straw is then dried by turning it upside down with a special tool called *Vaikkolvadi*. This GI reminds us of the GI details for handicraft products; it can be qualified as 'traditional rice'.

*History Sufficient for Qualifying a Product?*

Whatever the history of the product and its producers, or the uniqueness of its natural environment, it is only possible to register a GI for a product if the product is already reputed. The example of Coorg coffee is a useful one, as the history of coffee in the area could provide the necessary justifications for registering a GI. Coorg was for a long time autonomous and populated by a community benefiting from rules of use specific to the environment, because of the exceptional character of its ecosystem, which is very rich in biodiversity, thanks to a unique forest cover. A certification trademark thus has been applied for Coorg coffee by the Coffee Board. It consists of a logo, a bee, symbol of Coorg, and the geographical name Coorg. In fact, the Coffee Board has adopted a strategy of differentiating between coffees from different regions in India. However, it has precisely to do with the source of the coffee in the sense of indication of source and not in the sense of origin as required for the concept of GI, because according to the Coffee Board, the products do not reveal a quality linked to the geographical origin, partly because of the predominance of robusta beans, which are considered to be inferior in quality to arabica. The people in this industry insist upon the generic quality, through quality grading, for example, in their dealings with the international market, as they are not yet convinced about the specific quality of localized coffees. The opening of the domestic market could on the other hand enhance the status of the cultural and natural origin, which is without any doubt specific[35] because the reputation can be local or national.

*Reputation of Products Meeting Export Standards*

Europeans seduced by Indian spices developed their trade based on quality standards. The place of inspection became the names of those products. However, the checking was done to make sure that the generic quality was respected, in terms of factors like size and colour, rather than any specific quality attributed to the geographical origin.

The GI Malabar pepper designates a variety of pepper with a very strong taste, hot, cultivated in an extremely large zone, in the south-west

---

[35] For a complete study of the potential for a GI to protect the name of Coorg coffee, see the literature from the project Biodivalloc, ANR Biodiversity, Marie-Vivien, D., Garcia, C. A., Kushalappa, C. G. and Vaast, P. 'Trademarks, Geographical Indications and Environmental Labelling to Promote Biodiversity: The Case of Agroforestry Coffee in India', *Development Policy Review*, 32(4) (2014): 379–398.

coast of India called the Malabar Coast, from a very ordinary species, the *Piper nigrum*. Even though the name Malabar refers to the production zone, the uniqueness of Malabar pepper lies in its long history, which is described in great detail in the GI application, since the Malabar Coast is lacking in specific natural factors.

The geographic milieu where this pepper is cultivated is not described. On the other hand, the cultivation methods are described in detail: Black pepper is grown in soil that is neither too dry nor susceptible to flooding, moist, well drained and rich in organic matter. The plants are propagated by cuttings, tied up to neighbouring trees or climbing frames at distances of about 2 m apart; trees with rough bark are favoured over those with smooth bark, as the pepper plants climb rough bark more readily. Competing plants are cleared away. The roots are covered in leaf mulch and manure, and the shoots are trimmed twice a year. On dry soils, the young plants require watering every other day during the dry season for the first three years. The plants bear fruit from the fourth or fifth year, and typically continue to bear fruit for seven years. The harvest begins as soon as one or two berries at the base of the spikes begin to turn red, and before the fruit is mature.

Processing includes still-green unripe berries of the pepper plant blanching briefly in hot water for one minute, both to clean them and to prepare them for drying. The heat ruptures cell walls in the fruit, speeding the work of browning enzymes during drying. The berries are dried in the sun or by machine for several days, during which the fruit around the seed shrinks and darkens into a thin, wrinkled black layer around the seed.

Malabar pepper is classified under two grades: garbled and un-garbled. The garbled variety is black in colour, nearly globular with a wrinkled surface, the deepest wrinkles forming a network in the dried fruit. The un-garbled variety has a wrinkled surface and the colour varies from dark brown to black.

The first GI registered by the Spice Board of India, Malabar pepper, underwent a long and laborious examination procedure. From the very first letter sent by the GI Registry,[36] a great deal of supplementary information had to be provided, especially regarding the TK used and the uniqueness of the geographical environment. The Spice Board

[36] Rule 31.

replied by indicating that its pepper is sold at a higher price than that of Vietnam or Indonesia and that the quality of Malabar pepper does depend not only on the variety's intrinsic quality but on post-harvest techniques which create the grade of pepper which is internationally accepted.[37] To be granted the Malabar grade, the pepper must fulfil various technical criteria and regulations, specified in the 'AG Mark grade specification for Spices, 1969', promulgated by the Spice Board, specifying peppercorn weight, volatile oil content and other relevant factors for each grade.

Frequent reminders from the GI Registry asking the Spice Board to complete the description of agro-climatic conditions[38] indicate that influence of natural factors seems to be doubtful, or at least not clear enough. The reply of the Spice Board that 'the term Malabar Pepper is essentially an international accepted grade of pepper due to the intervention by the Spice Board in the arena of spice trading' seems to indicate that the link between Malabar pepper and the Malabar region is based on human factors and the Spice Board's knowledge of the spice trade, where spices are accorded different grades depending on their generic quality.[39]

Even though the reputation of the indication Malabar pepper is unquestionable, whether the specialized knowledge of grading is localized or not remains to be determined. The registration of a GI can be justified only if no pepper outside this zone uses the same appellation to designate its grades, with the consequence of Malabar pepper being a generic denomination.

The specialized techniques of grading are also used for cardamom. Thus, the GI Alleppey green cardamom refers to the place of grading, the Alleppey port in Kerala, on the south-west coast of India, from whence it is dispatched to Europe. Alleppey Green is a grade name corresponding to a generic quality, determined by its colour, its size, chemical components and its oil value. It is available in two categories: 'bold' or 'extra-bold'. In the past, Alleppey monopolized the sales of cardamom for export and consequently its name was naturally

[37] Statement 23 November 2006, Spice Board.
[38] For example, in a letter dated 19 March 2007, the GI Registry, based upon the large number of reminders sent, indicates that a period of one week is given to the Spice Board to respond to this question.
[39] Letter from the advocate of the Spice Board to the GI Registry, 23 May 2007.

associated with a specific quality used in international standards, even though the production zone was much wider than Alleppey town and spanned the Western Ghats.

It is essentially the cardamom of the Mysore variety which is used for Alleppey green cardamom. Alleppey green cardamom refers to the dried pods which are green in colour, striated, with three loculi where there are the aromatic grains, reputed for their perfume and their sweet and fruity oil.

Cardamom is a shade-loving crop, grown extensively at elevations of 800–1300 m under a warm and humid climate, on loamy soils rich in organic matter, with adequate moisture and well-distributed rainfall.

The quality of the cardamom and its green colour, a distinctive trait which is described as the soul of Alleppey green cardamom results from post-harvest techniques: washed thoroughly in water and then taken for drying. Curing is essential to bring down the initial moisture level. The room temperature in which the cardamom is stored between 40°C and 50°C for the first 10–12 hours, and then increased to 55°C in order to reduce splitting of capsule and loss of vital volatile cardamom oil.

The post-harvest techniques have hardly anything to do with natural factors and, on the contrary, make use of 'artificial' techniques, such as oven drying. The same post-harvest techniques are used to process Coorg green cardamom, for which another GI has been registered. These techniques are not specific to the geographical area because of the drying process, which is widespread, and the lack of specific natural factors. The link to the origin thus seems to be only the knowledge and expertise used in the classification of different grades.

To conclude, in the case of Malabar pepper or Alleppey green cardamom, history is the essential factor justifying the registration of these GIs. The geographical area whose name protected as GI played an important role in the history of transport of these products. As in the case of handicraft products based on local knowledge, here too their rootedness to the origin has to be checked. The protection as GI, however, stops the names from becoming generic, which is what happened in the case of Mokka coffee. Today, Mokka coffee refers to the taste of a coffee produced all over the world, while originally Mokha was the port in Yemen from where this coffee was shipped.

## The Unsolved Issue of Delimitation of Geographical Area

*The Extension of the Geographical Area of Basmati*
The definition of the geographical area was the main ground of the oppositions against APEDA Basmati GI's application. Initially comprising the states of Punjab, Haryana, Delhi, Himachal Pradesh, Uttarakhand and part of Uttar Pradesh and Jammu and Kashmir, the six opponents from Madhya Pradesh claimed to include the state of Madhya Pradesh in the geographical area. Twenty-three documents have been annexed, comprising many scientific documents of early 20th century showing that Mushkin, a recognized variety of Basmati, called red Basmati, was cultivated in the Malwa region of Madhya Pradesh; that there is the same quality of soil in Madhya Pradesh than in Uttar Pradesh, that temperature in Madhya Pradesh is adequate for Basmati cultivation, that farmers have been cultivating Basmati for decades, with the help of certification of seed agencies. The opponents continue with the fact that there is no universal consensus on which areas are traditional. If one were to go with the transitory and unscientific definition of traditional, in 1947, Haryana would not have been considered a 'traditional Basmati-cultivated area'.

APEDA opposed the inclusion of a new area as if the Basmati rice grown in Madhya Pradesh has all the required characteristics, physical and other characteristics alone do not determine a geographical indication. According to APEDA, the elements of reputation and consequent public perception are equally determinant factors, which do not exist for Basmati rice from Madhya Pradesh. The GI Registry Order agreed with the opponent and considered that 'the applicant is the guardian of the product which must include each and every cultivated area where it is grown, being vital to demarcate *actual* producing area'.

The case raises the issue: what is the link between a product and its origin? Is it only an indication of source, with the consideration of the actual area of cultivation or a GI, with a qualitative link based on the reputation of the geographical area? Is it the historical area of production or area of production at the time of registering the GI? Tradition versus modernity? Basmati not being a geographical name, the issue is even trickier, as there might be a serious risk of Basmati being qualified as generic, considering both the extension of Basmati definition to evolved varieties and to a greater geographical area.

## The Extension of the Geographical Area of Coorg Cardamom

The GI Coorg green cardamom covers the districts of Coorg, Hassan, Chickmagalur and North Kanara in Karnataka state. Can the GI name, which is more restrictive than the defined zone which includes three other districts besides Coorg, refer to natural factors having so little similarity among them? Numerous studies of landscapes and ecosystems tend to show that Coorg district has certain specific qualities which are absent elsewhere.[40] In the GI application itself, the historical description mentions that though cardamom was also cultivated in Hassan and Chickmagalur district, it is the cardamom cultivated in Coorg district that is most reputed in terms of quality and quantity. This inclusion strategy could perhaps have been instigated by the wish to include producers from neighbouring districts. It can also be explained by the wish to add dynamism to production of a crop damaged by pests, but it does not confer uniqueness to the product, which weakens the GI.

## Proof of Origin through DNA Tests on the Varieties?

The interaction between plant varieties and GIs led the GI Registry to insist that GI applications should contain 'objective' descriptors of the product such as DNA markers. The first example is given by Coorg orange. The consultative group asked the applicant to submit a DNA test, a 'fingerprint', to identify the variety.[41] The Biocentre of the Department of Horticulture of Karnataka supplied this test.[42] The GI office asked that the same test be done for Navara rice. The GI office thus seems to systematically insist on this test, even though the variety is not primordial as in the case of the GI Malabar pepper. This request gave rise to heated debates between the advocate of the Spice Board, the Spice Board and the GI Registry, and delayed the GI registration for the pepper.[43] Despite this insistence in practice, the assistant registrar of the GI Registry, when questioned about this point, said that in the absence of such a provision in the legal texts, it is not compulsory.

These tests help to differentiate the varieties according to their genomes but do not help to define the geographical origin of the products. So is

---

[40] Garcia et al., 'Biodiversity Conservation in Agricultural Landscapes: Challenges and Opportunities of Coffee Agroforestry in the Western Ghats, India'.
[41] Letter from the GI Registry, 13 June 2005.
[42] Mr Ramakrishnappa, Biocentre, interview.
[43] The exchange, recorded in the GI file lasted almost two years.

the GI ultimately registered for only one variety? In any case, the DNA test regulation has only added to the confusion between GIs and plant varieties. There is also the additional risk that population varieties which cannot be identified through these tests will be excluded.

## The Link to the Origin through Local Varieties/ Breeds in France

The French GIs for non-vineyard[44] farm products reveal a strong correlation between GIs and local varieties or breeds. Numerous AOC producers have chosen threatened traditional, local varieties for their products, illustrating the positive contribution of local varieties/breeds for consolidating the link to the origin. However, to avoid any confusion caused by the use of eponymous designations, which could be prejudicial for producers and consumers, there are clauses in the French law settling such disputes.

### Different Choices Regarding Varieties/Breeds

*Local Varieties*

It is generally acknowledged that in France, local varieties and local breeds constitute a link to the geographical area because, as noted by F. Roncin, they have either resulted from local knowledge and savoir faire or they have resulted from adaptation to a specific geographical environment, or both at the same time'.[45]

P. Marchenay[46] stresses the fact that in traditional systems, it was habitual to cultivate one or various populations of a particular variety

---

[44] We note that the reform of the Common Market Organization for wine is for the designation of grape varieties in the European wine labels.
[45] Roncin and Boulineau, 'Valorisation Des "Légumes De Terroir" Par Les Signes Officiels D'identification De La Qualité Et De L'origine (Aop-Igp), Comment Est-Ce Réalisable?', 3.
[46] Bérard and Marchenay, *Produits De Terroir: Comprendre Et Agir*, 35–40; Laurence Bérard and Philippe Marchenay, 'Local Products and Geographical Indications: Taking Account of Local Knowledge and Biodiversity', *International Social Science Journal*, 58, no. 187 (2006): 118; Bérard and Marchenay, *Les Produits De Terroir, Entre Cultures Et Règlements*, 92–94.

which were rarely fixed. This initial situation seems to be hardly compatible with current regulations. For example, in order to commercialize seeds and plants of vegetables species and of arable crops, the variety has to be registered beforehand in the official catalogue of species and plant varieties cultivated in France which means that the (DHS) criteria—distinctiveness, homogeneity and stability—shall be fulfilled. But local types are 'too' heterogeneous varieties and cannot be commercialized even if they are PGIs/AOCs products, with the exception of the PGI Petit épeautre de Haute Provence, which represented straw cereals derived from population varieties.[47]

P. Marchenay illustrated the relation between AOCs and varieties using several French examples. The AOC Coco de Paimpol is based on the use of a pure and fixed line issuing from the local bean variety *Phaseolus vulgaris*. The case of AOC Piment d'Espelette, derived from the pure and fixed line of the local population variety, *Capsicum annuum*, is the same. The AOC Oignon doux des Cévennes is derived from a homogenized population variety only partially representative of the local genetic pool (round shapes). For all these products, the AOC specifications indicate the possibility of using seeds obtained from the farm.[48]

Besides the issue of 'legality' of the seeds used, there is also the issue of whether the diversity of cultivable varieties through AOCs should be encouraged or not. Thus, the AOC Figue de Solliès has selected only one variety, the black Bourjasotte, while in 1945, in an inventory of the varieties of Solliès-Pont region, about 10 local types were described legalizing a drastic decrease in diversity. On the other hand, the AOC Noix de Grenoble uses of three varieties: Franquette, Mayette and Parisienne. The AOC Noix du Périgord is derived from four varieties: Marbot, Franquette, Corne and Grandjean. The AOC for olive oils are also often the result of cultivation of local varieties, such as the Tanche variety, used for producing Olive de Nyons.

A particularly interesting example where the diversity of local varieties is maintained is that of Châtaigne d'Ardèche. For centuries, local society in Ardèche was organized around chestnut groves. When the

---

[47] See the specification: http://www.inao.gouv.fr/repository/editeur/pdf/CDCIGP/CDCPetitEpeautreDeHauteProvence.pdf.
[48] See http://www.inao.gouv.fr, to access the decrees recognising AOC.

industry began deteriorating, new varieties resulting from the hybridization of plants of different regions, more suited to certain technical and marketing criteria, were proposed, but this innovation would have radically changed the manner of cultivating chestnut groves, shifting production from the domain of agro-forestry to intensive orchard farming. The producers thought of an AOC which would simultaneously protect local varieties, a mode of cultivation and the landscape. From a census of 66 local varieties, the AOC Châtaigne d'Ardèche selected 19 main varieties, also taking into account the specialized knowledge required to cultivate them. The AOC also specified that hybrid varieties were ruled out.[49] However, the European Commission considered that a common characteristic between the different varieties of chestnuts had not been established and refused to register the AOC at the European level.[50] To counter this argument, the producers decided to use the 'local ecotype concept' found in the 66 varieties in order to show their common characteristics. The code of practices now provides that chestnuts come exclusively from old local varieties of *Castanea sativa* species selected over the centuries in different production areas of Ardèche, thanks to the interaction between local natural conditions and human skills.[51]

The cultivation of varieties in different places highlights the impact of the geographical environment on the specificity of the product. For example, the AOC Lentilles vertes du Puy and the PGI Lentilles vertes du Berry are derived from the same Anicia line obtained from the *Lens esculenta puyensis* variety.[52] The name of the mother variety thus directly refers to Puy, probably because it has originated from Puy.

---

[49] See art. 4 of the Decree of 28 June 2006 concerning the appellation of origin 'Chestnut Ardèche': 'Chestnuts from local varieties of the species Castanea sativa Miller listed in the technical regulations provided for in art.1 of this Decree. The hybrids are prohibited.' This French inventory is largely inspired by the work published by Bérard and Marchenay, *Produits De Terroir: Comprendre Et Agir*, 35–40.

[50] Letter from the European Commission européenne, General directorate for agriculture and rural development, 9 October 2009 and interview April 2010.

[51] Decree n° 2010-1290 du 27 octobre 2010 relatif à l'appellation d'origine contrôlée 'Châtaigne d'Ardèche', http://www.legifrance.gouv.fr/.

[52] Shabnam Laure Anvar, 'Semences Et Droit: L'emprise D'un Modèle Économique Dominant Sur Une Réglementation Sectorielle' (Université Paris I Panthéon-Sorbonne, 2008), 67.

This variety has been recently introduced in Berry, where lentils started being cultivated in the beginning of 1950 and expanded rapidly.[53] The cultivation of the Anicia line in its place of origin—Puy—where it is an endemic crop, and there is a long tradition of lentil growing, gives a superior *typicity* to the product. This explains why Lentilles vertes du Puy is an AOC, demonstrating its strong link to the origin, while Lentilles vertes du Berry is a PGI, because it is a non-local variety which has been introduced recently.

*Widespread Varieties*
Numerous AOC products have been derived from widespread varieties such as the AOC Chasselas de Moissac (from Chasselas B grape varieties) and the AOC Muscat du Ventoux (from the Muscat de Hambourg grape varieties). The orchards which produce the AOC Pomme du Limousin are planted with the Golden Delicious variety or its mutants. The AOC Pomme de terre de l'île de Ré is derived from eight widespread varieties.

*Local Breeds*
Local breeds of cows, goats and sheep are gaining in importance in cheese AOCs. The breed is specified in the description of production conditions, including the Salers breed (for the AOC fromage Salers, tradition Salers/ Salers cheese, Salers tradition), the Tarine breed or the Abondance breed (for the AOCs Beaufort, Abondance and Reblochon) and the Montbéliarde breed or the French Simmental breed (for AOCs Comté, Mont d'or and Bleu de Gex). For other AOCs, the question is on the agenda, even though it is not clearly mentioned in the production conditions that the breed has to be used exclusively. These cases include preferences for the Vosgienne breed (for Munster AOC) and the Normandy breed (for Livarot, Pont l'évêque or Camembert de Normandie AOCs.)

## Conflicts Regarding Appellations

*Legal Provisions*
The praiseworthy aim of AOC/PGI is to preserve the diversity of plant varieties and animal breeds, but the confusion between plant varieties

---

[53] See the specifications of the PGI 'Lentilles vertes du Berry', www.inao.gouv.fr.

or animal breeds and the product designated by AOC or PGI must be avoided. This requirement is clearly codified in European and French law, unlike in the Indian law. Article 6.2 of regulation no. 1151/2012 stipulates: 'A name may not be registered as a designation of origin or a geographical indication where it conflicts with the name of a plant variety or an animal breed and is likely to mislead the consumer as to the true origin of the product'.

Names that are wholly homonymous with names of plant varieties or animal breeds for comparable products may not be registered if it is shown that the variety or breed is in such commercial production outside the defined area prior to the date of application and that consumers would be liable to confuse the products bearing the registered name and the variety or the breed.[54] Therefore, for endemic varieties or for varieties little cultivated outside their cradle of origin, the homonymy between the name of the variety and the PDO/PGI is not a ground for refusal of the PDO/PGI.

In France, the legal burden is upon the AOC applicant to 'present and develop eventual interactions between the name proposed as AOC with the name of breed'.[55] Indeed, the name of any cultivated species and plant varieties shall be registered in the official catalogue of cultivated species and plant varieties created in France in the beginning of the 20th century.[56] Regarding new, evolved plant varieties, often protected by IPR laws, the intellectual property code states that the name for the new plant varieties cannot be registered as trademark in a country which has adopted the UPOV convention.[57] Even though the rule does not deal directly with PGIs, the registration of a plant variety right creates a prior right. However, to get approval for AOC/PGI, steps were taken to rid the varieties or the breeds of their names. It was successful, thus conferring primacy upon AOC/PGI.

---

[54] Regulation (CE) no. 1898/2006 of 14 December 2006 on implementation of the regulation (CE) no. 510/2006, JOUE L.369/1.
[55] Guide of the AOC/PDO applicant, Version no. 5, 30/03/2009, p. 9.
[56] Decree of 22 January 1960 establishing a catalogue of species and varieties of crops, OJ 28 January 1960, p. 955. Since the decree of 22 January 1960, the listing of species and varieties of crops is mandatory for marketing, whether for new varieties or existing varieties.
[57] See C. prop. int. art. L.623-15.

*Examples of Conflicts in France*

The question comes up mostly for animal breeds, which tend to be named after their region of origin. Thus for the meat AOC Maine-Anjou to be acknowledged, the UPRA breed's name Maine-Anjou was changed to Rouge des prés. According to P. Marchenay, this situation is doubtful and should not be repeated, and in fact, it seems that this is an isolated case.

Another custom was to insert a linking term between the name of the product and the breed's geographical name, as in the case of PGI Veau du Limousin, denomination which is different from the name of the breed, limousine. M.A. Ngo alleges that though this solution is legally valid, it seems inappropriate because in reality, in the market there will be 'veaux du Limousin', who have originated from the Limoges region but are not necessarily from the limousine breed, and 'veaux Limousin', who are from the limousine breed but whose origins could be elsewhere.[58]

In the case of the AOC Bœuf de Charolles, the breeders have chosen the geographical name of the cradle for the AOC distinct from the name of the breed 'bœuf charolais'. Yet, according to L. Bernard, the appellation Bœuf de Charolles does not correspond to a designation traditionally used by producers, but the reputation of the animals of this eponymous region has been established since a long time. There are two main reasons: the local tradition of placing great importance on selecting quality meat and the herbage quality, which helps create an excellent product, thanks to the fattener's expertise.[59] Nevertheless, the breed *boeuf charolais* from anywhere as well as the AOC Bœuf de Charolles coexists, which can confuse certain consumers.

For this reason, the AOC application Quetsche d'Alsace was rejected by INAO,[60] justified by the fact that the 'quetsche d'Alsace' variety can be cultivated elsewhere in Lorraine but also in very small quantities in the Rhône valley. Moreover, the variety is registered in the official catalogue

---

[58] Mai-Anh Ngo, *La Qualité Et La Sécurité Des Produits Agro-Alimentaires* (L'Harmattan, 2006), 393.

[59] Bérard and Marchenay, 'Local Products and Geographical Indications: Taking Account of Local Knowledge and Biodiversity', 119.

[60] 'Quetsche d'Alsace, Une renaissance de qualité', M. Arnould, 5 September 2009, http://www.lalsace.fr/fr/region/alsace/article/1943255,208/Une-renaissance-de-qualite.html, consulté le 11 September 2009.

of species and plant varieties cultivated in France, leading to the assumption that the appellation was unavailable.

To conclude, the Indian situation, where there is a similarity between varieties, names and appellations constituting GIs, is quite rare in France because of the tradition of naming grape varieties without taking recourse to geographical names. It is also possible that in India more ancient local varieties are cultivated. While France has numerous local varieties, they are the result of selection, following which they meet the DHS criteria, compulsory for the marketing of seeds. The multitude of GIs for local varieties in India thus testify to a strong link to the origin, even though the issue of excluding producers, who in good faith have been using the same name for the same variety when cultivated outside the region of origin, needs to be settled because of the tendency of varieties to spread elsewhere.

For agricultural products as well as handicraft products, a study of the Indian's GI Act implementation reveals the importance of history and local specialized knowledge.

# Part II

## The Peculiarities of the Role of the State for the Protection of GIs in India, Compared to France and Europe

While TRIPS classifies GIs as private IPRs,[1] State intervention in GIs in many countries such as India has been expanded from the WTO-driven minimum role of framing GI recognition and protection to include various public policy considerations. Indeed, in India, the State and its agencies play an important role in the process of filing GI applications, including being the applicant of the GI. Therefore, through their position as the applicant, the State is involved in the definition of the content of the GI application and in the authorization of producers to use the GI.

In France, GIs were first a tool of public policy from the government through the Ministry of Agriculture and its specialized body, the INAO, but the substantive reform of 2006 provides for a step backward in State involvement and a transfer of activities from the State to the producers' organizations. It reinforces the role of the producers in the building of the GI specification and it provides for the disengagement of INAO in the inspection and control activities.

---

[1] See the qualification of GIs as private rights given by the panel of WTO opposing EU to US, WT/DS174/R, 15 March 2005.

Yet, both countries' experiences concur to the salient role of the State, which is also found in the international protection system of the Lisbon Agreement and in the regional European system.

# 5

# The Influence of WTO on the Role of the State in the International Protection of GIs

## The Role of the State in the Pre-WTO System

Countries that traditionally protected appellations of origin had created a legal framework based on the crucial involvement of the State under the Lisbon Agreement on the international protection of appellations of origin.

The Role of the State in the Lisbon Agreement System

*Automatic Protection*
The effectiveness of the Lisbon Agreement system depends on certain rules of substantive law and detailed formalities of international registration. The Lisbon Agreement creates a Special Union between signatory countries.[1] As soon as the appellation of origin is recognized and protected as such in the country of origin, it is protected in all countries' members of the Lisbon Agreement, except in the countries which have rejected it within a period

---

[1] Art. 1 of the Lisbon Agreement.

of one year.² D. Gervais, writing for New World countries, considers the Lisbon Agreement is very appealing as it allows for objections against registration of an appellation.³

A major principle of the Lisbon Agreement resides in the fact that the decision on whether a link exists with the origin is taken at the nearest place to the origin, that is, in the country of origin. This unique system is based on the fact that appellations of origin are basically local, which is different from patents. According to J. Derruppe,⁴ 'insofar as there is a right to the appellation based on the recognition of certain attributes related to the geographical environment, the conditions of this right shall be based on the law of the country of origin' Yet later, any court of any country can invalidate an appellation of origin following an action by an interested party, what happened in France regarding the appellation of origin 'Bud'.⁵

*The Role of the Authorities of the Countries*

The countries which are signatories to the Lisbon system participate via their authority, which acts as their sole representative and is involved at all stages of the registration procedure of appellations of origin. The registration of appellations of origin shall be effected at the international bureau, at the request of the authority of the countries of the Special Union, in the name of any natural persons or legal entities, public or private, having, according to their national legislation, a right to use such appellations.⁶ Consequently, individuals cannot send their applications directly to the international bureau.

In case of objection by a foreign country, the administration acts as an intermediary between the international bureau and the stakeholders.⁷

---

² Art. 5(3) of the Lisbon Agreement.
³ Daniel J. Gervais, 'Traditional Knowledge: Are We Closer to the Answers? The Potential Role of Geographical Indications', *ILSA Journal of International and Comparative Law* 15, no. 2 (2009): 564.
⁴ Jacques Derruppe, 'Appellations D'origine, Indication De Provenance', in *Répertoire De Droit International* (Encyclopédie Dalloz), 106 cited in Rochard, *La Protection Internationale Des Indications Géographiques*, 308.
⁵ Order of the Tribunal of Grande Instance of Strasbourg, 30 June 2004.
⁶ Art. 5(1) of the Lisbon Agreement.
⁷ Art. 5(5) of the Lisbon Agreement.

Legal action required for ensuring the protection of appellations of origin may be taken in each of the countries of the Special Union under the provisions of the national legislation: at the instance of the competent office or at the request of the public prosecutor, by any interested party, whether a natural person or a legal entity, whether public or private.[8] This arrangement is unique in the field of intellectual property.

In spite of the advantages of the Lisbon Agreement, the number of countries that endorse it is very low and, consequently, marginal in comparison to the number of WTO members. It is not so much the State's role that explains this low endorsement, but rather the strictness of the definition of appellation of origin used.[9] Indeed, a new draft, revised Lisbon Agreement is under negotiation to broaden the scope of the Agreement with the introduction of the concept of geographical indications, in order to attract more signatories.[10] The revised Act draft maintains the role of the State via its competent authority in the international registration of appellations of origin while proposing as an amendment the possibility that the application is filed directly by the beneficiaries or a legal entity which has legal standing to assert the rights of the beneficiaries in the appellation of origin or the geographical indication.[11]

## The Role of the State in the Protection of Foreign GIs in Europe

The European Regulation 2081/92 provided protection in Europe for GIs from foreign countries, that is, countries non-members of the EU.[12] It was necessary to comply with the condition of equivalence of foreign country regulations with the EU's one, which means that the role attributed to the State of the EU countries will, de facto, be the one of the State of foreign countries. This provision has been challenged by the United States and Australia and the EU had to amend its regulation.

---

[8] Art. 8 of the Lisbon Agreement.
[9] Rochard, *La Protection Internationale Des Indications Géographiques*, 318.
[10] See document LI/WG/DEV/7/2 of 22 March 2013.
[11] See the Draft New Act of the Lisbon Agreement on Appellations of Origin and Geographical Indications at http://www.wipo.int/edocs/mdocs/mdocs/en/li_dc/li_dc_3.pdf.
[12] Art. 12 of Regulation no. 2081/92.

*The Principle of Equivalence*

The principle of equivalence means that the third country is able to give guarantees identical or equivalent to those of the European regulation concerning the content of the GI specification and the inspection arrangements. Indeed, the European system is based on very detailed and specific technical specification. The second basic element of the European concept of GIs is the need for State-supervised controls to ensure products are genuine. The inspection structure may comprise one or more designated public authorities and/or private bodies. As of 1 January 1998, private certification bodies had to comply with standard EN 45011 or an equivalent standard.[13]

Thus governments, including those of foreign countries, were required to incorporate in their domestic regulation controls to ensure compliance with the GI specification.

*The Principle of Reciprocity*

A foreign country wanting to register its GIs in Europe had to provide protection equivalent to that available in Europe to GIs coming from Europe. Protection given to PDOs/PGIs by the EU regulation is high, and corresponds to the added protection given to wines and spirits according to the TRIPS Agreement.

Conditions of reciprocity and equivalence required by the erstwhile European regulation indicated a particular vision of GIs. This was evident in State agricultural and territorial development policies, and was very different from the principle of independence of IPRs.

*The Unique Role of the State in GIs Compared to IPRs*

The European regulation was primarily intended to bring together a heterogeneous right among EU member states. To achieve this objective, the regulation establishes a two-tier system based on subordination of the duties to be accomplished at the member state level to those at the European Commission level. The State is the accepted go-between linking these two levels. Thus, contrary to a European trademark that can be filed directly with the OHIM by any natural and legal person, the system of GI protection in Europe relies on the transmission, by EU member countries, of PDO/PGI applications to the EU Commission.

---

[13] Amendment of Regulation no. 2081/92 by Regulation no. 692/2003.

The same role was assigned to the 'foreign country' for transmission of GIs application to the EU.[14]

Thus, formerly, when a group or a natural or legal person in a foreign country wanted to register a GI in Europe, he would make an application for registration to authorities in his country. If it was found that the EU regulation requirements were fulfilled, the application would be forwarded to the European Commission, along with a description of the legal provisions and the usage on the basis of which the designation of origin or the GI is protected or established in the country.[15] The EU Commission would then send back its decisions regarding the acceptance or rejection of the application to the authorities in the country.[16]

*The Transmission of Objections*

The 1992 version of the European regulation had no provision for foreign countries to use the objection procedure. This was allowed only in 2003. Just as in the case for filing of applications, objections were compulsorily routed through the State.[17]

Although the provisions for GIs seemed identical in EU and other countries, the condition of equivalence was bound to upset the United States and Australia, who lodged a complaint against the discriminatory nature of the EU regulation vis-à-vis foreign GIs.

---

[14] The terminology of the regulation also uses the term 'State' to designate the third country.
[15] Art. 12 bis of Regulation no. 2081/92.
[16] Art. 12 ter.
[17] Articles 12 ter and 12 quinquies of Regulation No. 2081/92 provided that any natural or legal person legitimately concerned, whether from a WTO member or a third country whose law is equivalent to European regulation, may object to the proposed registration by sending a duly substantiated statement to the State wherein they reside, which shall forward it to the Commission. The Commission shall examine the admissibility of objections and where an objection is admissible, the Commission shall decide, after consultation with the State that transmitted the opposition, taking into account the traditional fair practice and of the risks of confusion.

## The Impact of the WTO Panel on the Role of the State

On 18 August 2003, the United States and Australia filed a complaint in front of WTO DSB, against the European regulation no. 2081/1992. The panel's reports were adopted by the DSB on 20 April 2005. The EU did not appeal.[18]

### The Decision of the DSB of WTO

The complaint made by the United States and Australia was based on discrimination against US citizens who wished to claim their rights over their trademarks against European GIs, such as the certification trademarks Idaho potatoes and Florida oranges are often cited as examples.[19] The first allegation the United States and Australia had against the EU regulation was non-compliance with the requirement of national treatment, which is a common principle of international law incorporated in TRIPS Agreement (Articles 3 and 4) and GATT (Articles I and III).[20] National treatment obligation means that each WTO member shall confer to the nationals of other WTO members' treatment no less favourable than that it accords to its own nationals with regard to the protection of intellectual property.

*The Content of the Decision*

<u>The requirement of an 'intermediary' state for foreign gis is denounced</u>

The report of the panel denounces the EU regulations as being discriminatory against applicants from foreign countries. Even if the same applied to applicants in Europe and from foreign countries, in the case of the European States, their respective governments were already

---

[18] *European Communities—Protection of trademarks and geographical indications for agricultural products and foodstuffs,* Reports of the panel WT/DS174/R and WT/DS290/R, 15 March 2005, adopted by the DSB on 20 April 2005. Citations are from report WT/DS174/R.

[19] Evans, G.E. and M. Blakeney, 'The Protection of Geographical Indications after Doha: Quo Vadis?', *Journal of International Economic Law,* 9, no. 3 (2006): 596.

[20] See Section III.A. 3.19 a) and b) page 4 of the report regarding the allegations of the United States.

The Influence of WTO on the Role of the State  151

governed by EU regulations applicable to all EU member countries. Authorities of EU member countries were thus obliged to forward the application to the European Commission, whereas it was not compulsory for GI applications from outside countries, since the EU regulation did not apply to them.

Foreign producers could not force their government to transmit their application. Consequently, the panel ruled that the EU regulation treated applicants from foreign countries less favourably than those from EU member countries.

The requirement of 'government' control over foreign GIs is denounced
For the same reasons, the panel overruled the mandatory participation of the governments of third countries in control structures. If, indeed, the Government of the foreign country did not designate and/or did not agree with control structures or monitor them, the producers could not get protection under EU regulation. The government of a foreign country was not required to apply the provisions of the EU regulation, thus denying its citizens any means of action, whereas EU member countries were bound by the obligations of the EU regulation.

*New EU Provisions for GIs from Foreign Countries*
The new European Regulation No. 510/2006 on the protection of appellations of origin and GIs, whose provisions regarding the protection of foreign GIs have been maintained in the last Regulation No. 1151/2012, has modified the procedure for third country GIs.

Analysis of new provisions
Earlier equivalence and reciprocity requirements for foreign countries are no longer applicable. Thus, applicants from these countries may file their PDO or PGI claims directly with the EU Commission (Article 49.5), although passing the application through the government of a third country is still possible. Similarly, objection by nationals of non-EU countries may directly be submitted to the European Commission (51.1), and in the case of GIs from non-EU countries, any resolution of the objection is carried out through consultation directly between the parties (Article 51.3). Provisions concerning the Government involvement in controls for GIs from non-EU countries are different from those of European GIs. Thus, foreign countries are not required to

designate a competent authority responsible for official's controls, that is, the supervision of the entire mechanism for GI control, as is required for member countries. The only controls required are that compliance with the specifications be verified, which can be ensured by one or more public authorities designated by the third country and/or one or more product certification bodies. Concerning product certification bodies, as in the previous Regulation No. 2081/92, Regulation No. 560/2006 provided they shall be accredited in accordance with European standard EN 45011 or ISO/IEC Guide 65 (general requirements for bodies operating product certification systems).

A final point concerns using the EU PDO/PGI logo, which is not mandatory for products from foreign country, whereas it is for EU GIs (Article 12), since it would be difficult for consumers there to understand that a logo with 12 stars implies compliance with a European standard, but does not indicate that the product originates in the EU.[21]

In conclusion, suspending the principle of equivalence in this way has a positive impact on foreign countries which can then implement national legislation that is more flexible than that of the EU. Additionally, they can continue to enjoy the same recognition and equal rights in the EU as those enjoyed by European producers, provided that GIs from these countries meet EU criteria for registration of PDO/PGI. However, this poses a risk: it may happen that the European Commission receives, on the one hand, an application from Europe whose validity and claims are fully verified, and on the other hand, applications from foreign countries.

### The outline of initial GIs from foreign countries filed in EU

Contrary to the panel report's projection, no GI claim has to date been filed from either the United States or Australia. Finally, producers from developing countries appear more interested in registering their GIs in Europe.[22] It was the Colombian authorities who forwarded the request

---

[21] Norbert Olszak, 'Les Nouveaux Règlements Européens Sur Les Appellations D'origine Et Indications Géographiques Protégées Et Les Spécialités Traditionnelles Garanties', *Revue de Droit Rural*, no. 343 (2006): 3.

[22] Stéphan Marette, Roxanne Clemens and Bruce A. Babcock. 'The Recent International and Regulatory Decisions About Geographical Indications' (Midwest, January 2007), 27.

The Influence of WTO on the Role of the State    153

for registering the PGI Colombian coffee to the EU, and the designation of origin was granted on 1 October 2009 under the earlier European regulations. In 2013, new GIs were registered under the new regulation of 2006 replaced by the regulation of 2012, including a PGI for rice registered from Thailand, 'Thung Kula Rong—Thai Hom Mali rice' one from Vietnam: Nuoc Mam from Phu Quoc, one PGI from India, Darjeeling tea registered in 2011; a PDO from South Korea; and six PGIs and four PDOs from China, one of which being for pasta 'Longkou Fen Si', meaning pasta.[23] Many GIs are still under examination: a PGI application for Kangra tea from India; three PGIs from Turkey with one for sweets 'Antep Baklavasi' and one PDO from Turkey; one PDO from Brazil, Camarão da Costa Negra; a PGI Ceylon tea from Sri Lanka; a PGI argan oil from Morocco; and two PGIs for coffee from Thailand. It is interesting to note that these applications for GI included both applications filed by producers directly with the European Commission and those filed by the Government of the country.[24] In particular, the Chinese GIs were filed within the framework of an administrative cooperation between the EU and China.

*The Protection of GIs through Bilateral Agreements: A Central Role for the State*
Numerous GIs are protected in the EU under bilateral agreements as part of a free-trade agreement. For example the EU-Canada Comprehensive and Trade Agreement, EU-Korea Free Trade agreement, EU-Singapore Free Trade Agreement, Trade Agreement between the EU and Colombia and Peru, Comprehensive Association Agreement between the EU and Central America, Deep and Comprehensive Free Trade Agreement between the EU and Ukraine and many are under negotiations.[25]

For example, South Korea, as part of a Free Trade Agreement signed with the EU on 15 October 2009,[26] included a list of 58 GIs that would gain from protection given by Regulation No. 1151/2012 (in return

[23] See http://ec.europa.eu/agriculture/quality/door/list.html.
[24] Interview, Direction Générale pour l'Agriculture, Commission européenne, Bruxelles.
[25] http://ec.europa.eu/agriculture/gi-international/index_en.htm, consulted 15 June 2015.
[26] http://trade.ec.europa.eu/doclib/docs/2009/october/tradoc_145180.pdf.

protection of a list of European GIs). In accordance with the Free Trade Agreement, the Agricultural Products Quality Control Act (the Korean law on GIs) was examined by the European Commission and found to be satisfactory, which led to the registration of all the listed product designations proposed.[27] These GIs were then published and open to opposition as required by Article 7 of Regulation No. 510/2006.[28] This procedure of protection of GIs with bilateral agreements signed by the State resembles the mechanism in Regulation No. 2081/92: the conditions of equivalence and reciprocity, and the role of the State. The reciprocal recognition of GIs through bilateral agreements reinforces the principle that States are within their rights to decide which of their GIs should be registered internationally. It is a move towards the consideration that the country of origin, in which the place of production is embedded, is more legitimate to decide upon the existence of such link with the origin. It goes against the principle of territoriality of IPRs. The GI thus continues to be a unique IPR, since it is unlikely that States could include trademarks or patents to be protected in a bilateral agreement in this way!

## The Consequences for International Governance of GIs

According to C. Charlier and M.A. Ngo, the decision of the DSB can be interpreted as the condemnation of an attempt by Europe to force international harmonization of regulations on GIs based on the European model, with the aim of guaranteeing European GIs a high degree of protection at the international level.[29] The same interpretation is given by M. Handler who quotes the Australian trade minister's comments criticizing the principle of reciprocity on the grounds that 'it is not up to the EU to decide whether a particular term claimed by EU producers should be protected within Australia's territory as a GI.[30]

---

[27] See Article 10.18.
[28] Communication—Indications géographiques de la République de Corée, 2008/C 141/15.
[29] Christophe Charlier and Mai-Anh Ngo, 'An Analysis of the European Communities: Protection of Trademarks and Geographical Indications for Agricultural Products and Foodstuffs Dispute', *The Journal of World Intellectual Property*, 10, no. 3–4 (2007): 181.
[30] Michael Handler, 'The WTO Geographical Indications Dispute', *Modern Law Review*, 69, no. 1 (2006): 79.

Yet, the consequence of the panel decision is thus the absence of harmonization of GI laws at the international level.

*Dependence of Titles Undermined, Territoriality of Rights Asserted*

The panel asserts that GIs are IPRs, which are considered to be private rights. However, in assessing the national treatment obligation, the panel considered the national origin of the legal title, the GI, and not the nationality of the applicant for the GI, unlike in other IPRs. In fact, foreign producers established in the EU have the same rights as European producers. The panel agrees that the vast majority of producers of GI products in the territory of one WTO member country are nationals of that country. It is not a random phenomenon occurring in a particular case, but a feature of the design and structure of the GI system.

This strong link between the product, the producer's nationality and country of origin could have resulted in the dominance of the decision taken by the country of origin regarding the GI's validity when going towards international protection. However, the panel's findings tend to subject the GI to the general principle of territoriality of IPRs, which implies that every country where protection is sought has the sovereign right to decide to either register or reject a GI.

The specificity of a right based on local assessments explains the inclination of the European system of 1992 to believe that authorities of the country of origin are better able to assess whether a GI qualifies for protection than authorities of foreign countries, because such an evaluation requires familiarity with a host of factors (7.248).

The panel's ruling undermines the idea of a multilateral system of specific protection that would allow automatic or facilitated recognition in foreign countries as soon as protection is granted in the country of origin.

*The Freeze in the Negotiations of the Multilateral System of Notification of GIs*

The panel's findings echo the difficulties encountered in the negotiations for the establishment of a multilateral system of notification and registration of GIs for wines eligible provided by Article 23.4 of the TRIPS Agreement. The negotiations, recorded in the Doha Declaration (Section 18), were started in 1997 and are still ongoing. The positions and protagonists are the same as those for the litigation before the DSB.

The United States supports the minimum proposal, known as the joint proposal (the name is based upon the large number of countries that support it).[31] It is influenced by the trademark system, and the role of the State is limited to basic registration procedures similar to those for other IPRs. The basic principle is to create a database of GIs from different countries. Participation is entirely voluntary, and the database will contain information on the name protected as a GI, the concerned WTO member, the date on which the GI was protected by the member, the expiration date and, if applicable, any agreement involved[32] and, finally, following the last proposal of 2005, the identification of the area relevant to the GI.[33] Any objection is resolved at the national level because it is not considered necessary to establish a new procedure for resolving disputes internationally.[34]

The joint proposal is based on a tradition of protecting GIs through the trademark system and constructs a multilateral system that is minimally least constraining, not really supporting the protection of GIs as required by Article 24.3.

On the other hand, there is the maximum concept of protection as set forth under the Lisbon Agreement and the European mechanism, characterized by the State's involvement in defending the interests of its producers in the international phase.[35] The first EU (1998) proposal outlined a multilateral system which necessarily involved all WTO members, with all the existing GIs being already recognized and protected in their country of origin, along with applicable laws and proof of compliance with the definition of the GI.[36]

---

[31] The group of the proposed joint proposal has fluctuating contours and has increased significantly. Japan signed the first proposal submitted in 1999 (IP/C/W/133) with the United States and will be part of the 17 signatories countries of the proposal of 2002 (IP/C/W/5, 23 October 2002): Argentina, Australia, Canada, Chile, Colombia, Costa Rica, El Salvador, Ecuador, the United States, Guatemala, Honduras, Japan, Namibia, New Zealand, the Philippines, the Dominican Republic and China have not, but will sign the last proposal of 2005.
[32] See IP/C/W/5, 23 October 2002.
[33] IP/C/W/10, 1 April 2005.
[34] TN/IP/W/9, 13 April 2004.
[35] Evans and Blakeney, 'The Protection of Geographical Indications after Doha: Quo Vadis?', 607.
[36] IP/C/W/107, 28 juillet 1998.

The EU proposal regarding an objection is in stark contrast to the joint proposal, in that the differences and objections are resolved at an international level through direct negotiations between the concerned countries in terms of 'absolute' grounds of refusal, known as reserves. The 'relative' grounds of refusal shall be resolved at the national level. Possible reasons for absolute refusal include non-compliance of the GI with the definition of the TRIPS Agreement (Article 22.1), the question of homonyms (Article 22.4) and the generic nature of the GI (Article 24.6). Relative grounds include the existence of prior rights (Articles 24.4 and 24.5).[37]

The system implies a two-tier logic of examination. Acceptance of an application, after success at the first stage of the examination of absolute criteria at the international level, reduces further questions about the validity of the GI (related to these criteria) in each country where protection is sought. These legal effects also apply to all WTO members, regardless of whether they are part of the system or not. However, the obligations of the participating members go beyond this: the registration of a GI on the multilateral register constitutes a rebuttable presumption of its eligibility for protection. The European proposal is therefore based on the State's role of representing producers in the international phase.

Hong Kong shares this concept of rebuttable presumption and has made a 'middle' proposal. This proposal is based on an entirely voluntary principle of participation, just as in the joint proposal. Any conflict between competing GIs is settled at the national level, in the same way as for the joint proposal. Registration would provide prima facie evidence of ownership of the GI, its conformity with the TRIPS Agreement and the protection it enjoys in the country of origin.[38] The presumption does not apply to the recognition of GIs as a non-generic name or to the issue of homonyms. All other grounds of validity of a GI would be dealt with at the national level, leaving little scope to move to the international sphere. The middle proposal assigns the State the role of an agent for the registration of its own GIs in a multilateral notification system. However, this proposal confirms that the

---

[37] TN/IP/W/11, 14 juin 2005.
[38] TN/IP/W/8, 23 avril 2003.

protection regime for GIs at the international level, at least with regard to wines and spirits, is distinct from other legal regimes of IPRs.

In conclusion, the WTO panel in condemning the State's role in transmitting GI applications for their international protection weakens the concept of the Lisbon Agreement of an international system that assumes the country of origin is better able to review the existence of a link between the product and its geographical origin.

# 6

# The Decline of the Role of the State in France and Europe

State's involvement together with private operators is at the core of GIs in some WTO countries such as France, even though State's involvement is declining since a major reform initiated in 2006.[1] Reform has strengthened the tasks entrusted to producers by organizations in charge of the defence and management of AOCs/PGIs, including all operators as members. Moreover, the reform is motivated by the idea that control efficiency is improved if it is managed by third-party organizations that are independent and impartial, and not by the State via its specialized body, INAO, as was the case previously. The European regulation itself in 2006 following the decision of WTO amended the control system. However, France has gone further and implemented a real reduction of government role in the protection of GIs, even though GIs are still influenced, quite naturally, by public authority.

---

[1] Ordonnance no. 2006-1547 du 7 décembre 2006, JO no. 284 du 8 décembre 2006, p. 18607 texte no. 48 et Décret no. 2007-30 du 5 janvier 2007, JO du 7 janvier 2007, p. 400, texte no. 16.

## Application for GI Registration by the Producers

Previously, the government authorities in France used to exercise the mandate of defining the content of GI specifications. This led to numerous revolts, and finally to the recognition that producers must be entrusted with the task of determining the specification's scope.

### The Failure of the Definition of GIs by the State

*Failure of Administrative and Judicial Phases*

The history of appellations of origin in France bears witness to the government role in determining the technical content of the appellation of origin, something that was essential in the period of administrative definitions. For the record, the Law of 1 August 1905 allowed the use of public administration regulations to determine the definition of food, beverages and other such products. M. Plaisant and Fernand-Jacques defended the State intervention, considering it the only authority capable of solving the numerous conflicts between producers, be it in Bordeaux or in Marne.[2]

Following the Law of 6 May 1919, the State relinquished its charge of determining the content of the appellation of origin in favour of the courts subsequent to complaints from aggrieved winegrowers. Judges could take the help of independent experts appointed by them. The Law of 6 May 1919 does not require the intervention of a group of producers, as a single person can lodge an action. In practice, however, it is often the unions or associations that are invited by the courts[3] to participate in the task of official delimitation.[4]

Although the definition of appellation of origin here is primarily determined by the uses of the appellation of origin by producers on which judges will base their decision, the decisions far away from practices of producers not including production conditions will lead to much discontent among them, especially for wines. Administrative and judicial

---

[2] Plaisant and Fernand-Jacq, *Traité Des Noms Et Appellations D'origine*, 30.
[3] Norbert Olszak, *Le Droit Des Appellations D'origine Et Des Indications De Provenance* (Paris: Tec&Doc, 2001), 80.
[4] Plaisant and Fernand-Jacq, *Traité Des Noms Et Appellations D'origine*, 41.

proceedings were then discarded in favour of AOC procedures (as these entailed more involvement for producers) since the intervention of the governing State and the judiciary was deemed unacceptable by them. They felt the State was responsible for the chaos and injustice resulting from heterogeneous decisions.[5]

## The Principle of Producers' Organizations

*History of the Participation of Producers' Associations*

A major innovation in the legislative decree of 30 July 1935 was to hold consultations with producers through relevant winegrowers' associations. The success of the first dialogue between these producers and public authorities showed the way forward.[6] Following this, production conditions for appellation wines and spirits were determined by the National Committee for the Appellations of Origin for Wines and Spirits (known as INAO since 1947) after obtaining the opinion of concerned producers' association.[7] Although INAO is a public institution, it primarily comprises producers, who constitute the majority of the national committee, with only 25 per cent of the members consisting of officers from the administration and qualified persons designated by the Agriculture and Finance Ministries.[8] This distribution in the composition of the INAO Committee exists even today, and it advocates the inclusion of representatives from consumer groups.[9]

The procedure for recognition of an AOC normally begins with a request by an association of producers, even though this point is not clearly established by law, which states that only INAO can propose a recognition 'following a notification by concerned producers' association'. However, it was decided for AOCs for food products that 'application

---

[5] *Une Réussite Française: L'appellation D'origine Contrôlée*, 24.
[6] Ibid., 25.
[7] Art. 21 du décret-loi du 30 juillet 1935.
[8] This phase of protection of appellations of origin under the aegis of the national committee is often referred to as the professional stage; see Bienaymé, 'L'appellation D'origine Contrôlée', 421.
[9] Order on the composition and nomination, 8 February 2007, JO 11 February and of March 2007, JO 21 March for the permanent council.

for recognition of AOC would be endorsed by an association', in order to meet the obligations of the EU regulation for PDOs and PGIs.[10]

Significantly, the administration, in this case the Ministry of Agriculture, finds itself divested of the power to decide the content of the appellation of origin in relation to the 1935 law. Although the ministry does have veto power, it is no longer in a position to modify the content of the appellation, which is now the sole responsibility of INAO.[11]

European regulation on GIs was built on the premise that only a group of producers may apply for a PDO or PGI registration. For the purposes of this regulation, 'group' means any association, irrespective of its legal form or composition, of producers or processors working with the same agricultural product or foodstuff. Other interested parties may participate in the group.[12]

A single natural or legal person may apply for a GI only where it is shown that the person concerned is the only producer in the defined geographical area willing to submit an application and that the defined geographical area possesses characteristics which differ appreciably from those of neighbouring areas or the characteristics of the product are different from those produced in neighbouring areas.[13] As noted by N. Olszak, these conditions are not required for a PDO/PGI filed by groups, which amply highlights the rarity of individual recognition.[14]

The form and substance of the group are not defined extensively. This allows flexibility to respond to the diversity of legal structures encountered in the various member states. Producers and processors are logically in the forefront, whatever the stage at which they participate. Dealers or distributors can be involved as part of the group of other interested parties. However, the group may only ask for a PDO/PGI for

---

[10] INAO, Rapport d'activité pour 2000, p. 14, cité dans Norbert Olszak, *Appellations D'origine Et Indications De Provenance* (*Indications Géographiques*) (Répertoire pénal Dalloz, 2008), 27, section 192.

[11] CE, 30 juil. 1997, no. 147826: 'Under Article 21 of the Decree of 30 January 1935, the government, before a proposed decree concerning the delimitation of the production area or production conditions of a wine with an appellation of origin cannot change the terms of the proposal before it without rendering its decision of incompetence'.

[12] Art. 5 of Regulations (CE) no. 2081/92 and no. 510/06.

[13] Art. 2 du Regulation (CE) no. 1898/2006.

[14] Olszak, *Le Droit Des Appellations D'origine Et Des Indications De Provenance*, 81.

products it produces or obtains, which implies a strong link between the members of the group and the product.

The examination of a PGI introduced in France in 1992 was relatively similar to those for AOCs, and was carried out by INAO in conjunction with the national commission for labels and certifications of agricultural products and foodstuffs of the Ministry of Agriculture.[15] In fact, only products that had obtained an agricultural label or a product compliance certificate (CCP) could benefit from a PGI.[16] Labels for agricultural products assert that a product have a distinct set of qualities and characteristics previously defined in a given specification that provide improved quality.[17] The best known is the Label Rouge.

A major point that foreshadows the 2006 reform was that only one group of producers or processors, regardless of its legal status, was entitled to apply for a label or CCP.[18] Thus, the application was required to include the identification and status of the group applying for the label, particularly specifying the conditions for accession to the group.[19]

## The Role of Producers' Organizations after 2006

The French reform of 2006 formalizes the producers' organization of AOC products by unifying different AOC and PGI application procedures.

### The Drafting of the GI Specification

The management and defence organization (the organization) of the AOCs and PGIs[20] shall be recognized by INAO.[21] To this end, the organization forwards its statutes to INAO and, where applicable, in order

---

[15] According to Decree no. 2003-851 du 1er septembre 2003, JO 6 septembre 2003 which replaced the decree no. 2000-826 of 28 August 2000 related to substantive examination of PDO and PGIs applications, JO, 30 août 2000, p. 13403.

[16] Art. L.642-1, former C. rur.

[17] Art. L.643-2 de l'ancien C. rur.

[18] Ibid.

[19] Art. R.643-13 de l'ancien C. rur.

[20] The dispositions concerning ODGs apply to all the signs of quality and origin, including Label Rouse, appellation of origin, PGI or traditional specialty guaranteed. In any case, in regard to the present project, I will only focus on the ODGs that correspond to products which benefit from an AOC or a PGI.

[21] Art. L.642-17 C. rur.

for INAO to assess the balanced representation of various categories of operators.[22]

Wines with an appellation of origin benefit from a special regime: the representativeness of the organization is only for producers, even though other operators such as processors are involved in the production conditions as well.

The tasks of the organization are of general interest,[23] and include the definition of the product, its rules of production and the important points to control.[24] An ODG is thus responsible for developing a proposal of specifications, the 'book of requirements' and choosing a body that will control the specifications.[25] The main role of operators, as defined in AOCs and PGIs, clashes with the practice of GIs in India.

The application for the AOC/PGI is sent to INAO and is subject to a formal examination by the concerned national committee, which may either request additional information or reject a poorly prepared application.[26] The national committee then appoints an inquiry commission[27] to examine every aspect of the proposal. It also arranges for field trips to personally meet applicants and anyone with likely objections. It then reports back to the national committee, as many times as is necessary, to validate the guidelines followed or to seek arbitration.

In addition, there is a parallel process of delimitation of geographical areas for AOC applications by appointed 'delimitation experts' responsible for defining the geographical area. These experts are researchers who have to work with the organization ODG under the auspices of the examination commission and focus only on defining the boundaries without worrying about specifications. The geographical area that is proposed is approved by the National Committee, which then calls for

---

[22] Art. R.642-33 C. rur.
[23] Art. L.642-22 C. rur.
[24] 'La Réforme Des Signes De L'identification De La Qualité Et De L'origine', (INAO, 2007), 4.
[25] Art. R.642-37 du C. rur.
[26] Olszak, *Appellations D'origine Et Indications De Provenance (Indications Géographiques)*, 28, Section 206.
[27] It is composed of members of the national committee: professional and skilled people with extensive experience, not necessarily in the same domain as the sign in question.

public consultation for a period of two months. Experts examine potential claims, following which the national committee may approve the geographical area in a conclusive manner.[28] The concept of delimited *terroir* is thus governed by a very meticulous procedure that is specific to France.

Subsequently, regardless of whether it is for an AOC or a PGI, the concerned national committee decides to launch a two-month process of opposition at the national level. Therefore, the procedure for the recognition of an AOC or the registration of a PDO/PGI consists of a detailed examination of the link to the origin. It has been implemented for wines since 1935 and for other products since 1990. The novelty of the reform is mainly to be found in the organization of producers and processors.

*The Prerequisite for Operators to Be Members of the Organization*
There can only be one ODG per GI where, by law, all concerned operators are required to be members. Does this imply a strengthening of the collective nature of GIs? The obligation to be a member of the ODG represents a rupture that must be highlighted. The *Conseil d'Etat* (France's highest administrative court) was requested to suspend the 2006 law by wine producers of Coteaux de Languedoc,[29] the association Société des producteurs et des amateurs de vins de *terroir* en Languedoc (Sopravit) on the ground of the fundamental freedom of association. The judge may suspend the execution of an administrative decision, provided there is a serious doubt regarding the legality of the decision whose suspension is requested,which was not the case here as the 2006 reform ordinance was adopted according to Article 73 of the Agricultural Regulation.[30]

Essentially, membership is made mandatory to allow the ODG to be run in a more democratic manner and to ensure that all stakeholders help with the tasks of drafting the GI specification. The principle of mandatory membership must indeed be coupled with provisions

---

[28] See 'Guide Du Demandeur Igp' (INAO, 2009) et 'Guide Du Demandeur D'aoc/Aop' (INAO, 2009).
[29] CE, 12 févr. 2007, no. 301131, Assoc. Sopravit, see N. Olszak, 'La réforme des AOC et les libertés. Note sous CE, ord. réf., 12 février 2007, no. 301131, Association Sopravit et autres', *Gazette du Palais, Spécial 'Droit agraire'*, 15 août 2007, 227, p. 14.
[30] Art. L.521-1 du Code de justice administrative.

regarding representativeness of operators. In fact, a better representation of operators strengthens the collective nature of the GI by allowing for technical content which more fully expresses the aspirations of all concerned stakeholders.

In any event, this development strengthens the move to a PDO/PGI that is determined more by producers than by the State.

## The Remaining Role of the State in Scrutiny

The State guarantees an impartial examination of AOC/PGI applications. In France and Europe, as in India, the examination of the GI conducted by the State bears both the constitutive name of the GI and the technical content of the specification, unlike rules governing trademarks, including collective and certification trademarks. Moreover, the State must implement procedures to identify any objection so that third parties get the opportunity to represent their rights.

### Substantive Examination of the GI Applications Shared Between EU Commission and Member States

*Examination of PDO/PGI*
Under the subsidiary principle, the tasks of examination and organizing objections at the European level are divided between member states and the European Commission. An agency at the EU level could have been set up when the EU regulation was changed in 2006 and in 2012, not only to oversee the examination procedure but also to directly receive GI applications. This did not happen, however, which risks to make the system heterogeneous among European countries, particularly because of the enlargement of the EU.[31]

Thus, where the registration application relates to a geographical area in a given member state, the application must be addressed to that member state which shall scrutinize the application by appropriate means to check that it is justified and meets the conditions of this

---
[31] Norbert Olszak, 'Actualité Du Droit Des Signes D'origine Et De Qualité (Appellations D'origine, *Labels*)', *Propriété* Industrielle 6 (2006), 20.

regulation.[32] Applications for AOC/PGI in France are examined by the INAO before being sent to the EU Commission. The Commission scrutinizes the application to check that it is justified during a period that should not exceed 6 months. Where the application meets the conditions laid down in the regulation, it is published in the Official Journal of the European Union (OJEU),[33] and if successful, the procedure culminates in the PDO/PGI being registered in the EU Community register. If the product does not comply with the conditions and a PDO or PGI is refused following an examination by the Commission, it loses its right to the appellation of origin or PGI it had been granted in France.[34] It is thus a two-level examination procedure.

*Objections*

Just as in the case of the examination, the procedure for objections is organized at two levels. The first is at the level of the member state, where the objection can be lodged by nationals of the State applying for the registration, followed by a second level of comment at the level of the Commission where objections can be lodged only by nationals of States other than that applying for the registration.

Within three months (previously six months) from the date of publication in the OJEU, any member state, third country or any natural or legal person having a legitimate interest and established in a third country may lodge a notice of opposition with the Commission.

In the case of persons established or resident in a third country, such objection shall be lodged with the Commission directly,[35] while objections raised by member states are directed to the authorities of that member state. The latter then sends these concerns to the Commission, in keeping with the role assigned to the State within the framework of the international protection given to PDO/PGI in Europe. The Commission then invites the interested parties to engage in appropriate consultations, and only if no agreement is reached, will the decision be taken by the Commission.

---

[32] Art. 49.2 of Regulation (CE) no. 1151/2012.
[33] Art. 50.1 of Regulation (CE) no. 1151/2012.
[34] Art. L.641-10 C. rur.
[35] Art. 50.1 of Regulation 1151/2012.

The question arose as to whether a member state was obliged to forward objections to the Commission. It was held that the State was only required to take those measures necessary to address the objections, and could decide not to transmit those that fell within its national jurisdiction to the Commission. It represents a formulation of objections made primarily by the States and not by individuals, reflecting thus the traditional role of the State in the international protection of GIs. In fact, it is possible for a State to take a decision to object to a registration as illustrated by the case of Darjeeling PGI application, where Germany, France, Italy, Austria and the United Kingdom, as States, lodged objections. The consultations to reach an agreement to these objections were conducted by the State of India. Even if the tea industry in Europe was behind such objection, the State was the authority competent for the procedures.

## Supervision of Control Mechanisms

Since 2006, and the EU Regulation No. 510/2006, the nature of controls has been specified and opened the door to private certification bodies as an alternative to controls exerted by public authorities, opportunity seized by France. This strengthening of control mechanisms was designed to meet the expectations of consumers as well as the general public.

### The Pre-reform Situation in France

In France, before the 2006 reform, the control processes for AOC products which were eligible for approval were different from control procedures for PGI products that needed to be certified.

### The previous approval procedure of the AOC

At that time, products which benefited from an AOC were subject to an approval procedure which included controlling production conditions as well as products.[36] Granting approval was the responsibility of INAO, which could delegate all or part of that authority to an organization under its approval. In practice, the AOC producers' associations carried out checks on production conditions, while the accredited organizations carried out tests on the product. The screening of the product focused on characteristics that could be identified in an objective manner,

---

[36] Art. L.641-2 alinéa 2 former C. rur.

for example, through the moisture content for lenses, whereas the organoleptic evaluation was more subjective. The procedure was defined at the initiative of the INAO for each AOC. Thus, the Rural Code included a series of specific provisions for olives, nuts and wine.[37]

Approval of AOC products can include a 'declaration of AOC capability' which focuses on infrastructure for production at the farm. A check is then made before any production takes place, verifying capabilities and material resources needed to meet AOC conditions.[38]

### The erstwhile certification of PGIs and labels

The former Rural Code provided that checking for compliance with specifications of PGI products was the responsibility of INAO, which was free to delegate it to an approved certification body.[39]

Due to the link between a PGI and agricultural labels or conformity certificates, PGIs were controlled by private certification bodies required to guarantee impartiality and independence, not supposed to be producers, manufacturers, importers or sellers of similar products.[40]

*The New EU Provisions*

European Regulation 510/2006, now replaced by EU Regulation 1151/2012, has completely reshaped the organization of control by differentiating between what fell within the ambit of public authority and what could be delegated to private agencies. Historically, the role of public authority in the organization of controls was pronounced by the ECJ which, following the Exportur case, decided that the quality requirements or production standards should be controlled by a public authority. There was an attempt to defend this position before a panel, which ultimately saw little success as there was little evidence to convince the panel of the benefit of a system founded on public, rather than private, monitoring.

The WTO panel criticized the government's participation in the control system, but not the level of control required by European regulation. The

---

[37] Olszak, *Appellations D'origine Et Indications De Provenance* (*Indications Géographiques*), 32, section 238.
[38] Art. R.641-8 former C. rur.
[39] Art. L.641-6 former C. rur based on the decree no. 96-193 of 12 March 1996 concerning the certification of food and non-food crops and unprocessed and decree of 2003.
[40] Art. L.643-5 former C. rur.

panel agrees with Europe that WTO members are entitled to aim for objective assessment of product conformity, provided that they implement this objective in a WTO-consistent manner. Inspection bodies need not be established for the sole purpose of conducting inspections of the PDO/PGIs: public inspection authorities may be general public administrators dealing with public policy issues while private inspection bodies may engage in a number of other activities.

The level of control required by the EU is thus compatible with the TRIPS Agreement, at least according to the technical requirement. This conclusion is important as such a control is a basic principle of the European legal framework for GIs which ensures compliance with the specifications. According to C. Charlier and M.A. Ngo, denouncing such a requirement would have led to the complete collapse of the European system.

Since then, the years following 2000 witnessed profound changes in the issue of controls that are now part of the general EU food law.[41] The new system provides for control at two levels: the first is at the macroscopic level, and enshrines the principle of a formal system of an overall control of PDO/PGI, the so-called 'official control'. The second, at a microscopic level, concerns the monitoring of compliance with the specifications for each PDO/PGI. These provisions have been influenced by the decision of the DSB of the WTO, which condemned the State involvement in control structures in foreign countries.[42]

Macroscopic controls

The concept of official controls was introduced in 2006 with the EU Regulation 510/2006. Member states designate the competent authority or authorities responsible for officials' controls,[43] with INAO serving this function in France.[44] The purpose of this provision is to retain overall

---

[41] Establishing the European Food Safety Authority and laying down procedures in matters of food safety; see Regulation (CE) no. 178/2002, 28 January 2002, JO L 31, 1ᵉʳ fév. 2002, 1–24.

[42] See Olszak, 'Les Nouveaux Règlements Européens Sur Les Appellations D'origine Et Indications Géographiques Protégées Et Les Spécialités Traditionnelles Garanties', 1–6.

[43] Regulation (CE) no. 882/2004 related to general rules applicable to official controls and art. 36.1 of Regulation (CE) no. 1151/2012.

[44] Art. R.642-2 C. rur.

State control of PDO/PGI, in terms of the responsibility for the overall GI system, with official controls covering the overall verification that a product complies with the corresponding PGI specification. Very interestingly, the regulation of 2012 has introduced the obligation for States of the monitoring of the use of registered names to describe product placed on the market.[45] For this, member states shall carry out checks of product placed on the market, based on a risk analysis, and shall take necessary measures.[46]

The microscopic level
Verification of compliance with the specifications for each PDO/PGI is ensured by the competent authorities of the member state and/or by one or more control bodies operating as a product certification body, an independent third party to which the competent authority has delegated certain control responsibilities[47] accredited in accordance with European standard EN 45011 or ISO/IEC Guide 65.[48]

Member states are thus free to assign the control of the specifications to competent authorities within their administration or to private independent bodies or to both. The term *certification body* was introduced by the 2006 regulation and marks the inclusion of AOC/PGI in the general standards for product certifications.[49] Where the public authorities have chosen to verify compliance with the specifications, they shall offer adequate guarantees of objectivity and impartiality.[50]

*The French Reform of 2006*
The French reform of 2006 introduced the principle of control by independent private third-party bodies uniformly for AOC and PGI, whereas INAO was responsible for controls regarding AOC. France thus took advantage of the new European regulation of transferring control, which is not mandatory, from public authorities to private authorities, and thus

[45] Art. 36.3 of the EU Regulation 1151/2012.
[46] Art. 38 of Regulation (CE) no. 1151/2012.
[47] Art. 37.1 of Regulation (CE) no. 1151/2012 and Regulation (CE) no. 882/2004.
[48] General requirements for bodies operating product certification.
[49] Gonzales_Vaqué, 'Indications Géographiques Et Appellations D'origine: Interprétation Et Mise En Oeuvre Du Nouveau Règlement no. 510/2006', 795–813.
[50] Art. 36.2 of Regulation (CE) no. 1151/2012.

reduced public spending. This desire matched the opinion of civil society, which was apprehensive that the controls, although officially under the authority of INAO, were in practice delegated to producers' associations and were viewed as not being sufficiently impartial.

Henceforth, INAO, in the capacity of a competent authority according to the European regulation, is responsible for a macroscopic level of control,[51] namely:

- Accreditation of control bodies,
- Approval of control plans and
- Regulation of control bodies.

To this end, an approval and control board CAC, Conseil des Agréments et des Contrôles [in French]) was created in INAO which sought to supervise official controls that determine control principles. This high-level control is the guarantee that the entire control system adheres to the objectives of European and French regulations.

At the microscopic level, a third-party body oversees the control of compliance with the specification on the basis of the control plan in a competent, impartial and independent manner.[52] The certification bodies are developing a control plan for each AOC/PGI specification, in consultation with the concerned producers' organization.[53,54] The control plan incorporates individualized control carried out by operators in regard to their own activities, and internal controls carried out by the ODG. It also indicates the external control to be made by the inspection body and includes a list of measures to be taken against violations. Finally, it provides the procedures for issuing the clearance that recognizes the ability of the operator to control production factors that will allow them to meet the specification.[55]

---

[51] Art. L.642-5 C. rur, see 'La Réforme Des Signes De L'identification De La Qualité Et De L'origine'.
[52] Art. L.642-27 C. rur.
[53] Art. L.642-29, art. R.642-54, art. R.642-39 C. rur.
[54] Art. R.642-37 C. rur.
[55] Art. R.642-39 C. rur.

The certification body sends the control plan to the INAO[56] board that is responsible for approvals and controls, and then sends it to the ODG which, in turn, will communicate it to operators.[57] It takes action against violations of specifications and can, after having allowed operators to record their views, suspend or withdraw a certification.[58] The certification bodies inform INAO of any decision resulting in the operator losing the right to use an AOC or a PGI.[59] All costs incurred towards monitoring compliance with the specification shall be borne by operators.[60]

In conclusion, INAO no longer act as the first-level control, although it is now responsible for the supervision of control procedures monitored by private bodies.

*Exceptions Procedures for AOCs*

Until July 2013, for those AOCs that desire it, the control of compliance with specifications is carried out not on the basis of the control plan but on the basis of an inspection plan, and not by a certification body but by an inspection body which offers guarantees of competence, impartiality and independence, and functions on behalf of and under the authority of INAO.[61] The belief is that an inspection body works more closely with INAO than a certification body.[62] We observe here a residual interest of the State in the control of specifications, but it tends to be more of an exception.

In the case of inspection plan, however, the power to take measures against violations rests with INAO.[63]

With the concerned rules having been specified, the organoleptic tests were retained for the AOC. Thus, an organoleptic tasting is carried out by a commission comprising professionals and experts who are skilled in

[56] Art. R.642-39 C. rur., art L.642-10 du C. rur.
[57] Art. R.642-55 C. rur.
[58] Art. L.642-30 C. rur.
[59] Art. R.642-55 C. rur.
[60] Art. L.642-27 C. rur.
[61] Ibid.
[62] Art. L.642-27 which states that all costs incurred by the necessities of monitoring compliance with the specifications shall be borne by the operators, control is provided by a certification body or an inspection body and by the National Institute of Origin and Quality.
[63] 'La Réforme Des Signes De L'identification De La Qualité Et De L'origine.'

the relevant conditions, to ensure an independent and impartial examination of the products.[64]

AOC-specific provisions were implemented mainly in order to achieve a smooth transition. N. Olszak justifies this difference by the following pragmatic requirements: if for certain signs of quality for foodstuff products one had the habit of turning to product certification, this was not the case for many appellations of origin of wine, and it was necessary to encourage the transition to the new system without being weighed down by the red tape and costs involved in an accreditation process.[65]

## Action for Infringement

INAO, as a public institution, has the power to litigate and bring a civil action on behalf of producers' associations which, in turn, can also bring civil actions in case an infringement on an appellation undermines the interests of an industry. It is a French practice that was not reflected in European law until the last amendment of the European legal framework in 2012 which introduced ex officio protection for GIs in all European member states.

### Ex Officio Protection of GIs in Europe

The ex officio protection[66] of GIs has been introduced in the EU Regulation 1151/2012, which means that member states shall take appropriate administrative and judicial steps to prevent or stop the unlawful use of GIs that are produced or marketed in that member state. To that end, States shall designate the authorities that are responsible for taking these steps in accordance with procedures determined by each individual member state.[67]

Such ex officio protection has been introduced as a result of a decision of the EUCJ regarding an action to restrict the usage of the term 'Parmesan', which is a translation of the Italian PDO Parmigiano-Reggiano.[68] This case opposed the European Commission to Germany,

---

[64] Art. L.642-27 C. rur.
[65] Olszak, *Appellations D'origine Et Indications De Provenance (Indications Géographiques)*, 31, sections 227–228.
[66] Following a question at the European Parliament, January 2013.
[67] Art. 13.1.
[68] Case Parmesan C-132-05 Order of 26 February 2008.

where the Commission requests the court to declare that, by formally refusing to proceed against the use, on its territory, of the name 'Parmesan' on the labelling of products which do not comply with the requirements of the specification for the PDO 'Parmigiano-Reggiano', thereby favouring the appropriation of the reputation of the genuine, community-wide protected product, Germany has failed to fulfil its obligations. While it is not contested that Parmesan is an evocation of Parmigiano-Reggiano and consequently such use of the word 'Parmesan' for cheese which does not comply with the specification for the PDO 'Parmigiano-Reggiano' must be regarded as infringing the protection provided for that PDO under EU regulation, the ECJ ruled that a State, other than the member state from where the PDO or PGI originates, has no obligation to take on their own initiative the measures necessary to penalize infringements. The court considered it is the responsibility of interested parties, and by extension of producers, to complain. In this case, the court found that German law ensures effective protection of rights of producers by guaranteeing them the possibility to appeal against any conduct that is likely to prejudice a PDO/PGI. The court thus rejects the Commission's argument that the violations of Article 13 of Regulation No. 2081/92 should be subject to statutory measures and not just private actions brought before national courts.[69] Such interpretation of the court is now invalidated with the explicit reference to the ex officio protection.

*The French Experience*

Producers in France have since long been empowered to defend their rights to appellations of origin since wine-related trade unions have obtained, after protracted legal battles, a recognition for intervention of groups as claimants to protect the general interest of the industry.[70] However, the State also has powers related to lawsuits. Thus, under the Decree-Law of 1935, the National Committee for Appellations of Wines

---

[69] EUCJ, 26 Feb. 2008, aff. C-132/05, Commission c./ Germany: JO C 92 12 April 2008, p. 3. See Le Goffic, 'Le Parmesan, C'est Râpé! (Commentaire De L'arrêt De La Cjce Du 26 Février 2008)', 1–7, and Joanna Schmidt-Szalewski, 'Protection Communautaire Des Dénominations Géographiques', *Propriété industrielle*, 6, no. Juin (2009): 1–4.

[70] Ch. Réunies, 5 avr.1913, S.1920.1.49, Olszak, *Appellations D'origine Et Indications De Provenance (Indications Géographiques)*, 7.

and Spirits could contribute to the protection of appellations of origin in France and abroad, cooperate, to this end, with associations formed to defend these appellations and take legal action to defend the same (Article 23). It was the same for the National Committee of Appellations of Origin of Cheeses (Article 5, Law of 1955). It is natural that the INAO assumed this task, all the more since the Lisbon Agreement provided a similar mechanism.[71]

In conclusion, the French tradition of State intervention demonstrates the specificity of the AOC in France. Recent development, however, shows the decline of State intervention in favour of private stakeholders. The State was relegated to the role of general guarantor, an institution that yet provides a public character to the GI, albeit to a lesser extent. The competence of public authorities to determine the contents of the GI is also declining, following the transfer of the task of defining specifications to operators who are members of the ODG. This transfer seems beneficial in France if we put together the difficulties generated by the definition of appellations of origin by the State. On the other hand, the government is very reliable regarding the examination of applications for AOC/PGI in France, where it is seen as very meticulous and guarantees the specific function of GIs: the existence of a link between the product and its origin. However, is this really a public authority? But the INAO Committee is composed of a high number of professionals which gives it a 'neo-corporate' character. These professionals seek to promote their ideas and interests, a fact that could risk affecting the perception of the entire institution of AOCs and PGIs. Such a risk could at least be countered by the welcome reforms of control that are independent and impartial.

At the European level, it is striking that after the introduction of the private certification bodies for the inspection of GIs in 2006, there is in 2012 a step back to public intervention, with the introduction of the ex officio protection of GIs against its unlawful use and the provision that the costs of the verification of compliance with the specifications may be supported in part by the member states[72] while 2006 regulation provided for the costs to be borne only by operators.

---

[71] Art. L.642-5, 8 C. rur.
[72] Art. 37.1 of the EU Regulation No. 1151/2012.

This declining trend in State action in France seems thus a little anachronic to the European evolution. French public action decline is far from the reality in the Indian scenario, where the involvement of the State as applicant is strong, unexpected, added to the State's task of substantive examination of GI applications.

# 7

# The Interventionism of the Indian State

As in the EU, the State is responsible for scrutiny of the GI application and opposition's procedures. The State set about promoting GIs in India with complete commitment, conviction and dynamism. Seminars were organized under the direction of the GI Registry to raise awareness of the concept of GIs, and State officials immediately began to start protecting GIs with renewed, almost messianic fervour, even up to the point of wanting to use the system to protect the 'chakra', the cotton spinning wheel which was the symbol of Gandhi and the struggle for independence. GIs in India can also be organized in collaboration with the CII, which plays a supportive role to the State.[1] Many other agencies are created to help the development of GIs: for example, the Federation of Indian Micro and Small & Medium Enterprises (FISME) is planning to set up an intellectual property facilitation (IPF) centre in Bangalore, Hyderabad and Delhi.[2] Moreover, daily and business newspapers

---

[1] National Seminar-Cum-Workshop of Stakeholders of Geographical Indications on 18–19 September 2008, New Delhi, in coordination with Confederation of Indian Industry.

[2] http://www.deccanherald.com/content/305142/intellectual-property-facilitation-centre-soon.html, consulted on 15 April 2013.

regularly report every registered GI. However, the Indian State discharges a function that is entirely unexpected: the filing and registration of GIs in its name, even though it does not manufacture the product. Even in the case of applicants who are producers, the State provides great support for registration of GIs (Figures 7.1 and 7.2).

**Figure 7.1**
*Nature of the applicant: 153 GIs registered for Indian products, December 2011*

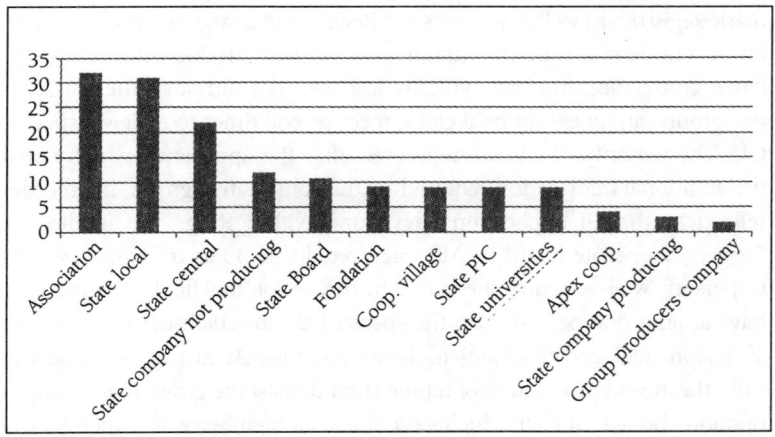

**Figure 7.2**
*Within the State bodies: 153 GIs for Indian products, December 2011*

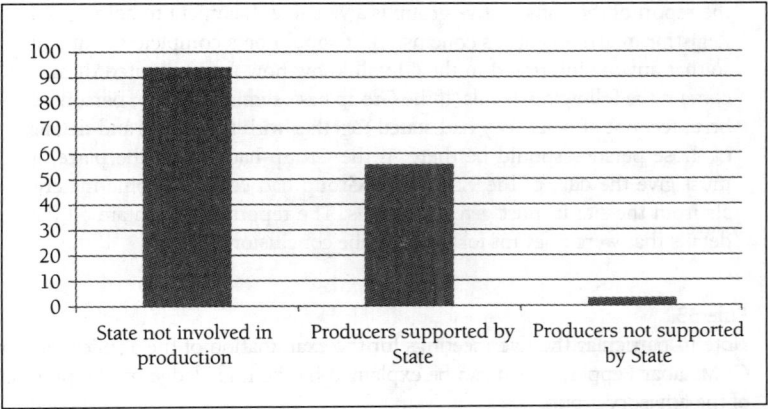

## The Role of the State in Scrutiny

GI Registry examines the application and constitutes a consultative group of not more than seven representatives or persons chaired by the Registrar of GIs. The members of this group are from institutions such as universities or well-known organizations and are experts in the field.[3] The Controller General of Patents, Designs and Trademarks is always a member of the consultative group, although in practice he can be replaced by the trademark Registrar, as well as the assistant Registrar in charge of the GI Registry. Producers demonstrate the 'uniqueness' of their product during consultative group meetings that typically last one day, although the consultative group can, in exceptional cases, meet several times to review a specific GI.[4] The majority of GIs are registered after the applicant has submitted the additional information required by the consultative group. In an order related to the GI application Payyanur Pavithra Ring,[5] the Intellectual Property Appellate Board (IPAB) interpreted rule 33 as referring *inter alia* to persons well-versed in the varied intricacies of 'this field'. It is better to have at least one person from the special field to which the goods relate. That alone will lend credibility to the proceedings. An artisan or a producer from the area of production of repute should assist the group in forming an opinion about a GI claim. Inclusion of such a member with expertise will undoubtedly further the Objects and Reasons and will ensure the protection of the artisans and craftsmanship. Further IPAB order points out that

> the report of the consultative group is a valuable document to help the GI Registrar in arriving at his conclusion. It should be a complete document so that anyone interested in the GI will know how it was granted. It may contain the following details. If the Group has examined certain persons, a brief account of what they had stated together with the names and details of those persons should be there. If the Group had visited the place, it must give the date of the visit. If the Group had collected some materials from the site it must give the details. The report must contain all the details that were relevant for drawing the conclusion.

---

[3] Rule 33.
[4] Note in particular the five meetings for the examination of the application for GI Malabar Pepper, which can be explained by the knowledge on the product of the advisory group.
[5] Order (No. 255 of 2012), 14 November 2012.

If the application is accepted, it is published in the Official Journal of Geographical Indications and subject to potential opposition, as for any IPR. A hearing may be held by the GI Registry.[6] If the GI is accepted by the Registrar, it is recorded on Part A of the register of GIs, unless the Central Government decides otherwise.[7]

Rectification of a GI registered can be requested to the Appellate Board or to the Registrar by any person aggrieved.[8]

There has been several applications for cancellation of GIs, one against the GI Darjeeling and one against the GI Tirupati Laddu, with orders of the Registrar or of the IPAB. Both rectification applications have been rejected on the principle of absence of locus standi of the applicant for rectifications which was not an aggrieved person (see Chapter 8).

# The Support of the Indian State to the Applicant/Proprietor

A third of the Indian GIs are registered in the name of their producers. Apart from certain applicants who are sole producers, applicants are producer groups that have the legal status of an association or a cooperative governed by the Society Act of each Indian State. However, following a complete review of the files and/or interviews with applicants, in many cases it appears that the State was involved in the protection of those GIs as well. There are, however, a few GIs that are actually the result of a purely private initiative from producers.

## Exceptional Cases with Little Involvement of the State

*Producers' Associations*

### The All India Agarbathi Manufacturers' Association

The All India Agarbathi Manufacturers' Association (AIAMA) was founded in 1949 and owns the GI Mysore Agarbathi (incense sticks). The group comprises 400 members, 300 of whom are located in Bangalore

---
[6] Section 14.
[7] Section 16(b).
[8] Section 27.

and account for about 90 per cent of the goods manufactured under the name Mysore Agarbathi.[9] AIAMA is very active and organizes regular seminars for its members. The initiative of application for registration was taken by younger members of the association who hoped to implement an active marketing policy for products using GI registration as a tool. A special committee comprising 11 members was established for the management of the GI. This committee decides on the nature of the products which will be allowed to use the GI.

According to AIAMA, the GI will help create product awareness, improve the packaging and put into practice a quality policy.[10] AIAMA is the sole authority that oversees and manages the production of Mysore Agarbathi and the use of the GI.[11]

The 'Payyanur Pavithra Ring Artisans and Development Society'
The GI Payyanur Pavithra ring has been applied by the Payyanur Pavithra Ring Artisans Society, created especially for registering the GI as the body was recognized by the law only six months after the application date. Oppositions to this applicant by artisans have conducted the IPAB to take an order and cancel the registration (see Chapter 8).

*A Sole Private Producer*

Reliance, one of the largest private Indian companies, filed for four GI applications for petroleum products (fuel, gas, diesel, LPG) as a sole producer. This led to a major controversy because of the nature of the applicant and the nature of these products, which ultimately led to Reliance withdrawing the GI applications in September 2009, four years after they were filed.

## GIs Applicant Linked or Supported by the State

*Legal Entities Partly Managed by the State, the Sole Producer*

Even though there is no longer any difference between 'state-owned companies'[12] and 'private companies' following the introduction of the

[9] Mr Hussain Razwan, President of AIAMA.
[10] Mr Septagiri, Director of the enterprise Sarathi, President of the GI Management Committee, AIAMA.
[11] See GI file.
[12] Interview with Rahul Singh, Professor, NLSIU, Bangalore, 7 May 2008.

Competition Act of 2002, it would seem that consumers have a somewhat more hallowed image of state-owned companies as opposed to private enterprises.

The state-owned companies that produce GI Mysore silk (Karnataka Silk Industries Corporation [KSIC]) and Mysore sandal soap and Mysore sandal oil (Karnataka Soaps & Detergents Ltd [KSDL]) are industries that have manufactured these products for a long time. They benefited from technical and production facilities that were inherited from the Maharaja of Mysore, including equipment that was often imported from the United Kingdom and represented a technological innovation in its time. As a result, these companies were pioneers in the manufacture of the above products.

The weaving plant was established in 1912 by the Maharaja of Mysore in order to meet the wants of the royal family. The factory soon increased its installed capacity from 10 weaving machines to 44, all imported from Switzerland. Following the independence of India, the Department of Sericulture of the erstwhile state of Mysore took over control of the factory. In 1980, the silk weaving factory was merged with the KSIC, whose board of directors comprised exclusively of employees of the Government of Karnataka. KSIC sells its products exclusively through its own shops, following a franchise model. Following the registration of the GI, KSIC changed its brand name from a simple 'KSIC' to one that included 'Mysore Silk' and the words 'heritage weaves'.[13]

KSIC proclaims itself to be the sole producer of Mysore silk. The GI defines the method of manufacture which corresponds exactly to that of KSIC and the geographical area is limited to the city of Mysore. KSIC registered the GI to boost its declining sales, thanks to the fight against imitation goods that were estimated to have taken over more than 60 per cent of the market share.[14] Misuses lead to a need to define authentic goods, but the definition of what Mysore silk is according to KSIC is not shared by everyone, and has led to objections (see later).

KSDL is a public company owned by Karnataka, and was formed and registered in 1980 under the Company Act of 1956. It was formed by merging the Mysore Sandal Soap Factory, established by the Maharaja of Mysore in 1916, and the oil company established in 1944. KSDL is

---

[13] http://www.ksicsilk.com.
[14] Mr Vijayan, General Director, KSIC.

considered to be one of the largest producers of sandalwood oil in the world.[15] The geographical area demarcated in the application for the GI covers the city of Bangalore, home to the KSDL plant, and not the erstwhile Mysore Presidency which also forms part of the state of Karnataka. The GI is based on the name Mysore Sandal Soap and KSDL's defining logo, which is a lion with an elephant head. The description of the manufacturing method, the geographical area and the inclusion of the company's brand in the GI's logo comes from the fact that KSDL is the only producer that complies with the specifications of the GI.

In conclusion, although these companies are government entities in terms of control and funding, they can be classified as commercial enterprises. This thus brings up the question of the legitimacy of their ownership of the GI, since they can be considered as one among the numerous producers. Although these government enterprises, inheritors of the businesses of the Maharaja, were the first to manufacture the product in question, other producers of these products may now exist, and as a result, the registration of the GI led to their exclusion, due to a specification that is limited to a manufacturing process specific to the state-owned company and a geographical area corresponding to where the plant of the public enterprise is located. Thus, it is significant to note that the applications for the GIs Mysore sandal oil and Mysore silk have both given rise to objections (see later).

*State Participation in a Religious Organization*

Tirumala Tirupati Devasthanam (TTD) is a Hindu religious organization in charge of the management of the Tirumala temple and owns the GI Tirupati laddu. The TTD is governed by the TTD Act, a specific law created in 1932 which provides that the temple is administered by a board comprising representatives from the central and state governments.[16] The TTD is the only producer of Tirupati laddu, generatingt considerable controversy in India. This is also the first case of a GI being registered in the name of a religious body for a religious good (see later).

---

[15] http://www.mysoresandal.co.in/index.html.
[16] The A.P. Charitable & Hindu Religious Institutions & Endowments Act (1987), *The Tirumala Temple*. Tirumala: Tirumala Tirupati Devasthanams. 1981, http://en.wikipedia.org/wiki/Tirumala_Tirupati_Devasthanams#cite_note-Tirumalatemple-2, consulted on 22 November 2009.

## Associations/Cooperatives Supported by the State

The State supports directly, or through its agencies, to numerous GIs submitted by producers' groups.[17] The CII is increasingly partnering with the State in a mission to protect GIs. The CII is a nonprofit NGO in the industrial sector which plays a major role in the economic development of India. Established in 1889, it was one of the first professional organizations in India, and arguably the largest. Its members include more than 7800 direct affiliates from the public and private sectors, and its extensive network includes 90,000 companies as indirect members The CII has identified potential products and has supported filing procedures in several states, such as Andhra Pradesh and Chhattisgarh.

Primary cooperatives

Most cooperatives that own GIs are in the handicrafts sector, more specifically in the textiles sector. There are two levels of producers' cooperatives. Village cooperatives that are often concerned with a specific product form the first level; they are known as Primary Handloom Weavers' Cooperative Societies or Primary Handicrafts Cooperative Societies. The second level comprises more inclusive cooperatives that are formed and managed by the State, and are known as Apex Cooperative Societies.

The Puri Creative Handicraft Cooperative Society, which co-owns the GI Pipli appliqué work, is a primary cooperative of 63 artisans (including 18 men and 45 women) who are direct members and 243 are associate members. Bodies that help in its development include the Directorate of Handicrafts & Cottage Industries of the state government and the Development Commissioner (Handicrafts) of the central government, Ministry of Textiles. The Orissa State Cooperative Handicrafts Corporation, an apex cooperative society, is one of its main customers.[18]

The GI Pochampally Ikat is jointly owned by a cooperative, the Pochampally Handloom Weavers Cooperative Society, a first level cooperative established in 1955 with the objective of providing saris to official government handicraft stores (emporiums) and an association, the Pochampally Handloom Tie & Dye Silk Sarees Manufacturers'

---

[17] Simply reading the official GI Gazette does not allow one to know the actors who have been involved in editing the file.
[18] GI file.

Association, which comprises a group of master weavers. This GI was registered with strong government support.[19]

The application for the GI was initiated by the Andhra Pradesh Technology Development & Promotion Centre (APTDC), an autonomous institution created by the Confederation of Indian Industries (CIIs), the Government of Andhra Pradesh; Technology Information, Forecasting and Assessment Council (TIFAC, an autonomous organization under the Department of Science and Technology, central government); and the Central Government Textiles Committee. The work of documenting and drafting the GI application was carried out by APTDC's office for intellectual property, with funding provided by the National Bank for Agriculture and Rural Development (NABARD). Since an association and a cooperative already existed, the GI application was filed on their behalf.

Moreover, the Pochampally Ikat Foundation, which is part funded (40 per cent) by the state government was created specifically to develop and use the GI for advertising and marketing. The foundation also aims to provide legal support for any future action. One of the projects of the foundation is the Handloom Park which promotes rural development in Pochampally, with a focus on training, a necessity in view of the alarming decline in the numbers of weavers.[20]

The APTDC provides technical assistance for the registration of other GIs, such as the GI silver filigree of Karimnagar, registered in the name of the Karimnagar Silver Filigree Handicrafts, Mutually Aided Cooperative Welfare Society.

Another interesting case is the GI Kondapalli Bommalu, which was filed by two applicants, one of which is the Lanco Institute of General Humanitarian Trust, part of a large industrial group in the energy field located in the State of the GI. The organization has joined forces with a cooperative of producers and traders called Kondapalli Wooden Toys Manufacturers Mutually Aided Purchase and Sales Cooperative Ltd to file for the jointly owned GI. The foundation actively promotes handicraft production by building, for example, modern manufacturing workshops.

---

[19] http://textilescommittee.nic.in/pochampally-GI.pdf.
[20] Interview with Chary H.K., Director of the Pochampally Handloom Park Pvt. Ltd, July 2007.

It has collaboration with the Design and Technical Development Centre (Bangalore), the Crafts Council of India and the National Institute of Fashion Technology. The state government has granted 100 acres to the cooperative to plant trees for manufacturing the goods.[21] Support for filing the GI can thus be seen as a humanitarian gesture that benefits local artisans of the region, while allowing the foundation to be a co-owner of the GI.

<u>An association benefiting from light state support</u>
Two GIs Navara rice and Palakkadan Matta rice indicate how the government agencies consider GI as a legal tool to protect Indian heritage. P. Narayanan Unny, a trained and enterprising farmer and owner of the Navara Eco Farm, which has passed through three generations, was keen to preserve the legacy of traditional rice cultivation in Navara. Mr Narayanan Unny's farm, spread over an area of 8 acres, is the largest producer of Navara rice with a production of 4–6 tons per year. He first thought of filing a patent for the rice variety. However, following an involved exchange with various government agencies and the CII, of which Navara Rice Farmers Society is a member, he filed an application for a GI.[22]

This GI application for Navara rice was filed on the behalf of Mr Narayanan Unny and three farmers working on his farm. In response to the point made by the GI Registry stating that a group of producers from a single farm was not entitled to file a GI application, the applicant's name was changed to that of Navara Rice Farmers Society, an association created specifically to file the GI application.[23] The GI Registry also wanted additional clarification on how the interests of all producers of Navara rice were taken into account.[24] The association comprised less than 20 members in 2008, while Mr Narayanan Unny estimated that there were between 100 and 200 Navara rice producers in all. Moreover, producers would have to convert to organic farming

---

[21] http://www.business-standard.com/india/news/kondapalli-toys-to-get-ip-protection/248170.
[22] *Hindu*, 18 March 2008.
[23] Letter from GIR, 21 December 2005.
[24] Letter type GIR according to rule 31, 24 February 2005, letter type according to rule 32, 1 November 2006.

methods, as required by the GI specifications, in order to be part of the association.

The applicant founded an association, while for the GI Palakkad Matta rice, it was the company Palakkadan Matta Farmers Producer Company Ltd, comprised of only 10 producers, of the total of 5000 producers growing this rice. The chairman of the company is Mr Narayanan Unny, and only producers can be members. The choice of the legal framework is justified by the desire of producers to make profits, like any commercial enterprise.[25] Indeed, Matta rice is considered a commercial product sold as common foodstuff, whereas Navara rice is used for medicinal purposes, which does not fall within the scope of trade but comes under the purview of 'an overall well-being of body and soul'. Moreover, the GI Navara rice seeks to preserve and conserve this dwindling resource, which, according to Mr Narayanan Unny, implies that the ownership of the GI must be with an association rather than a company.

The transfer of a GI to an association

The GI Aranmula metal mirror was first filed on behalf of the government entity Parthasarathy Handicraft Centre. In fact, the Department of Chemical Sciences, Mahatma Gandhi University, based in Kerala, in collaboration with the central government's Department of Science and Technology had initially taken the initiative to register the GI. To do this, Dr Suresh Kumar Saha, a scientist from TIFAC, a unit of the Department of Science and Technology, and Dr Ibnu Saud, a scientist at the University, visited Aranmula and interacted with artisans in order to document the GI application.[26] In the course of the procedure the application was, subsequently, transferred to Aranmula Viswabrahmana Kannada Nirman Society, which is an association of producers.

The 28 producers from six to seven families are members of the association headed by Mr Selvaraj, the son of a very influential artisan in the area. According to the GI statement of case, only members of the Viswabrahmana community are allowed to manufacture the mirror. According to a producer, only eight members of the association know the secret alloy composition. However, it appears that producers who are not members of the association manufacture mirrors that are 'not

---

[25] Statement issued during the GI application procedure.
[26] Letter from Mahatma Gandhi University, August 2003.

authentic' and sell them cheaper.²⁷ Becoming an authorized producer is not legally restricted but instead is regulated culturally as only members of specific communities can become artisans.

A local association

The GI Allahabad Surkha guava was registered in the name of a local association known as Allahabadi Surkha Amrood Utpadak Welfare Association—Allahabad. The GI was registered following the initiative of the Uttar Pradesh Diversified Agriculture Support Project, a body registered under the Society Act, which was created for the protection of the guava and submitted the first applicant for the GI.²⁸ In reply to a GI Registry request to explain how local producers were protected, the name of the applicant was changed to that of the association of producers.

Foundations funded by UNIDO

The Chanderi Development Foundation, registered under the Societies Act of 1973, was established with the support of the United Nations Industrial Development Organization (UNIDO) with the aim of protecting products from Chanderi as well as the commercial interests of its weavers in various international fora, including the WTO. One of the main objectives of the foundation is the registration of GIs, a fact that is also mentioned in its statute of incorporation. The foundation is headed by a governing body made up of four master weavers and seven weavers. The statutes allow several categories of members, and can include any individual who can prove domicile in Chanderi for 15 years.

Membership conditions seem restrictive, subject to approval by the 'managing committee'. Yet Mr V.K. Jain, the counsel for the Chanderi Foundation, states, in his report to UNIDO on recommendations on the implementation of the GI, that 'all weavers and others associated with Chanderi are automatically members of the foundation'. The statutes of the NGO, The Heritage, which filed the first application for the GI Basmati, were drafted by the same lawyer and showed the same inconsistency.²⁹

---

[27] Interview, April 2007.
[28] Mathew Prasad, Coordinator, letter to GI Registry, 24 September 2007.
[29] The file was provided by the lawyer Vinay Jain. The GI application is still not published because of a conflict with the Government which considers The Heritage's GI application illegitimate.

The Kota Doria Development Hadauti Foundation, the owner of the GI Kota Doria, is another example of a foundation established with the support of UNIDO. It is an inter-professional association that includes a representative selection of weavers, dyers and manufacturers of looms. Members are designated by stakeholders from different villages in accordance with a process implemented by UNIDO.

Both Chanderi Foundation and Kota Doria Foundation were created specifically for the registration of GIs, even though their activities are not limited to its management.

# The Registration of GIs in the Name of the State

## Autonomous Statutory Bodies Proprietor of GIs

### Commodity Boards

The annotated edition of the GI Act mentions the Coffee Board, Tea Board and the Spice Board as examples of applicants.[30] These Statutory Commodity Boards are attached to the Ministry of Commerce which is responsible for the marketing of commodities. They are termed 'statutory' as they were established under laws specific to each board, at the time India attained independence so as to effectively develop and promote commodities.[31] The functions of the boards are diverse, ranging from the production to the marketing of products, with specific emphasis on export marketing.

Statutory Commodity Boards are managed by a committee comprising representatives from central and state government ministries, Members of Parliament and various professionals (farmers, producers, etc.); these members are appointed by the central government. These boards

---

[30] The Geographical Indication of Goods (Registration and Protection) Act, 1999, *Bare Act with Short Comments* (Professional Book Publishers, 2005), 8.
[31] There are five commodity boards under the authority of the Ministry of Commerce, for five products: tea, coffee, tobacco, rubber and spices. See http://commerce.nic.in/aboutus/aboutus_commodityboards.asp.

are described as 'autonomous bodies',[32] but the connection with the government is strong at the institutional and functional levels.

The Department of Commerce set up a very active policy in 2003 to regulate the registration of GIs by the boards in order to avoid another case like that of Basmati, and to help protect the heritage of India. A choice phrase used by the minister was 'Selectivity is essential for maintaining exclusivity', indicating that only products that merit protection should be protected by GIs, not all products.[33]

The Tea Board, proprietors of GI Darjeeling as well as the GIs Nilgiri tea and Assam tea, controls and manages all the tea that is produced in India. It wields considerable regulatory power and is involved in every aspects of the production, including pricing, marketing and control quality.

The Darjeeling tea plantations are structured as commercial enterprises and managed by planters who are members of the Darjeeling Tea Association (DTA), formerly known as the Darjeeling Planters Association. Thus, DTA's membership included 67 planters in 2006, spread over 83 plantations that make up the region of Darjeeling. All the planters are in the process of becoming members, concerned with land issues, as the farmers do not own land that is leased from the State.[34]

The Tea Board licenses the use of its certification trademarks to DTA members[35] and other traders or exporters who wish to use the logo.[36] The trademark licence agreement gives the Tea Board an increased control over use of the trademark and, consequently, on the quality of tea. Considering that the certification marks were renewed, it seems that there was the desire to retain control, through the marks, over the entire sector to protect the designation Darjeeling, with the help of various legal systems throughout the world.[37]

---

[32] See the different websites of the boards, such as that of the Coffee Board and the Indian Ministry of Commerce.
[33] http://commerce.nic.in/PressRelease/pressrelease_detail.asp?id=128, India Identifies Number of Products for Geographical Indications, 22 June 2006, New Delhi.
[34] Sandeep Mukherjee, DTA.
[35] Ibid.
[36] See the rules of use of the certification trademarks Darjeeling and logo, consulted at the Office of the DTA, May 2006.
[37] Interview with Mrs Aditiya Ray, Tea Board, May 2006.

In the case of spices, the Spice Board initially identified more than 60 spices from which it selected some spices with a link to the origin, namely, some peppers and cardamoms. As a consequence, the Spice Board now owns the GIs Alleppey green cardamom, Coorg green cardamom, Malabar pepper, Tellicherry pepper, Byadagi chilli and Guntur Sannam chilli.

The Coffee Board owns two GIs for the GI Moonsoned Malabar coffee: one for robusta coffee and one for arabica.

The Coir Board (Coir Industry Act, 1953) is a statutory body which functions like the Statutory Commodity Boards, except that it comes under the authority of the Ministry of Agriculture.

In conclusion, producers do not directly apply for GIs in cases where Boards are the owners. The GI is registered in the name of the Tea Board and not in the name of the DTA, which is an organization of tea growers. Even though these boards may include representatives of various stakeholders of the industry, they are appointed by the government and hold office with members of the government and Parliament.

*The Agriculture and Processed Food Products Export Development Authority (APEDA)*

Other state agencies that come under the power of the Ministry of Commerce are involved in the protection of GIs, including the APEDA, a statutory body that can be also qualified as an autonomous body.

The Ministry of Commerce requested APEDA, in 2006, to identify potential GIs for mangoes. APEDA later filed an application for the GI Basmati in November 2008. In order to do this, APEDA had to change its status which, in its previous form disallowed any activity within India, as it was originally mandated to carry out export activities. The Act of 6 March 2008 on the APEDA amended the Act of 1985 to expand its duties to undertake, by such measures as may be prescribed by the central government, the registration and protection of the IPRs in respect of special products in India and outside of India such as Basmati. APEDA considers it is rightly positioned as it is an Indian body who can work in all states of India.[38] The Ministry of Agriculture participated in the definition of the legal content of the GI application. This application was subject to many oppositions.

---

[38] A.K. Gupta, Vice-Chairman, APEDA, interview 20 February 2013.

## Autonomous Organizations of Indian States

### Boards

Governmental bodies of a state may have the legal attributes of a board, such as in the case of Chhattisgarh Hastshilp Vikas Board,[39] an organization of the State Government of Chhattisgarh that was created in 2001 to develop handicrafts in the State. This board owns three GIs related to tribal handicrafts of Chhattisgarh.

### Government enterprises responsible for marketing of handicrafts

A number of states have established government enterprises to develop, protect and market their handicrafts and textiles. These articles are then sold through emporiums (state-owned shops). These enterprises are only required to support artisans from the State; they are not allowed any involvement in the production process. Their management is controlled by members appointed solely by the state government. A good number of these people are selected from within the State.

For example, the Karnataka State Handicraft Development Corporation (KSHDC), created in 1964 as a commercial enterprise (Company Act of 1956), is dedicated to the preservation, development and marketing of the handicrafts from Karnataka.[40] It is funded by the Government of Karnataka, which appoints the directors. There are seven of these directors, six of whom are selected from within the Government and one chosen from among the artisans. The KSHDC undertook to inventory products originating in Karnataka that have a link with the origin, and five products were selected from this list, including Channapatna toys and dolls, Bidriware, Mysore rosewood inlay, Kasuti embroidery and Mysore traditional paintings. Officers from the KSHDC conduct quality check, provide technical support to producers and assist in procuring raw material. They also provide broader and more general support, such as assistance for housing, access to schools and health care facilities, to producers who are registered with KSHDC.[41] The KSHDC is widely known through its brand name, which is made up of a logo with the name Cauvery, a mark that has been duplicated on a number of fake

---

[39] http://www.cghandicraft.com/index.asp.
[40] Mr Umashankar Apali, Manager Export, KSHDC.
[41] Ibid.

products. In fact, its authentic nature is recognized more through this KSHDC trademark, than through the GI.

Another example is the Andhra Pradesh Handicraft Development Corporation, founded in 1982, which has filed for three GIs, including Nirmal furniture, Nirmal paintings and Andhra Pradesh leather. The corporation is 75 per cent funded by the Government of Andhra Pradesh, while the remaining 25 per cent is funded by the central government.[42]

Finally, the GI Phulkari was filed by the Punjab Small Scale Industries and Export Corporation, a Government of Punjab enterprise registered under the Company Act of 1956. The goal of the corporation is to market handicraft from Punjab through its numerous stores spread across the State and support small-scale handicraft businesses, both Government-owned and private, in terms of financial and technical assistance.[43]

*State Cooperatives*

In the textiles sector, Apex Cooperative Societies, or cooperatives societies considered to be at the top of the primary cooperatives pyramid, are also known as State Cooperatives. They were created by the state government to help resolve production and marketing challenges faced by weavers. These apex cooperatives also play a role in protecting the heritage of the State.[44]

For example, the Orissa State Cooperative Handicrafts Corporation Ltd has legal status similar to that of a corporation. Its members are drawn from the central and state governments and statutory bodies. Membership is also open to any cooperative from the handicrafts sector, to any person having contributed significantly to the promotion of handicrafts, and to any master craftsman, subject to the approval of the managing committee.[45] Seventeen stores were opened under its aegis in Orissa and elsewhere for the sale of handicrafts from the State. This cooperative owns the GIs Konark stone carving and Puri Pattachitra.

---

[42] See http://www.lepakshihandicrafts.gov.in/corporate-profile.asp.
[43] See http://www.psiec.gov.in/index.html.
[44] See, for example, a presentation of the 'Andhra Pradesh State Handloom Weavers Cooperative Society Ltd.', an 'Apex Cooperative Society' in Andhra Pradesh. http://www.apcofabrics.com/aboutus.html.
[45] See http://61.8.135.28:8081/utkalika/getMenuList.do.

## State Agencies for Intellectual Property

GIs have been filed on behalf of agencies specializing in intellectual property. These agencies, or patent information centres (PICs), were established by TIFAC (Technology Information, Forecasting and Assessment Council, an organization of the Department of Science and Technology of the Central Government), whose objective is to analyze advances in technology at the global level and recommend the most appropriate technology for the Indian scenario. PICs were established in twenty states in India by 2008,[46] usually as association registered under the Society Act of the state as for example the PIC of Himachal Pradesh.

The PICs conduct research on prior art during patent application, develop initial points for drafting patent applications and educate professionals on issues related to patents. In view of their technical competence, the PICs were requested to help prepare the specifications of GI applications. To this end, PICs contact producers, collect information, draft technical points and define the geographic area. GIs registered under PICs include those for handicrafts such as Muga silk of Assam or agricultural products such as Malda Fazli mango.

PICs are also in the process of developing producers' associations in the field, in hope of educating them on GIs, which will subsequently allow them to become authorized users. However, no transfer of ownership takes place in favour of these producers' associations.

The registration of GIs on behalf of PICs shows the closeness of technical specifications in GI applications to the descriptions of inventions in patent applications. Some confusion between GI and patents remains, as can be seen in cases where the Indian press refers to a product being patented when its name was actually registered as a GI.[47]

## Institutes/Universities

Agricultural universities funded by the states have also filed GIs. Thus, the much awaited GI on Alphonso mango was filed by Dr Balasaheb

---

[46] Andhra Pradesh, Assam, Chhattisgarh, Gujarat, Kerala, Madhya Pradesh, Manipur, Rajasthan, West Bengal, Himachal Pradesh, Punjab, Sikkim, Tripura, Uttranchal, Uttar Pradesh, Haryana, Goa, Tamil Nadu, Karnataka and Jammu and Kashmir.

[47] *Tribune*, online, Sunday, 26 August 2007, Chandigarh, India, 'Patent for Assam "muga" silk', 'patent Kashmiri handicrafts' dans http://www.kashmirtimes.com/archive/0708/070811/front.html.

Sawant Konkan Krishi Vidyapeeth, a university in Maharashtra. The GIs Wayanad Jeerakasala rice, Vazhakkulam pineapple and Pokkali rice were jointly filed by the Kerala Agricultural University and producer associations. The GI for Gir Kesar mango was filed by Junagadh Agricultural University. The involvement of universities in the registration for GIs is a recent phenomenon and can be explained by the technical knowledge of the product they have.

A contentious case that would lead to several objections revolves around the Craft Development Institute (CDI), an autonomous institute established in February 2004 by the Development Commissioner for Handicrafts, Union Ministry of Textiles, and the Department of Industries & Commerce (Directorate of Handicrafts) of the Governments of Jammu and Kashmir. The CDI showcases a collective activity between the central and Jammu and Kashmir governments. The institute is run by an executive committee made up of members of the central and state governments, as well as people drawn from government agencies. The CDI is involved in developing new designs, carrying out training and protecting regional handicrafts[48] and was created mainly to assist in the registration of IPRs such as GIs.[49] This is illustrated in the case of the three GIs, Kashmir pashmina, Kashmir Sozani craft and Kani shawls, all of which were subject to objections, a fact which brings into question the legitimacy of CDI as an applicant for GIs.

## The Government

### The Government of the Union of India

All GIs filed by the central government come under the purview of the Development Commissioner for Handicraft of the Union Ministry of Textiles. This ministry is responsible for all handicrafts, with the exception of weaving, which comes under the purview of the Development Commissioner for Handloom. The Office of the Development Commissioner for Handicraft was established in 1950 to develop handicrafts in every state in order to increase the activities of the sector and boost the income of artisans, whether at an individual or collective level.

---

[48] http://www.cdisgr.org/about_cdi.html.
[49] Letter from CDI to the GI Registry, 19 March 2007.

It stresses an improvement in quality and productivity, an increase in exports and the preservation of cultural heritage.[50]

According to some authors, the bulk of these funds, which were previously misused, are now invested in extensive and innovative programmes that have changed the very nature of the Government intervention. Specifically, designers and experts are getting involved in programmes for development of clusters. The results are impressive, and many of the products that have benefited from these programmes are now on display in international trade fairs.[51]

The National Institute of Design created an inventory of handicraft products that are eligible for GI protection. Consequently, many applications for GIs were registered in the name of the central government for products as diverse as bronze casting, patchwork, woodwork, stones and jewellery and embroidery.[52] The Development Commissioner for Handicraft of the Union Ministry of Textiles is the sole proprietor of these GIs.

*The Government of the States of the Union*

The governments in some states in India have also registered GIs in their names.

The Department of Horticulture, Government of Karnataka

Following a circular from Union Commerce Minister asking that all local traditional species be identified and protected, the Department of Horticulture, Government of Karnataka, proceeded with the registration of GIs. In addition, awareness on GIs was disseminated through a seminar organized by the GI Registry.[53] The GIs Coorg orange, Mysore betel leaf,

---

[50] See the affidavit provided to the GI Registry during the examination process of the GI Ganjifa cards of Mysore, Sundara Murthi, 31 August 2007.
[51] Liebl and Roy, 'Handmade in India', 68.
[52] Coconut shell crafts of Kerala, screw pine crafts of Kerala, Madalam of Palakkad, Ganjifa cards of Mysore, Navalgund durries, Karnataka bronze ware, Swamimalai bronze icons, Temple jewellery of Nagercoil, blue pottery of Jaipur, Molela clay idols, Kathputlis of Rajasthan, appliqué (Khatwa) work of Bihar, Sujini embroidery work of Bihar, Sikki grass products of Bihar, leather toys of Indore, Bagh prints of Madhya Pradesh, Sankheda furniture, agates of Cambay, bell metal ware of Datia and Tikamgarh, Kutch embroidery and Thanjavur art plate.
[53] Mr Ramakrishnappa, Department of Horticulture.

Nanjangud banana and the three GIs on jasmine were registered by the Government of Karnataka. Moreover, the Department of Horticulture has a technical centre known as the Biocentre, which grows healthy plants for farmers. The office of GI asked this centre to carry out DNA tests that were required to check agricultural products.

The Department of Handloom and Textiles, Government of Tamil Nadu

The Department of Handloom and Textiles of the Government of Tamil Nadu is the proprietor of GIs on textiles from the State, including the famous Kancheepuram silk. The application for the GI was documented with the help of Department's Kancheepuram district branch.[54]

The Department of Science, Technology & Environment, Government of Goa and the Goa Cashew Feni Distillers & Bottlers Association

The Government of Goa (through the Department of Science, Technology and Environment) is the co-proprietor of the GI Feni with the Goa Cashew Feni Distillers & Bottlers Association. According to Mr D. Rangnekar, the association of producers (distillers and bottlers) was established by the Goan government to file for the GI. Out of the 3000 or so bottlers and distillers in Goa, only 19 are member of this association. Producers of cashew nuts are not part of this association because of a lack of vertical integration in the industry. According to Mr Rangnekar, the Goan government decided to be a co-applicant for this GI as it wanted to be among the states that own a GI.

# Trends

## The Link between the Kind of Applicant and the Product Type

The issue is to understand whether there is a relationship between the nature of the product indicated by GIs and the kind of applicant. The case of tea is notable in this regard. The Tea Board of India which

---

[54] According to A. Mohamed Jamaluddin, Managing Director, Tamil Nadu Handloom Development Corporation Ltd.

controls tea throughout the country and owns tea-related GIs (Darjeeling tea, Assam tea and Nilgiri tea) does not own the GI Kangra tea, which is registered by the PIC of Himachal Pradesh. In some cases, it is the central board that controls a given product, whereas in the other case, we observe a territorial ownership approach, since it is the state government where the plantations are situated that owns the GIs. Similarly, in the case of the GI Karnataka bronze ware, it was the central government that applied for the related GI, even though the Government of Karnataka is quite active in registering GIs.

## The Inclinations of Co-applicants

The structures in place in India lead to a trend where GIs are filed by a large number of applicants, a group that often includes state government entities. Thus, the GI Pipli wall work is registered in the name of Orissa State Cooperative Handicrafts, an apex cooperative of Orissa that includes seven primary cooperative and nine producers' associations, adding up to 16 applicants. An application for the GI Paithani sari and fabric was filed by the government body Maharashtra State Handloom Corporation and six other co-applicants. Another government organization, the UP Export Corporation, owns the GI Lucknow Chikan craft together with six other co-owners, including a foundation and two producers' associations. Similarly, the famous Benares silk GI is jointly owned by the Textiles Ministry of Uttar Pradesh, an apex cooperative, and six producers' associations. The rationale behind the registration of GIs by several co-applicants is possibly to include the maximum number of stakeholders in the practice. The following chapter will discuss the concept of the 'authorized user' in detail, something that seems to be misunderstood in India.

# 8

# The Legitimacy of the Involvement of the Indian State

The Indian government often plays an active role as a GI applicant, or as an important partner in GI registration. This is in stark contrast to European or French rules regarding GI applications, which are initiated by a group of producers. Such intervention needs to be analyzed in light of the Indian GI Act and its objectives.

## The Ambivalence of the Applicant/Proprietor of GIs

This strong State presence is analyzed in the context of the Indian GI Act which is characterized by the principle of dissociation between the applicant (called the 'registered proprietor' once the GI is registered) and the registered authorized user of the GI. The applicant is meant to represent the interests of the producers, which is the cornerstone of the system, ensuring that legitimate producers are not excluded from the GI. However, the capacity of producers to be represented varies greatly according to the nature of the applicant.

## The 'Applicant–Proprietor/Authorized User Pair'

*The Applicant/Proprietor*

The applicant shall be any association of persons or producers or any organization or authority established by or under any law for the time being in force representing the interest of the producers.[1] The term *producer* means any person who if such goods are agricultural goods, produces the goods and includes the person who processes or packages such goods; if such goods are natural goods, exploits the goods; if such goods are handicraft or industrial goods, makes or manufactures the goods, and includes any person who trades or deals in such production, exploitation, making or manufacturing, as the case may be, of the goods.[2] It is remarkable that traders can qualify as applicants when it comes to handicrafts and industrial products.

This definition incorporates the WIPO Model Law definition, which broadened its purview to register GIs for traders, but did not make a provision for mandatory representation of producers. As regards the legal nature of the applicant, the WIPO Model Law introduced the concept of 'any competent authority' included in Indian law. The applicant is then qualified as a 'registered proprietor' following the registration of the GI. The filing process is the same for an applicant who is an Indian citizen or from a foreign country.

### The legal nature of the applicant

The first part of Article 11 of the GI Act defines the legal nature of the applicant. Thus, any association of persons or producers or any organization or authority established by or under any law may apply for a GI. The definition of authority is given by the Supreme Court of India which referred to the dictionary: an authority is a public administrative agency corporation having quasi-governmental powers and authorized to administer revenue-producing public enterprise and the definition.[3] Every authority is created under a statute and functioning within the territory of India or under the control of the Government of India. All

---

[1] Section 11.
[2] Section 2(1).k.
[3] Case Rajasthan State Electricity Board vs Mohal Lal (1967) 3 SCR 377.

constitutional or statutory authorities on whom powers are conferred by the law.[4]

The representation of the interests of producers

The second part of Article 11 stipulates that the applicant shall represent the interests of producers. Details must be furnished along with the GI application, including information on producers who are nominated in the application, and who have been identified individually or collectively.[5] An affidavit must be filed to indicate how the applicant represents the interests of any association of persons or producers or any organization or authority established by or under any law![6] The strange construction of the rule should probably be interpreted in terms of Article 11 and may be seen as representing the interests of producers and not the representation of organizations qualified as applicants.

The GI Registry often requests additional information on this condition of representation of producers' interests during the examination procedure.[7] A requirement frequently formulated by the consultative group is added to this request, asking, 'What are the steps to be taken for the protection of local artisans?'

An order of the Intellectual Property Appellate Board (IPAB) dated 14 November 2012 on the opposition against the GI applicant of Payyanur Pavithra ring GI has brought clarity about the provision of the representation of producers. According to the board, Section 11(2)(e) requires a statement 'containing such particulars of the producers of the concerned goods, proposed to be initially registered with the registration of the Geographical Indication'. The Act clearly requires the submission of the particulars of the producers. At any rate, the application should show that the association represents the interest of the producers of the goods who are desirous of the registration of GI. Therefore, the least that the applicant should do is to name those producers, whether they make or manufacture the good or whether they trade or deal in the making or manufacture of the

---

[4] Smt. Ujjam Bai versus State of Uttar Pradesh, AIR 1962 SC 1621.
[5] Rule 32(5).
[6] Rule 32(6)(a).
[7] See point 3(f) of the model letter established by the GI Registry according to Rule 32 of the GI Act.

good. The IPAB states that this would appear to be a sine qua non for entertaining the application for registration.

The definition of the word 'producer' is wide and includes any person 'who trades or deals in such production, exploitation making or manufacturing' of the goods. Yet the IPAB continues with the statement that while undoubtedly the definition is wide, the persons who really need the protection are the artisans and the actual craftsmen and the growers, they might also be the most vulnerable. Even if 'a producer' includes the person who deals in this goods or selling those goods, the main object of the Act is to protect those persons who are directly engaged in exploiting, creating or making or manufacturing the goods. They have the hands-on experience of the GI products.

Compliance of the applicants/proprietors' legal nature with the law

Section 11 identifies three types of applicants: an association (which not necessarily comprises producers, as an association of persons is also mentioned), an organization (a general term that is not fully defined) and an authority established under a specific law. According to one scholar, in practice, it is the concerned trade association which has the major responsibility of protecting the GI.[8]

Some Indian applicants are entities that can easily be qualified as complying with the definition of Section 11. For example, the term *authorities* clearly refer to Commodity Boards, according to an order ruling against an application for rectification of the GI Darjeeling (see *infra*), the Assistant Registrar qualified the Tea Board as an authority established by and under the Tea Act, a statutory body, that has 30 members drawn from different stakeholders of the tea industry and 15 regional sub/regional offices. PICs and universities could also come under this category even if it does not seem so evident. As for cooperatives, they can be classified as associations in terms of legal status, as they are registered under the Society Acts of each state. Commercial enterprises, whether they are government or private, are more difficult to qualify. It seems unlikely that they could be included in the

---

[8] 'In practice, it is the concerned trade association which has the major responsibility of protecting the geographical indication. IPRs, therefore, will strengthen the hands of the trade associations dealing in the products comprising geographical indications'. Mishra, 'Intellectual Property Rights and Food Security', 11.

category of organizations. Consequently, it would appear that private enterprises as well as government enterprises find no place in the definition of the applicant's legal nature.

Conversely, it certainly looks like the Act did not anticipate that the Government would register GIs. This is therefore a major innovation brought about by practice. The presence of an applicant as the State was therefore unexpected, and if seen strictly according to the law, it might not be so legal (see Table 8.1).

**Table 8.1**
*Compliance of applicants with the first part of Section 11 of the GI Act regarding the legal nature of the applicant*

|  | Association | Organization | Authority Established by the Law |
|---|---|---|---|
| Applicants in conformity with the definition | Producers' association Apex cooperatives Village cooperatives | Religious organization | Commodity board State PIC State universities |
| Applicants whose conformity is doubtful | Government enterprise Private enterprise |  |  |
| Applicants not provided for in the law | Central government State government |  |  |

In addition to this formal analysis of a legal provision where it cannot be proven that the restriction of the kind of applicant was voluntary, it seems essential to consider the second part of the definition of the applicant, which seems fundamental with regard to the spirit of GIs. This is the applicant's obligation to represent the interests of producers.

*The Registered Authorized User*

<u>The required consent of the proprietor</u>
The obligation of producers who wish to use the GI to register themselves as 'authorized users' with the GI Registry is an innovation created by the Indian law. The application for registration of the producer as authorized user must be effected jointly by the registered owner and the producer. An opposition procedure is open from the

date of publication of the application for registration of the producer.[9] The producer is then registered in Part B of the register of GIs.

Authorized users have exclusive right to use the GI.[10] It seems fairly clear that this right is exclusively granted to the authorized users and not to the registered owners.

According to the GI Act, where two or more persons are authorized users of GI which are identical with or nearly resemble each other, the exclusive right to the use of any of those GIs shall not be deemed to have been acquired by anyone of those persons as against any other of those persons, but each of those persons has otherwise the same rights against other persons as he would have if he were the sole authorized user. The notes in the section, which is an integral part of the law, use a more precise terminology, namely that two or more authorized users of a GI have co-equal rights. In the event of the death of an authorized user, his/her right on the GI shall devolve on his/her successors.

Although some GI applications specify the identity of producers, it is usual to see the words 'to be provided on request' entered in the section 'List of association of persons/producers/organization/authority' of the GI application form. This information can be found in the GI application file that is available in the GI Registry. If references to producers are not furnished, the GI Registry notifies applicants using a form letter requesting a 'statement containing such particulars of the producers of the concerned goods proposed to be initially registered. The statement may contain such other particulars of the producers ... including a collective reference to all the producers of the goods in respect of which the application is made'.[11]

The procedure for the registration of authorized users is identical to that for registering GIs. The application for the registration of an authorized user includes a declaration indicating how the producer makes the goods designated by the GI. Any third party may express an objection against an application to register an authorized user.[12]

---

[9] Section 17, Section 56 of the Rules.
[10] Section 21(b).
[11] Point 3(e) of the model letter established by the GI Registry according to Rule 32 of the GI Act.
[12] Section 17.

The consent of a GI's proprietor seems necessary to register producers as authorized users, despite unclear provisions in the GI Act. On the one hand, the law maintains that an application for the registration of a producer as an authorized user shall be made jointly by the registered proprietor and the proposed authorized user.[13] Consequently, form GI-3 used for producers application provides for joint application. On the other hand, the law asserts that a copy of the letter of consent from the registered proprietor of the GI may accompany the application, and where such consent letter is not furnished, a copy of the application shall be endorsed to the registered proprietor for information.[14] This last point suggests that the GI Registry must inform the proprietor that a producer has made an application for registration as an authorized user. This would suggest that the registered proprietor might not be aware of such a request. However, because forms are used on a regular basis, the proprietor's consent is deemed necessary. Some examples of GIs reinforce this viewpoint. For example, the Chanderi Development Foundation recommends the authorized users to be registered at the GI Registry.[15]

Another example is given by the GI Orissa Pattachitra. Form GI-3 has been applied on 24 September 2012 for an application with 14 names of producers, presented by the Social Action Forum for Manav Adhikar, New Delhi. A statement of case of those the applicant claims to be producer is enclosed together with a copy of consent letter/no objection certificate (form B) from the registered proprietor. The statement of case is exactly the same as the one filed for the GI application with the name of the authorized replacing the name of the applicant of the GI. Moreover, one of the producers has furnished an affidavit that he has been involved in the production of Orissa Pattachitra for 25 years, and has achieved acclaim in India/overseas as being a national/state awardee. All the producers applying have the same statute of national awardee of state merit. Is it that only producers granted awardee are allowed to produce the GI good? This would mean an additional condition that those laid down in the GI specification.

Cooperatives may apply to be registered as authorized user for the benefit of all their members, if the weavers are selling in the name of the

---

[13] Rule 56(1).
[14] Rule 56(2).
[15] See the statutes of the Foundation.

cooperative and not in their own name as for example, the Kancheepuram Annai Kasthuribai Women Silk Handloom Weavers Coop.[16]

The influence of the trademark law

The condition for registering producers as authorized users was not included in the draft bill prepared by the intellectual property law consulting firm K & S Partners.[17] It was inserted by M.V. Ravi, the final editor of the GI Act, who is currently the controller general of Patent, Trademark and Design. At the time of drafting the law, he was the joint registrar of Trademarks, a fact that may also explain the influence of the Trademarks Act on the final version.

In fact, in relation to 'regular' trademark (i.e. which is neither a collective nor a certification trademark) in the former British trademark law, trademark licences were not authorized, only the company directly involved was eligible to use the brand. From 1938, licensing of trademarks, called 'permitted use', was authorized with a system of registration of the users of the mark, the registered users. Since 1999, the definition of 'permitted use' has been expanded to include both the registered users and licensed users of the trademark who were no longer required to be registered.[18]

Introduced in 1999, a collective mark belongs to an association and is used by its members according to regulations which specify the persons authorized to use the mark, the conditions of membership of the association and the conditions of use of the mark.[19] The explanatory notes included in

---

[16] See the GI authorized user Registration Certificate No. 16, Application on 4 November. 2009, Form GI-3 8 déc 2009.

[17] Project drafted by Rajendra Kumar, K&S Partners: Art. 6(1). In respect of a geographical indication relating to certain goods, the producers carrying on their activity shall have the right to use that geographical indication in the course of trade, with respect to the said products if such goods possess the quality, reputation or other characteristic attributable to that origin.

[18] K.C. Kailasam, *Law of Trademarks and Geographical Indications* (New Delhi: Wadhwa & Co., 2003).

[19] Trade Marks Act, 1999, Art. 61(2): ... distinguishing the goods or services of members of an association of persons which is the proprietor of the mark from those of others. Art. 63. (1) An application for registration of a collective mark shall be accompanied by the regulations governing the use of such collective mark. (2) The regulations ... shall specify the persons authorised to

the legislation specify that an authorized user is a member of an association authorized to use the registered collective mark of the association.[20] Once a user is authorized by the association, there are, strictly speaking, no more procedures for registering with the Trade Marks Registry.

However, the concept of registered user of the regular trademark, or the concept of authorized user of the collective mark, does not apply to the certification mark. Users of the certification mark are benefiting from the certification control provided by the owner of the trademark who cannot himself be involved in marketing or producing the certified product.

The term 'registered authorized user' used in the GI Act thus combines the concept of registered user of the regular trademark to designate the user registered with the Trade Marks Registry to that of authorized user of the collective trademark to designate a member of the association who is authorized to use the collective mark. One might conclude that the concept of registered authorized user, specific to GIs, means that the user of the GI should be registered with the registrar of GIs and a member of the association that owns the GI. What happens then to producers when the applicant of the GI is not an association? The relevance of this mechanism was, until very recently, challenged by the absence of registered authorized users.

The absence of registered authorized users until 2010

Registered authorized users have the right to use the GI; this right of use is not expressly provided to the GI's proprietor.[21] The legal commentary

---

use the mark, the conditions of membership of the association and the conditions of use of the mark, including any sanctions against misuse and such other matters as may be prescribed.

[20] Trade Marks Act, 1999, Chapter VIII, Explanation I: For the purposes of this Chapter, unless the contact otherwise requires, 'authorised user' means a member of an association authorised to use the registered collective mark of the association.

[21] Art. 21, GI Act: (I) ... the registration of a geographical indication shall, if valid, give,

(a) to the registered proprietor of the geographical indication and the authorised user or users thereof the right to obtain relief in respect of infringement of the geographical indication in the manner provided by this Act;

on the Act indicates that authorized users alone shall have the exclusive right to the use of the GI[22] and this interpretation is confirmed by the doctrine.[23] Infringement proceedings can be initiated by the registered proprietor as well as by authorized users.[24]

Yet, this clear-cut provision seems to have been interpreted in different ways. For example, the then Minister of State for Commerce, Mr Ashwani Kumar, stated, in the course of a question hour in the Indian parliament, that the registration of GIs gave the registered proprietor and all authorized users the right of exclusive use of the GI and the right to initiate action in case of infringement.[25]

Although the law provides for registration of authorized users, no producer was registered with the GI Registry until April 2010. This was the case even when the GI application mentioned the names of producers. Since then, some authorized users have been registered,[26] but the law was not enforced for seven years.[27]

An initial explanation is based on the fact that the registration procedure is probably too complex, especially since producers are ignorant of the rules regarding GIs, or even their existence. Such a procedure is applicable neither to certification marks nor to collective marks. In a recent order of IPAB regarding Payyanur ring GI, the IPAB held that the actual artisans may not even know that an application had been filed for registration of the GI. So the IPAB gave directions for publication informing on GI. Indeed, after the publication in a prominent newspaper, and affixture of

---

(b) to the authorised user thereof the exclusive right to the use of the geographical indication in relation to the goods in respect of which the geographical indication is registered.

[22] Authorized users alone shall have the exclusive right to the use of the GI.
[23] Srivastava, 'Geographical Indications and Legal Framework in India'. 4030.
[24] Art. 21 of GI Act.
[25] Government of India, Ministry of Commerce and Industry, Lok Sabha unstarred question n°3824 to be answered on 16 May 2006.
[26] As for February 2013, there are 116 authorized user registered in India and 1558 applications received related to 20 GIs.
[27] According to this phone call, 108 authorized users were registered by the GI Registry, individuals as well as associations: 4 for the GI Lucknow chikankari, 31 for the GI Kancheepuram silk, 1 for the GI Pochampally Ikat, 28 for the GI blue pottery of Jaipur, 30 for the GI Bhavani jamakkalam, 6 for the GI Benares saris and 3 for the GI Kota doria.

public notice, the intervener filed his petition, and several persons also filed affidavits stating their interest. The IPAB considers it as no answer to them to say that they can always file a petition under Section 17 of the Act and get themselves registered as authorized users. The artisans like weavers, goldsmiths and other craftsmen may not be affluent or literate in English language, so the publication must be in the local language.

The IPAB then recommends to the committee to ascertain from the persons who have filed the affidavits, whether they are desirous of being registered as authorized users. If such applications under Section 17 are filed, they may also be considered. It is also open to the GI Registrar, if he is so satisfied, to register the respondent association and the trust (intervener) as joint proprietors. It is open to one of the artisans to apply as an authorized user or as a member of the society, what is left to his discretion.

In conclusion, the clear theoretical principle of proprietor–user seems largely unimplemented. The category of proprietor seems to dominate that of the authorized user. It is poorly understood because it is not known well, whereas property rights are treated as sacred in India, just as it was in France after the Revolution of 1789. Such sacralization of property right has led to many procedures in India against applicant of GIs (see *infra*), which suggest to get rid of such a concept as the author proposes in Part III of the book.

## Producers Represented by the Applicant–Proprietor

In the domain of GIs, contrary to collective and certification trademarks, the applicant–proprietor represents the interest of producers, thus ensuring that producers are not excluded from using an appellation they aspire to. Although the applicant's decision about the content of the GI specifications can lead to this exclusion, the consent of the GI proprietor as to whether GI can be used or not is also a determining factor. Many objections have been raised regarding the legitimacy of certain GI applicants, and one of the major arguments that tends to be put forward is that the interest of producers have not been taken into account by the proprietor (see *infra*).

The applicant's capacity to represent the wider pool of potential applicants is analyzed in detail by referring to GI files and interviews of different stakeholders. In particular, can the State, whose legal status does not comply with the law, represent producers and be the legitimate owner of a GI? Can it be claimed, following Yashwant Panwar, an IPRs expert in TIFAC, that due to the nature of GIs as collective rights, the Government has the responsibility to monitor the GI registration process?[28] Do the associations or organizations represent the producers in a better way?

*The State's Ambivalent Representation of Producers*

<u>The commodity boards representing all the producers of the industry but facing oppositions</u>
The Commodity Boards which administers all the producers in certain industries seem to know all of them and are responsible for constituting a list which includes as many producers as possible. For example, 10,000 small producers' companies are registered under the Coir Board which employs more than 80,000 workers using 85,000 looms.[29] Moreover, the Coir Board has approved 400 government cooperatives and 300 cooperatives uniting small producers who respect quality norms.[30] Such a repertory helps greatly in identifying GI users.

The Coffee Board has been providing technical assistance to coffee producers since 1950. This background justifies its legitimacy to register GIs. The Monsooned Malabar coffee users have thus been formally identified by the Coffee Board, which lists seven exporters in the GI application.[31]

As for the Tea Board, it has established itself as the suitable strategist for GI registrations because of its experience in protecting the Darjeeling appellation and certifications trademarks through legal actions. Yet, a rectification application had been filed under Section 27 of GI Act by Rajeev Saraf, defended by Vinay Kumar Jain for removal of 'Darjeeling Tea' GI,[32] on the ground that the Tea Board has no locus standi to file GI, as representative of stakeholders of Darjeeling tea export is not qualified to become a GI owner. According to the rectification applicant, the Tea Board is a commercial incorporation not a nonprofit, and is not meant to

---

[28] Delhi, interview, 13 November 2007.
[29] See file of the GI Alleppey Coir.
[30] Mr Govadrij, Deputy Director of the Coir Board.
[31] Dr Raghu, Coffee Board.
[32] Letter dated 3 February 2009.

protect the interest of farmers/growers of Darjeeling who are not member of the Tea Board. He claims that no scrutiny of the status of Tea Board was made at the time of GI application. As no authorized users are mentioned in the application, they are not registered. He thus considers that there is the deprivation of pre-existing legitimate legal rights of the basic farmers/growers of Darjeeling. Publication of GI should have been done in the geographical area. The assistant registrar vide order dated 28 September 2012 rejected the rectification application, inter alia, on the ground of absence of locus standi according to Article 27 and Rule 65 of the GI Act. Being a citizen of India according to the registrar is not enough to prove that he is harmed by the registration of a GI, rejecting the allegation of the rectification applicant that he is a citizen of India, a public spirited person and that every GI is enforceable against any citizen. The delay between rectification application and registration of the GI, five years, was also considered as too long.

During the EU registration process, Rajeev Saraf also opposed Darjeeling PGI application of the Tea Board. But the rectification applicant did not respond to the Tea Board communications to meet or to have discussions as was mandated under Article 7 of EU Regulation 510/2006. According to the assistant registrar, this clearly establishes a pattern vis-à-vis the applicant's misconduct in filling frivolous objections and not defending the same on merits. The lost time and harassed Tea Board as the applicant for rectification never turned up for hearing at the GI Registry was fined ₹10,000.

In spite of the legitimacy of these Boards' registration of GIs, their understanding of the GI concept is heterogeneous. The Spice Board misunderstood it since its reply to the consultative group's request asking it to consider the interests of the producers of Malabar pepper and Tellichery pepper[33] was: 'this application does not address the interest of the producers of Malabar and Tellichery Pepper since it has no bearing on the interest of these parties'.[34] The consultative group then asked the Board for modification again as 'this application takes into account the interest of all stake holders'.[35] Later the Spice Board began to promote itself as an ardent defender of producers' interests:

[33] The GI application for Tellichery Pepper has since been abandoned.
[34] Statement fournished by the Spice Board, 23 November 2006.
[35] Meeting of the Consultative group, 3 April 2007.

The Spice Board is implementing several schemes for helping the Malabar pepper growing farmers as per their requirements and our mandate. In future the Board will implement specific programs for the benefit of the said farmers. Moreover, the Board will take timely action in bringing the specific problems of the Malabar pepper farmers to the notice of the concerned authorities to solve their problem. Therefore the interest of the local farmers cultivating Malabar pepper shall be protected by the Spice Board.[36]

The Spice Board probably interpreted the obligation of representing producers as a ploy for establishing a financial and organic link between the Board and the producers. Moreover, the example of Malabar pepper GI shows clearly that the declarations of applicants are sufficient and do not require further investigation by the GI Registry.

The Commodity Boards, who a priori represent all the producers' interests, are legitimate proprietors of GIs because of their knowledge of products and their knowledge of the entire industry. However, the fact remains that the Boards have exclusive control over GIs and small farmers outside the 87 Tea estates identified by the Tea Board are excluded, not taking any advantage of the GI.[37] This raises a high issue of equity.

*The Statutory Body APEDA Representing All the Producers of the Industry but Facing Oppositions*

Regarding Basmati application from APEDA, it has been opposed by the same advocate, Vinay Kumar Jain (opp. 12), also counsellor of another opponent, Rakesh Kumar Jain (opp. 11). These opponents were the applicants of a first GI application for Basmati in the name of an NGO The Heritage, rejected after 6 years of proceedings.

Indeed, a GI application was filed on 19 August 2004 by the NGO The Heritage, advised by Vinay Kumar Jain, rejected in August 2010.[38] Registered under the Society Act of 1973, it was created specifically to proceed to the GI application. It included 10 members located in the district of Karnal, in Haryana State: four farmers, two merchants, two mill owner and two collecting agents.

[36] Letter from the Spice Board to the GI Registry, 17 August 2007.
[37] *Business Standard*, Manisha Pande, 12 January 2011, Discontent brews over Darjeeling tea label.
[38] All the facts concerning the GI application for Basmati filed by the NGO The Heritage are from the full application submitted by the legal counsel of The Heritage. The file is not accessible at the GI Registry.

The Basmati GI application of The Heritage provides a list of people involved in the production, promotion and marketing of Basmati rice. The applicant states that all producers are automatically members of the association, so they are not individually identified. However, the GI application includes a list of 108 members of the 'All India Rice Exporters Association', the list of 95 exporters of Basmati rice, the list of 272 intermediary agents (rice collectors) based in Taraori, the list of 76 mills and traders based in Taraori.[39] The GI application contains several inconsistencies regarding eligible Basmati varieties.[40] The geographical area includes seven districts of the state of Haryana and three districts of the states of Punjab and Jammu and Kashmir. The application then describes the different types of rice and the control mechanism. The historical part is documented with excerpts from the gazette of Karnal and refers to the epics Mahabharata and the Vedas, describing the common origin in Pakistan and India of Basmati rice. Finally, the GI application emphasizes the need for constructive efforts to protect the most important natural heritage.

The GI Registry requested additional information and an affidavit explaining how the interests of all producers of Basmati were taken into account, the guarantee that the entire production area was covered in the application, three copies of the map, and the mechanism to ensure that specifications are met. All this data was provided by the applicant. For its part, the consultative group asked the applicant to clarify several points of fact which were confused, missing, contradictory or clearly erroneous in the GI application as to the statutes of the association, the geographical area, the list of varieties, the description of varieties (phenotypic characteristics) and the description of the agro-climatic parameters.[41] The consultative group

---

[39] Taraori is a small town in Karnal district in Haryana State, renowned for the quality of Basmati rice and headquarters of the association The Heritage.

[40] Varieties described as traditional varieties in the GI application are the seven following varieties: Basmati 370, Basmati 386, Super Basmati, Type 3 (Pusa Basmati), Taraori Basmati (HBC-19), Basmati 217, Ranbir Basmati (IET-11348). Then the application references a list of notifications according to the Seed Act of eight varieties of Basmati, adding to the previous list the Haryana Basmati variety. Further, the application states that only five varieties have been listed under the Seed Act. For our part, we note that Super Basmati is not a traditional variety.

[41] The consultative group comprised the following members: S. Chandrasekaran, registrar of geographical indications; V. Natarajan, assistant registrar of

considered that the GI application did not ensure the equitable distribution of benefits to all producers as required by the GI Act, despite the claim that Basmati rice is the collective heritage of Indian farmers.

Vinay Kumar Jain requested an additional two months to respond to the requests.[42] The GI Registry said that 45 days was given to re-file the GI application.[43] Vinay Kumar Jain then complained of having received the findings of the consultative group very late and asked for a further period of six months. He also complained about the Government and its agencies, who failed to protect Basmati, and took the risk that it becomes generic.[44] In a subsequent letter,[45] he severely criticized the GI Registry, and in particular the very long period (of two years) required to set up the consultative group. Finally, a second GI application was filed by Vinay Kumar Jain on 1 March 2007, which conformed with the conclusions of the consultative group. Since then, however, various consultative group meetings have been held, without Vinay Jain being informed.[46] The GI application filed by The Heritage has been rejected by the GI registry after six years, in 2010. While the reasons for this rejection are the deficiencies and defects in the application, it is merely on the nature of the applicant and, more particularly, the representativity of the applicant. Regarding the fact that The Heritage is a society formed by only farmers, traders, commission agents and millers of Karnal district of the Haryana State and registered under the Society Registration Act, 1860 having registered office at Taraori, whereas Basmati rice is being produced in at least six states of India, the GI Registry considered that the society clearly does not adequately represent the interest of all the producers in the area other than Karnal district of Haryana.[47] The GI Registry considered that APEDA represented all the producers over the geographical area

---

geographical indications; Justice A. Ramamurthi (Retd), Member; Dr S. Jayaraj, Entomology Research Institute, Chennai; Dr S. Bala Ravi, M.S. Swaminathan Research Foundation in Chennai; Dr M.S. Venugopal, Agricultural College and Research Institute, Madurai; Dr C.R. Ananda Kumar, Head of Department of Plant Breeding and Genetics, Agricultural College and Research Institute, Madurai.

[42] Letter, 30 November 2006.
[43] Letter, 28 December 2006.
[44] Letter, 23 January 2007.
[45] Letter, 13 February 2007.
[46] Email from V. Jain, 19 July 2007.
[47] Grounds of Refusal of GI application, 16 July 2010, GI Registrar.

which covers several states, and maintained such statement during the opposition procedure where one of the grounds of the nine oppositions against Basmati GI application of APEDA, from Madhya Pradesh, from an individual from Haryana, from the NGO The Heritage and from Pakistan, concerns the nature of the applicant. According to the opponents, APEDA represents only few exporters of Basmati and not producers as a whole, whereas the GI Act requires that the applicant represent the producers. In its order issued on 31 December 2013, the GI Registry has decided that APEDA is a statutory authority established under an Act in 1985, and thus clearly falls under the 'authority established by the law' mentioned in the definition of the applicant in the Indian GI Act and that being a non-trading body, it is qualified to represent the interest of all the producers/stakeholders including farmers, millers, traders, exporters and importers of Basmati.

The GI Registry as well as APEDA and the Commodities Boards are placed under the authority of the Ministry of Commerce, which is conducting a policy of encouraging registration of GIs. Basmati illustrates the risk of collision, with the GI Registry favouring the application from APEDA versus the application from the Heritage and with the weak analysis from the GI Registry of the oppositions against APEDA's legitimacy to apply for a GI. Indeed, it is striking that the analysis of the capacity of representation of producers has been conducted during the examination procedure of the Heritage's Basmati application and neither during the examination of APEDA's application nor during the opposition procedure against APEDA's application. However, even if such risk of bias exists regarding the nature of the applicant, the recent order of the GI Registry rejecting APEDA's argument on the geographical area of Basmati shows a certain independence of the GI Registry towards the State's agencies.

The government's representation of registered producers, members of government cooperatives

The state governments seem to favour producers directly registered by them or producers of cooperatives supported by the government. The GIs registered by the Department of Handloom and Textiles of the Tamil Nadu Government, Arni silk, Salem silk and Kovai Kora cotton, first identify the different cooperatives supported by the State involved in production and then mention that other producers are also welcome.[48] What about the other producers? The Kancheepuram silk GI throws little light on the topic.

Twenty-three cooperatives are involved in the production of Kancheepuram silk and 60 per cent of the weavers are members of these cooperatives. Besides cooperatives, master weavers, who are independent, also take care of the rest of the production. The master weavers are generally tradesmen and their suppliers are individual weavers who are not members of the cooperative.

The GI's geographical zone includes only government cooperatives corresponding to the historical zone of the weaving of silk saris, around the temples of the town centre, but this area does not correspond to the current production zone. Indeed, the government does not seem to regard a GI necessary for private entrepreneurs like master weavers, because only cooperative saris guarantee superior quality and merit a GI. This reputation is confirmed by the practice of certain master weavers who put up a false cooperative sign in front of their shops to attract consumers.[49]

The Kancheepuram district's Department of Handloom office is responsible for registering users. At least a hundred weavers should have been registered from the government cooperatives as well as from the private sector, and in April 2010, this was apparently the case. The registration of one hundred producers may seem insignificant compared to thousands of producers, but it established the principle of including master weavers, provided they meet the requirements of the GI, such being located in the geographical area.

Another example that demonstrates the risk of other producers being excluded when the State is the GI proprietor is given by the GI Feni. According to D. Rangnekar, it is not certain that the Goan government represents all the participants. He noted that the government showed signs of embarrassment when the names of other distillers were disclosed.[50] During the GI examination, the proof of representation of

---

[48] 'Any other societies or associations that are already established or that will be established in future within the identified territorial limits (map) submitted to GI Registry will also become eligible to use the GI mark upon the said goods by complying with the requirements under law'.
[49] According to a master weaver.
[50] Rangnekar, 'Geographical Indications and Localisation: A Case Study of Feni', 1–63.

producers' interests was requested only to the association of producers co-applying for the GI and not the Goan government. Does the GI Registry consider the Goan government de facto representative of the interest of all Goan citizens and thus the Feni producers? The association replied in the affirmative by saying that it was the only registered body which defends the interests of the cashew industry.[51]

An important element characterizing GIs owned by the State is the wish to transfer the ownership of GIs to producers' associations so that producers become aware of the GI tool. For example, the Karnataka government plans to transfer the proprietorship of the Coorg orange GI to a local NGO,[52] involved in forest management which hopes to see orange producers benefit more from status. The Government expressed a similar wish at the time of the Kashmir pashmina GI registration (see *infra*). This gesture of the Government can be easily interpreted. The Government does not deem its role as the GI proprietor to be legitimate and would like producers to be beneficiaries of the GI. However, the issue of the transfer of proprietorship accentuates the importance given to being a GI proprietor while the debate was supposed to be about its beneficiaries, the users. Moreover, the transfer of the proprietorship of GI rights is prohibited by the law (Article 24). It is indeed the concept of proprietorship which is at stake (see *infra* Part III)!

Non-productive government enterprises

The link between the State proprietor of the GI and producers can be based on producers' accreditation. For example, the KSHDC registers individual producers who supply the corporation with goods on a non-exclusive basis. On the whole, about 10–15 per cent of Karnataka producers are registered in KSHDC. Around 900 of the 3000 total producers, that is, less than 30 per cent, are registered in KSHDC for the GI Channapatna toys and dolls. Similarly, only 40 per cent of objects produced under the GI Mysore rosewood inlay are marketed by KSHDC, and by KSHDC's own admission, this additional production

---

[51] Model letter from the GI Registry according to Rule 31, 26 December 2007, answered on 31 March 2008 by an affidavit stating that 'the applicant represent interests of all producers because it is the only body registered for representing the interests of the cashew nut industry'.

[52] Kodagu Model Forest Trust; *Kodagu* means Coorg in local language.

conforms to the GI specifications as well. The question is then to what extent producers not registered by KSHDC can use the GI. A letter sent by KSHDC to the GI Registry says that artisans who have not yet been approved by KSDHC can take the necessary steps to register free of cost and that they will be trained to meet the quality standards.[53] Although the GI proprietor is the government, it represents only its own registered producers and not all the entire group of producers of the product.

Proving the legitimacy of the state's intellectual property agencies

Producers' representation was a crucial issue in the case of GIs applications submitted by PICs. The GI Registry asked the PICs to provide proof of representation of producers' interests during the examination of the GI Kangra tea. The state governments issued a statement granting the PIC of its state the right to submit GI applications. Thus, a notification of the Himachal Pradesh government explaining the protection and registration policies regarding GIs declares that the PIC is the central agency responsible for submitting GI applications for products of its State.[54] Thanks to this permit, the Himachal Pradesh PIC could apply for Kullu shawl and Kangra tea GIs and the Assam PIC for the Assam Muga silk GI.

The Governmental Craft Development Institute of Kashmiri judged unrepresentative

The Craft Development Institute's (CDI) GI registration for Kashmir Sozani embroidery and Kashmir pashmina was contested by Kashmir Handmade Pashmina Promotion Trust (KHMPPT), an association created by the Wildlife Trust of India. Its purpose is to rehabilitate artisans who without any prior warning are forbidden from plying their craft because of the ban on the production of *shahtoosh* shawls (made from the wool of a Tibetan antelope, an endangered species). According to KHMPPT, the Kashmiri artisans who constitute the opposition are known for producing the most beautiful pashmina, sold in India since the beginning of the 19th century under the designation Kashmir Handmade Pashmina.

[53] See the GI file.
[54] N°SCSTE/F (1) 6/2004, 10 December 2004, consulted in the GI file.

According to KHMPPT, its planned GI application was rejected on the basis of CDI's previous application. In KHMPPT's opinion, the only reason the CDI had applied for the GI was to monopolize a right which in fact belonged to the KHMPPT artisans. KHMPPT also considered CDI's claims about protecting artisans' interest a falsehood because the CDI essentially consists of experts, researchers and high-ranking officials who are incapable of understanding the interests of artisans, while the 300 artisans fully oriented towards pashmina production are KHMPPT members. Moreover, it seems registering a GI in CDI's name is against the spirit of the GI law, which is to promote producers' economic prosperity. To conclude, KHMPPT highlights the risk of confusion between its own products and the products benefiting from the GI registered by the CDI since they are sold in the same sales circuits.[55]

The CDI replied by first of all asserting to KHMPPT that it was indeed qualified to be a bona fide user of the Kashmir pashmina GI. On the other side, the CDI, supported by the Pashmina Weavers Union, the Jammu and Kashmir Handloom Co-Operative Societies Union, the Jammu and Kashmir Shawl Makers Union, the Kashmir Chamber of Commerce and Industry, argued that local stakeholders involved in the production of pashmina were unaware of KHMPPT.[56] Registering a GI in the CDI's name in no way stopped the opposite party from being registered as an authorized user and neither did it grant the CDI monopoly, since, on the contrary, all the artisans of the opposition can become GI users. The CDI claimed that it was better placed to protect and promote the trade of pashmina, thanks to the Government's support and the involvement of high-ranking officials. Finally, the CDI pointed out that, thanks to its initiative Tahafuz, an artisan's association consisting of a large number of artisans was formed at the moment of filing the GI application.[57] The CDI asserted that it was only a catalyst in the protection and promotion of Kashmiri handicraft[58] and that GIs can be only registered by an association made up of artisans who are the guardians of traditional knowledge.

[55] Affidavit from the opponent, 26 June 2007.
[56] Affidavit from the Director of CDI, 22 October 2007.
[57] Letter from Anand, 1 December 2006.
[58] Affidavit from the Director of CDI, 22 October 2007.

Finally, a compromise was reached on 2008, resulting in the registration of the GI in the name of Tahafuz association. This conflict reveals that producers of the opposing association did not understand the concept of proprietor/GI user and regarded it as a mark identifying products of a producer. It is important to keep in mind the government's role as a catalyst (see *infra*).

Moreover, the three GIs applications submitted by the CDI for Kashmiri handicraft raises the question of cooperation between India and Pakistan, following the division of Kashmir during the Partition. Thus, the Traders Association of Pakistan filed an objection on the pretext that pashmina was also made in Pakistan,[59] and the president of the Chamber of Commerce along with Rawalpindi industry also lodged another objection. The High Commission for Pakistan, situated in New Delhi, communicated these objections to the GI Registry.[60] Pakistan was inclined to sharing a GI with India considering pashmina is a common heritage and would have liked to apply for a joint GI registration. India replied that this option was feasible if the quality of pashmina in Pakistan was on par with pashmina made in India. According to India, the thinnest pashmina comes from Srinagar in India.[61]

The opposition was rejected on a formal issue, as apparently the Pakistani opponent did not correspond to the GI Act's definition of an applicant.[62] This argument seems undefendable insofar as an association of traders and a Chamber of Commerce have been recognized as valid applicants for Indian GIs and the law does not discriminate on the basis of nationality. Anyway, as the opposition was received one day after the expiration date; the case was closed on 21 January 2008. Thus, following the decision of the registrar of GIs, the opposition was not registered, further testifying to the long-standing conflictual relationship between India and Pakistan.[63]

---

[59] Source: http://www.kashmirtimes.com/archive/0708/070811/front.htm.
[60] The Minister of State in the Ministry of Commerce and Industry (Shri Aswani Kumar, Questions at Lok Sabha).
[61] The Director of CDI, M.S. Farooqi stated that 'A joint GI is possible only if it is proven that Pakistani Pashmina is the same wool as ours. The finest Pashmina is found only in the Srinagar Valley'.
[62] 'Interview: G.K. Muthukumaar, Senior Associate, Anand and Anand', *The Financial Express*, 7 January 2009.
[63] Letter from M. Natarajan and M. Ravi to the Ministry of Commerce, 12 September 2008.

*Associations/Cooperatives as Ambivalent Representatives of Producers*
Associations have been identified as legal GI applicants, but do they fulfil the criteria of representing producers' interests?

Associations and cooperatives representing their members
The main question is whether producers have to be members of an association in order to use GIs, and, if that is the case, what constitute the relevant terms and conditions for becoming members of the association.

For example, to be a registered authorized user of the Mysore Agarbathi GI, the manufacturer should be a lifetime member of AIAMA, the GI proprietor. All the members of the association who wish to use the GI have to submit an application along with a sample of their product to AIAMA and pay taxes. The sample is then sent to Federation of Aroma/Agarbathi Manufacturing Enterprise (FAME), AIAMA's inspection body for analysis. Following the recommendations of FAME, AIAMA can issue a permit to use the GI, but the decision rests solely with AIAMA. The permit is granted for a year, for one particular product, and has to be renewed annually. It cannot be transferred or given away to a third party. AIAMA supplies a label in the form of a hologram to ensure traceability.

The question is what happens for a producer complying with the requirements of the GI specifications, but not a member of the association, who applies to be registered in the GI Registry as an authorized user. Will the association approve the registration of such producer? If not, then we can conclude that AIAMA uses GI as a collective mark reserved for its members. The conditions for becoming a member of the association are not difficult; however, a discretionary power which withholds or grants permission to producers to use a GI, irrespective of whether the standards of the specifications are fulfilled or not, may seem very far from the GI spirit and even from that of certification marks.

In some associations, membership is highly restricted, such as in the case of the GI Aranmula metal mirror. Though legally anyone has the right to be a producer, in reality, there are rigid cultural barriers, and in practice, only members of the Viswabrahmana community can become artisans.

Restricting the use of GIs to only members of the association corresponds to P. Narayanan Unny's vision, the president of Navara

Rice Farmers Society, proprietor of the Navara rice GI. In his case, membership to the association is determined by an adherence to the organic production methods indicated in the specifications. However, these methods are rarely implemented by anyone aside from the president of the association.

In the case of Palakkadan Matta rice, owned by the Palakkadan Matta Farmers Producer Company Ltd, the question is whether producers have to become shareholders in order to use the GI, and if it is easy for them to have shares in the company. According to the director, P. Narayanan Unny, about 3000 producers are in the process of becoming part of the company.

Even though the initiative of producers lead to Navara rice and Palakkad Matta rice GIs, the only reason the association and the company were created was to register a GI following the GI Registry objection to an application filed in the name of only a handful of producers.[64] However, P. Narayanan Unny is proud of the fact that it is producers who took the step to register this GI, where in most cases, GI applications are made by the Government or its agencies.

Associations were also not spared from opposition proceedings. The Payyannur Pavithra Ring Artisans and Development Society, bringing together various artisan families under the same umbrella, was considered as not representing the producers by the IPAB in an order dated 14 November 2012. The board considered that the members of the society were not even artisans, they were businessmen. Indeed, the application shows that of the seven original members of the society, only four are artisans and three are not. Even if the definition of the word *producer* is wide and includes any person 'who trades or deals in such production, exploitation making or manufacturing' of the goods, the applicant ought to have shown that 'the producers' of the rings as defined in the Act had a desire to form the association. There should be evidence to show that the association represents the interest of the producers. A mere claim that the society is called Payyannur Pavithra Ring Artisans and Development Society will not suffice. There should be evidence to show that the producers are desirous of coming together to protect the GI, which is clearly absent. The Payyannur Pavithra Ring Artisans and Development

---

[64] Interview, 26 April 2008.

Society itself in its application has stated that the task of manufacturing this unique Pavithra Mothiram was given to the Choovatta Valappil family and yet the intervener in the opposition, who is the secretary of Choovatta Valappil Tharavad Dharmadaiva Paripalana Trust. He filed opposition only after the publication was made. Others affidavits have been filed by artisans to object the rights of the Payyannur Pavithra Ring Artisans and Development Society, which has obtained the GI by the back door method by forming a society.

Because Choovatta Valappil family which was entrusted with the technique of making the ring had no notice of the GI application, the IPAB decides that such an application will defeat the purpose of the Act.

Foundations, associations: Representatives of public interest

Associations of public interest are not solely concerned about their members but the entire industry and represent the interests of all the stakeholders.

For example, the Chanderi Development Foundation recommends authorized producers, who are not necessarily members of the foundation, to the GI Registry.[65] The names of more than 3000 weavers are indicated in the GI application, but none of them have been registered. This shows the reference to producers in a GI application is not sufficient and that there is no bypassing the long-drawn procedures of individual registration. Yet, the Chanderi Development Foundation had to prove that it was qualified to represent producers, which it did by highlighting the objectives of the foundation noted in the statutes.

*The Crucial Problem of GI Registration in the Name of Producers*

GIs registered by companies, organizations and unique producers have been seriously criticized and opposed because they are not collective in nature.

The GI Registry raised the issue of appropriate representation during the examination of the Mysore silk GI application by the KSIC, who was asked to give the references of the producers involved. KSIC replied by providing the names of the company directors, which revealed that the organization of producers did not exist at all! This fact became the two oppositions' main ground.

The first opposition was filed by the company Chamundi Silks Textiles Ltd, a well-known brand for the sale of saris in Bangalore, which resulted

---

[65] See the statutes of the foundation.

in an amicable settlement. The second objection has been lodged by the Mysore Powerloom Silk Manufacturers Cooperative Society and the Karnataka Weavers Federation, which was alerted by Chamundi but whose objection was received after the deadline. The main ground of opposition of Chamundi is that the name Mysore silk is associated with the silk produced by a large number of producers and cannot be claimed exclusively by KSIC.[66] The KSIC cannot be described as the owner under Section 11.1 of the GI Act which provides that the GI applicant shall represent the interests of the producers. The second objection is based on the same arguments, set out with great clarity: the KSIC is not legitimate (has no 'locus standi') to apply for the GI because it does not represent the interests of producers. The opponent goes on to denounce the fact that the KSIC is fully owned by the Government of Karnataka, has only one manufacturing unit, is a sole producer and does not represent the other producers of silk in Mysore or in the state of Karnataka. The opponent considers that the KSIC has individual and not general interest, arguing that the application for GI registration was filed in order to obtain a monopoly in the manufacture of the product and increase its individual profits as a business. Thus, according to the cooperative, about 400,000 weavers will be unemployed out of 80,000 looms owned by craftsmen.

Another argument made by the first opponent, Chamundi, is that the name Mysore silk is generic and cannot be registered, based on a research report conducted by the Trade Marks Office citing a number of trademarks, including the words *Mysore silk*. Chamundi seeks to maintain the name free of use, inappropriate for a GI, even by the entire group of producers.

In response, the KSIC says it does not claim ownership rights over Mysore silk but it claims registration under Section 11 of the Act. The KSIC states it is legally authorized to protect the distinctive and unique characteristics of Mysore silk. The GI allows the applicant to take action against misuses because at present, the public is misled by unauthorized persons.

The KSIC argues that it is the only company that manufactures 100 per cent crêpe de Chine silk with a zari made of 65 per cent silver and that the product quality depends on the geographical area of production through a specific link that exists between the silk and its area of origin.

[66] Letter from Chamundi, 17 February 2005.

Yet, Chamundi believes that the name of Mysore does not refer to the city of Mysore where the KSIC factory is situated, but refers to the area covered by the former kingdom of Mysore and during the hearing of opposition, Chamundi had requested the geographical area to be extended to all districts of Karnataka state corresponding to the former kingdom of Mysore, a proposal rejected by the GI Registry.[67] However, Chamundi did not seek extension of manufacturing methods, while the cooperative and the association of producers emphasize in their opposition that the use of thread of 26/28 denier by KSIC is confusing because the crêpe de Chine or georgette can be manufactured in 18/20, 20/22, 22/24 or 28/30 denier and small producers using thread of 18/20 denier. Finally, following the hearing of opposition, a memorandum of understanding was signed between the applicant and Chamundi, who agreed to withdraw its opposition on the condition that it can still use the name Chamundi Silk to sell its products.[68]

It thus appears that the government enterprise is solely a manufacturer of Mysore silk and does not represent the community of weavers. The opposition was rejected by amicable arrangement, because, according to an informal discussion with the GI Registry, the KSIC, the government enterprise is within its rights because it comes from the government, and as such works for the interest of all, and also is the only one making quality products.[69]

The other GI held by a government enterprise, Mysore sandal oil filed by 'Soap and Detergents Ltd Karnataka', has also been the subject of an opposition. The opponent, Devu's enterprise, denies the uniqueness of the product on the grounds that Devu uses the same process as the KSDL in trade and manufacture of sandalwood oil and soap. The specification of the GI describes KSDL as the only producer of soap and sandalwood oil. However, according to a manager of KSDL, three companies are involved in the manufacture of such products, with KSDL providing 90 per cent of production. This virtual monopoly is explained by the need to obtain permission from the Government for the extraction of sandalwood oil, due to its status as a rare tree. It seems then that the government

[67] Interview with the Director of Chamundi, February 2007.
[68] Audience: 21 October 2005, postponed to 8 November 2005 and finally 25 November 2005.
[69] GI Registry, Mr Natarajan, Assistant Registrar.

enterprise set up with the GI has a legal monopoly in the objective to trace the course of its sales, low due to the outdated image of the brand.[70,71]

In conclusion, it appears that the strategies pursued by government enterprises are more brand strategies identifying the company. GIs are used here in combination with the old brands that reference the location of Mysore. Despite public funding and public governance, the KSIC and the KSDL are producers among others, representing only themselves, not all producers. Thus, it becomes difficult to share the vision of the GI Registry of a government company that represents the interest of all producers. Although the GI system was chosen because it is perceived as suitable for ancient traditional products, the collective nature of the rights is not respected. These GI applications seem to operate against the GI Act, which is to protect the interests of producers in a strict sense, as the owner has no right to use the GI.

The objections against a single industrial producer

The four GI applications involving petroleum products made by the company Reliance Industries Ltd were the subject of several objections. The first opposition, formed by Vinay Jain,[72] is based on the argument that a GI cannot be registered for the benefit of a single undertaking applicant and user because the application must be filed by a group of people. Additionally, there is no mention of other users who could benefit from the GI. According to the opponent, the GI applications from Reliance show an association between a recent activity, in this case petroleum refining, and a location, Jamnagar, but the spirit of the GI is to devote a long history associated with geographical origin.[73]

Another objection has been lodged by an Indian scholar from the London School of Economics working on GIs, Dev Ganjee. Although the majority of grounds of objection concerns the inability to characterize petroleum products as GIs, the question of the nature of the applicant was also discussed. According to the objection, using a name such as Jamnagar for a GI is contrary to the principles of fair competition because

---

[70] *Hindu*, 5 September 2002.
[71] Marketing Practice, 31 October 2006. http://marketingpractice.blogspot.com/2006_10_01_archive.html.
[72] Lawyer for the GIs 'Chanderi silk' and 'Basmati'.
[73] See GI file.

Reliance seeks only to strengthen its private rights to the name and not to protect any collective rights. This is a private company representing its own interests and not the interests of a group of producers.

These diverse oppositions show that the collective aspect of GI is considered by experts as a key requirement. GIs registered in the name of a single enterprise are consequently challenged. This is even though the GI Registry was willing to consider that the GI users could be the shareholders of the company Reliance![74]

In any case, the problem raised by GI registration for the benefit of a commercial nature is not so much its nature as commercial enterprise but it being the only producer, thus leaving the company unable to comply with the obligation of producer representation. Thus, T.C. James, Director of the Department of Industrial Policy and Promotion at the Department of Commerce of the Ministry of Commerce, noted that there was no prohibition in the GI Act to commercial enterprises filing GI applications, provided they represented the interests of producers. Indeed the GI Palakkadan Matta rice was filed by a commercial company whose shareholders are the producers. It seems then that the second part of Article 11, defining the applicant as a representative of producers, places a premium on a strict reading of the legal nature of the applicant.

### The controversy over a religious organization as the sole producer

Registration in September 2009 of the GI Tirupati laddu in the name of a religious organization, the TTD, has also been a source of controversy[75] being an individual entity whose monopoly on the production of laddus is not a doubt. One observer commented that, contrary to the GI Darjeeling tea, there are no producers who produce these laddus, bring them to the temple and could benefit from some of the huge profits of TTD. Instead, the TTD is the producer and the sole beneficiary, the laddus being produced by workers of the temple, employed by the TTD. The GI would be justified only if a community of qualified cooks around Tirupati laddu prepared them for the temple. Consequently, the intellectual property

---

[74] Interview with V. Natarajan, Assistant Registrar.
[75] The data presented here are from an article in the magazine *Frontline* and personal exchanges with experts in GIs in India. The specifications for its part refer only to the TTD under 'list of association of persons/producers/organization/authority' of the GI application.

experts are concerned about the registration of the GI as contrary to the spirit of the GI which, they say, is to protect, preserve and promote the collective rights of communities. They fear that the registration of the GI Tirupati laddu could be used as a precedent for the registration of GIs for the benefit of companies unique in their industry.

Subodh Kumar, of the APTDC, which played a major role in drafting the application for the GI Tirupati laddu, says on the contrary, that the GI Act allows an organization as a sole producer as well as a group of producers to own a GI. Moreover, according to Subodh Kumar, the ban on the marketing of fake laddus is only a weak objective of TTD, seeing GIs as pursuing primarily a holistic goal which includes the global recognition of the cultural heritage of Tirupati, thus allowing TTD to be recognized globally and to attract more pilgrims. These intangible goals are different from tangible objects towards which trademarks might be used. The then trade minister[76] himself seemed to be perplexed by the registration of such GIs.[77] The controversy reflects the importance given to the collective aspect of GIs, which is understood to refer to several producers who have some autonomy from each other and not to employees of the same entity.

Unexpectedly, the GI is also the subject of an action for annulment before the Chennai High Court on the grounds of the inability of any kind of sacred objects to be the objects of IPRs, as such objects are considered non-marketable![78] Particularly, in this case, the issue goes well beyond the individual character of the owner of the GI. Following the decision of the Chennai High Court which considered it was not competent for dealing the case, R.S. Pravinh Raj filed an application for rectification in front of the GI Registry and a plea for cancellation of GI in front of IPAB. R.S. Pravinh Raj's complaint is based on two grounds. One is that because TTD states in its application that 'The laddu gets its reputation not from its taste alone but from its sanctity as they are first offered as naivedyam to the Lord' (at pages 40, 60 and 64 of the GI journal No. 28), it is a serious prejudice to Articles 25 and 26 of the Indian

[76] Statement from Jairam Ramesh, 23 February 2009.
[77] V. Venkatesan, 'Bittersweet Status: The Grant of G.I. Status to Tirupati Laddu Is Criticised as Being against the Spirit of the Geographical Indications of Goods Act, 1999', *Frontline* 26, no. 21 (2009): 1–3.
[78] Madabhushi Sridhar, 'GI for Tirupathi Laddu: Whose Interests Protected?' *Sinapse, an intellectual property rendez-vous*, 16 March 2010.

Constitution, related to Freedom of Religion. For Raj, it is dangerous to allow private appropriation (especially in the form of IPR) of religious symbols. Second is that of the GI Act is violated, raising an issue that the TTD is a sole producer of the product.

The assistant registrar of GIs decided in an order dated 30 July 2012 that each and every person involved in the manufacturing of the product is deemed to be a producer of the product. It is an admitted version that the Tirupati laddu is not manufactured by the effort of single person. It is a product emerging from of the effort of employees of TTD. The essence of GI is to protect not only the interest of manufacturer but also that of consumer who are willing to pay more for a genuine product. The legislative intent is to protect the interest of the producer and general public from imitation, as the Tirupati laddu is having a well-known reputation and the producer is having every right to fence the product by getting all types of eligible intellectual property protection. Regarding the prejudice to Articles 25 and 26 of Constitution of India, assistant registrar for GI states that the Constitution of India authorized the religious institution for acquiring right in property.

The rectification application was rejected on the ground that the applicant 'lacks standing' in proving his locus standi in the registered GI, being a third party, working with National Institute of Interdisciplinary Science and Technology (NIIST-CSIR) and not involved in the same trade or manufacturing the similar GI product. The applicant is also residing at Thiruvananthapuram (Kerala) and do not connect the particular geographical area of the Tirupati Tirumala—Chittoor district (Andhra Pradesh). Moreover, because the rectification applicant was granted sufficient opportunity of hearing, but never turned up for hearing and wasted the precious time of the tribunal by filing frivolous, frolicsome and playful application and misused his official for status and emblem of his employer (NIIST-CSIR) shameful publicity, the assistant registrar was fined ₹10,000.

This desire to register the name as a GI and not as a trademark is a sign of the attractiveness of the GI concept. Yet, trademarks seem more adapted in this case, as according to the GI Act, registered proprietor is not allowed to use the GI, right exclusively granted to users which here indeed are not existing, considering that employees can certainly not be considered as users of GIs according to the GI Act. The fine of ₹10,000 is far too expensive, against the provision of the GI Act, which raises the issue of the equity of the GI Registry in handling rectification applications.

## The Rationale for the Ubiquity of the Indian State and Its Consequences

### Disadvantaged Producers

Although parliamentary debates reflect the commitment to use the GI Act to protect export goods, and in priority commodities, the influx of GIs in the field of handicrafts will change that. Indeed, apart from some GIs in the field of handicrafts for products destined for domestic and international markets, especially the products of the highest quality for niche markets, many of the GIs registered for handicrafts were for those with only a weak market or even no market. In all cases, the market is essentially national, reflecting the slow entry of India in the globalization of exchanges.

Kancheepuram saris are sold on domestic and export markets. Exports to Sri Lanka, Singapore, Hong Kong, England, Africa, Aden, Gulf countries, United States, United Kingdom, Italy, Germany and Russia are encouraged by the Indian Silk Export and Promotion Council.[79] However, in view of the cultural aspect of the sari, it seems plausible that its export is mainly destined for the large Indian diaspora. Moreover, the domestic market seems to be a priority because the GI will, according to the Ministry of Textiles, Government of India, help to fight against fake saris produced in China.[80] The risk of misuse of Indian textiles are primarily found in the domestic market, for example, production of counterfeit Chanderi saris is estimated at ₹60 crores compared to a production of authentic sari estimated at about ₹12–15 crores.[81]

This finding contrasts with the situation of commodities controlled by the Statutory Commodity Board, which are mostly destined for foreign

---

[79] Ibid., 37.
[80] Mr. Nayak, Director of the Textile Committee, ministère du textile, cité dans *Hindu*, 25 décembre 2005.
[81] Report from Vinay Jain.

markets. Even though there is an increasing domestic demand for coffee currently estimated at 30 per cent, the GI Monsooned Malabar coffee is fully turned to lucrative foreign markets. It is the same for Basmati rice, which is the only rice allowed to be exported following the global food crisis in 2008, when India banned all other rice exports.[82] The Darjeeling tea is another example of an exported product.[83]

However, even products that were thought assured of a niche market suffer from a decrease in demand. Thus, the Kancheepuram sari is facing a saturated market because of the price of gold used for zari. Combined with the abandonment of the traditional dress, that is, the sari, there was a decline in production and of the number of weavers, with about 5 per cent of weavers leaving the industry each year since 1987.[84]

The loss of market also justified the registration of GIs Mysore sandal soap and Mysore silk.[85]

Finally, for some products which are rare, like jewels of the temple, there often is not any real market, or if one exists, it is very limited. Similarly, the crafts of Bastar tribes seem primarily manufactured for community-based consumption.

The lack of market does not call into question the existence of the product's reputation, but rather the relevance of GIs as a tool for commercial exploitation and argues instead for the objective of preserving Indian heritage. GIs on traditional paintings of Mysore and Thanjavur are not threatened by any infringement, but, instead, a potential loss of knowledge.

With regard to agricultural products, local plant varieties may suffer from a loss due to the homogenization of varieties. Thus, Navara rice is less and less cultivated, despite a market that looks promising in the long run but that is not yet secure. The GI on Coorg orange illustrates the case of a culture which has completely disappeared.

[82] See www.apeda.com.
[83] Pradyot R. Jena and Ulrike Grote, 'Changing Institutions to Protect Regional Heritage: A Case for Geographical Indications in the Indian Agrifood Sector', *Development Policy Review* 28, no. 2 (2010): 217–236.
[84] Interview with A. Mohamed Jamaluddin, Managing Director, Tamilnadu Handloom Development Corporation Ltd.
[85] Marketing Practice, 31 October 2006, http://marketingpractice.blogspot.com/2006_10_01_archive.html.

The Legitimacy of the Involvement of the Indian State    233

This declining trend in some markets, following globalization, darkens the prospects of the artisans who for decades, with farmers, ranked among the most disadvantaged populations of India, a trend that globalization has not improved. Because of this uncertainty, the new generation does not generally want to keep working on the family business, whether that is agriculture or handicrafts. Thus, although the number of producers of Aranmula metal mirrors is stable, the younger generation prefers to continue his studies and work in better-paid occupations.[86] Similarly, the Handloom Park was created to help rural development in Pochampally, which had been undermined by the decline in the number of weavers.

Producers, often disadvantaged both financially and educationally, are often illiterate which explains their lack of knowledge about GI registration and the lack of registration as authorized users shown by the N.S. Gopalakrishnan's study on the GI Pochampally Ikat.[87] It is the case of the weavers of Pochampally Ikat, whose poor living conditions are cited in connection with a lawsuit brought against a manufacturer and seller of imitation saris, counterfeiting being perceived as a source of incalculable damage, removing the only source of income for these weavers.[88]

According to Sunita K. Sreedharan, an expert in the field of GIs, the industry sectors concerned by GIs are usually poorly organized,[89] whether in agriculture[90] or in the craft sector.[91] It is undeniable that in any case, the task of identifying individual producers for their registration as authorized users appears difficult to achieve. It was also the response of the Punjab Small-Scale Industries and Export Corporation, applicant

---

[86] Interview with Mr Gopakumar, artisan.
[87] Gopalakrishnan, Nair, and Babu, *Exploring the Relationship between Geographical Indications and Traditional Knowledge: An Analysis of the Legal Tools for the Protection of Geographical Indications in Asia*, 40.
[88] Citation from the complaint filed by the proprietors of the GI Pochampally Ikat Pochampally Handloom Weavers Co-op Society, in front of the Delhi High Court, no. 887/2005.
[89] National Seminar on Geographical Indications, Sunita K. Sreedharan, SKS Law Associates, New Delhi, 24 September 2009, Management of Geographical Indications.
[90] L. Achoth, 'Report on Surveys on Coffee Holdings and Coffee Market Chain in India in Relation to Mould Contamination in Coffee' (Bangalore: Coffee Board of India, 2005).
[91] Liebl and Roy, 'Handmade in India', 57.

for the GI Phulkari (a form of floral embroidery): 'there are thousands of artisans/manufacturers so it is impossible to ascertain the number of persons involved but enclosed is a list of manufacturers dealing with applicant and phulkari products'.

This state of poverty of the producers leads to the conclusion that in India, GIs are the IPRs of the poor.[92]

*The Dual Purpose of GIs Justifying the Intervention of the State*

The presence of these disadvantaged producers justifies the intervention of the State for the protection of GIs. The State is still a major economic player in India's 21th century. Moreover, the choice to register GIs for goods for which the market is weak or not threatened by misuses reveals the unexpected pursuit of an objective, the protection of products linked to Indian cultural identity. This objective has to be combined with that of improving the incomes of producers. GIs have therefore a dual purpose. 'GIs are in the nature of collective community rights and protection of a GI has significant economic and social implications for a developing country like India while at the same time protecting the cultural heritage represented by India's wealth of well-known GIs,' stated the assistant registrar of GI Registry in an order.[93]

In 2001, on the occasion of the inauguration of the new office of intellectual property in Chennai, the then minister of trade and industry Murasoli Maran announced that GIs were vectors of 'national, regional and local cultural identities providing added value to the products'. In a globalizing world, GIs represent more than a simple category of IPRs.[94] Indian academics themselves, such as Kasturi Das, talk about Indian cultural identity regarding GIs.[95]

---

[92] See the comment of an observer in the case of Tirupati.
[93] Regarding GI Darjeeling, 28 September 2012.
[94] 'These (GIs) indications were vectors of "national, regional and local cultural identities" providing value addition to the products. In a globalising world, geographical indications represented more than a simple category of intellectual property rights', 'Hon'ble Union Minister of Commerce & Industry Thiru Murasoli Maran Inaugurated Modernised Patent Office in Chennai', in Press Releases (Patent Office India, 2001).
[95] K. Das, 'Protection of India's Geographical Indications': An Overview of the Indian Legislation and the TRIPS scenario', *Indian Journal of International Law*, 2006, 46, 39–73.

According to V. Natarajan, more than products related to the origin, GIs represent the heritage of traditional knowledge, as suggested by the title of a symposium held in 2007: 'Protection of GI of products of heritage commercial value and with special emphasis on quality insurance, an overview'. It is also significant that V. Natarajan wants to create a museum of GIs.[96] The seminar talked about heritage products, without connecting to a particular place. Venkatesh Thuppil, a member of many consultative groups in charge of examining GIs, applauded this change and increasing appreciation of heritage, saying '[t]hanks to all those who have restored and retained great Indian tradition and culture and for making our people proud of our country. Let us celebrate India in its true spirit, through GI granted to all deserving wealth of India created by people of this country'.[97]

A certain imperialism results from this strategy of preserving national identity. V. Ravi claimed that 'with GI protection for thousands of Indian products the country can become invincible and be breadbasket for the globe. Within a generation, the sleeping giant called India will change face of global power politics'.[98] According to J.L. Racine, a French Indologist, success of GIs can be explained by the fact that the abandonment of protectionism by India, India seeks to protect himself as much as possible; it is the post postcolonial stage.[99] GIs are an attribute of national unity in a world where Indian products can be threatened by globalization, meaning that protection goes beyond a simple economic benefit and contributes to the restoration of Indian identity.

However, this goal was not identified at the time of passage of the GI Act, though it was very much influenced by the Basmati affair, which was as much a question of identity as an economic one.[100]

---

[96] 'GI road show', 3 December 2008, Bangalore.
[97] Ibid.
[98] See the intervention of V. Ravi, GI Registrar, WIPO National Seminar on the importance of intellectual property for the handicraft sector, organized by the World Intellectual Property Organization (WIPO) in cooperation with the Ministry of Textiles, Government of India, and the National Institute of Fashion Technology (NIFT) Hyderabad, India, 5–7 April 2005, www.wipo.int/export/sites/www/sme/en/.../topic5_ravi.ppt.
[99] Interview with J.L. Racine, Paris, 5 June 2008.
[100] http://commerce.nic.in/PressRelease/pressrelease_detail.asp?id=128, India Identifies Number of Products for Geographical Indications, 22 June 2006, New Delhi.

Finally, can India's GI Act be qualified as welfare legislation, as suggested by G.K. Muthukumaar? The GI Act would be put on the same scheme as the regulations for the protection of historical monuments and archaeological excavations, but it would apply to products.[101]

Combined with this objective is the one of improving the conditions of living for disadvantaged producers, as identified in the 'Statements of Objects and Reasons' section of the GI Act. It is recognized that the registration of a large number of GIs is essential to improve the living standards of farmers and artisans,[102] and this objective is always connected to the preservation of cultural heritage. Thus, the PIC of Himachal Pradesh stressed that the registration of the GI Phulkari 'will help to preserve and promote the integrity of this handicraft. It will promote economic prosperity of local artisans by boosting exports and will prevent the misuse and misrepresentation of the GI by unauthorised users'.[103]

Is this dual objective of GIs translated by the intervention of different actors? Protection of national heritage would be the responsibility of the Government, while the increase in producers' incomes would be taken in charge by producers. It does not appear that there is tension between these different objectives of GIs, which should necessarily be analyzed sequentially, with the urgency of protecting the national heritage explaining the prevalent role of the State.[104]

According to the Department of Horticulture of Government of Karnataka, only a public body is able to overcome the difficulty of documenting the specification as it is legitimate to collect data.[105] Similarly, V. Ravi pointed out the difficulty of describing the GI products, which have been the object of little research.[106] It an Order

---

[101] 'Interview: G.K. Muthukumaar, Senior Associate, Anand and Anand'.
[102] Ibid.
[103] http://www.pscst.com/en/services/patents.htm.
[104] Ruet, 'Réformes et nouvelle économie politique en Inde'. 206.
[105] Mr Ramakrishnappa, Département d'horticulture.
[106] See the intervention of V. Ravi, GI Registrar, WIPO National Seminar on the importance of intellectual property for the handicraft sector, organized by the World Intellectual Property Organization (WIPO) in cooperation with the Ministry of Textiles, Government of India, and the National Institute of Fashion Technology (NIFT) Hyderabad, India, 5–7 April 2005, www.wipo.int/export/sites/www/sme/en/.../topic5_ravi.ppt.

on Basmati case, the GI Assistant Registrar considered that the request from the NGO The Heritage to adjourn a hearing on the ground that the applicant does not have enough funds to travel from Delhi to Chennai is a prima facie evidence that the applicant is not capable to protect the interest of the Basmati rice producers. Coffee producers are waiting for the Coffee Board to be the applicant of GIs on coffee as in the case of coffee in Coorg. This is not the view of opponents of the GI for Kashmir pashmina who believe that producers are better able to document GIs.

The issue of GI users seems to be a concern that can be adjusted later. The intervention of the State seems transitional, as the government waits for the increasing capacity of producers. Thus, for the Department of Horticulture, Government of Karnataka, the GI Coorg orange belongs to no one; it belongs to the community, and no individual can claim rights to the name. The Department of Horticulture does not consider itself the owner of the GI but the guardian of the GI.[107] Similarly, the CDI considers itself a catalyst in the protection and promotion of handicrafts of Kashmir.[108] This State intervention is a sign of a society in transition.

The central government as well as the federated states are involved in the protection of GIs, and there has been some competition between states for the number of GIs they have registered. According to D. Rangnekar, this is what motivated the Government of Goa to apply for the GI Feni. The preservation of Indian national identity is being tested by the rise of internal regional identities.

In addition, the State intervention is due to its still remarkable presence in economic activity.[109] The Development Commissioner for Handicraft of the central government is responsible for economic issues, the organization and management of commodities are still placed under the control of boards, albeit in declining numbers, indicating in this case too, the transitional state of India.

The configuration of the State owner of GIs shocks practitioners and some scholars in India who consider it as a lack of democracy and as

---

[107] Mr Ramakrishnappa, Department of Horticulture.
[108] Affidavit from the Director of CDI, 22 October 2007.
[109] 'Handicrafts are a state subject in which the central government provides supplementary support'; Panini, 'Trends in Cultural Globalisation', 3913.

exemplifying the weakness of producer organizations. The GIs filed by associations do not seem to represent all producers but only their members, and they are unaccustomed to collective action.

The doctrine considers that only the genuine producers of GI products should be allowed to register GI and the double registration—that of registered proprietors and authorized users—is complicated and leaves dangerous room for exploitation of genuine producers. If the Government wants to facilitate GI registration, taking into consideration the poor status of GI producers of India, their role should be limited to the simple facilitator of registration and marketing promoter.[110] This view is shared by the administration; V. Ravi thinks that associations will over time become the voice of GIs.[111]

The question remains whether this is really a temporary situation or rather a characteristic of the Indian system that offers a new look at the legal nature of GIs, which worldwide involves the State. It seems in any case that this type of State intervention can be found in all developing countries, intervention that S. Bowen considers necessary in those countries.[112]

### The Risk of Bias of the GI Registry

The GI Registry is under the authority of the Ministry of Commerce, which is conducting a policy of encouraging registration of GIs. If the GI is accepted by the GI registrar, it is registered in Part A of the GI register, unless otherwise decided by the central government.[113]

---

[110] Exchanges with T.G. Agitha, Research Officer, HRD Chair on IPR, School of Legal Studies, Cochin University of Science And Technology, Kerala, India.

[111] See the intervention of V. Ravi, GI Registrar, WIPO National Seminar on the importance of intellectual property for the handicrafts sector, organized by the World Intellectual Property Organization (WIPO) in cooperation with the Ministry of Textiles, Government of India, and the National Institute of Fashion Technology (NIFT), Hyderabad, India, 5–7 April 2005, www.wipo. int/export/sites/www/sme/en/.../topic5_ravi.ppt: 'Over time, associations will become the voice of that GI'.

[112] Sarah Bowen, 'Development from Within? The Potential for Geographical Indications in the Global South', *The Journal of World Intellectual Property*, 13, no. 2 (2010): 231–252.

[113] Section 16(b).

Consequently, numerous exchanges take place between the GI Registry and the Department of Commerce, particularly for difficult cases. Examples here involve GI applications filed by Reliance for petroleum products or for the processing of the GI application for Pisco, the first GI application to be filed by applicants from third countries.[114]

This leads to the question of whether such a system can preserve the neutrality necessary for the substantive examination of GIs filed by the union government, states, commodity boards and government enterprises. Basmati illustrates the risk of collision, with the GI Registry favouring the application from APEDA versus the application from The Heritage. Even if the reasons for the rejection of the application from The Heritage are legitimate (see Chapter 8), it is striking that such an analysis of the capacity of representation of producers has not been conducted during the examination procedure for other GIs. Yet, recently consultative groups have been more cautious on this aspect. Following the GI application Basmati from APEDA, where a list of only traders and millers was provided with the statement of case, without any producers,[115] the consultative group has requested APEDA the mention of the producers of Basmati.

The GI Mysore silk is another example of a defence by the GI Registry of a GI on the grounds that it comes from a government enterprise. However, the GI on the Malabar pepper seems to be a counterexample—probably because of the maturity of the consultative group that met more than five times.

The role of the State as GI applicant thus runs the risk of interfering with the role of the State as an examiner of GI applications. Although it is meant to be impartial, the fact that the Ministry of Commerce is often

---

[114] Thus, on 6 December 2005, K. Saxena, Under Secretary to the Government of India, Ministry of Commerce and Industrial Promotion Policy, sent a letter to the GI Registrar to inform of the filing of the GI application for Pisco by the Embassy of Peru and requested immediate processing of the application. The GI Registry responded on 8 December that the recommendations were followed and that the application had already been considered in matters of form and that the advisory group would meet on 12 December. From 15 December, the Ministry of Commerce inquired about the decision of the advisory group (file at the GI Registry).

[115] See GIR website http://ipindiaservices.gov.in/GirPublic/ViewApplicationDetails.aspx?AppNo=145&Index=1.

both the supervisor of the GI Registry and the drafter of GI applications can lead to a tendency to favour applications filed by the State.

*Weak Controls Compensated by the Presence of the State?*
The issue of GI control has been little debated in India, with it being considered an issue to be resolved after the GI registration.[116] The Act is rather vague about the obligation to monitor GIs. The regulations of the Act, Rule 32(1).6.c request the particulars of the mechanism to ensure that the standards, quality, integrity and consistency or other special characteristic in respect of the goods to which the GI relates are maintained by the producers, maker or manufacturers of the goods.

The study of Indian GI applications shows that for about half of them, the inspection structure rubric is filed with 'under construction', usually in coordination with the Government. For just under one-third of GIs, among the members of the inspection structure is at least one member of the local government. Finally, some GIs are controlled directly by the applicant. This is the case with Darjeeling tea, Monsooned Malabar coffee, Alleppey coir, which are controlled by the relevant boards, or Mysore Agarbathi, controlled by the association that owns the GI.

The GI Registry and consultative groups have begun to pay more and more attention to the issue of controls and, repeatedly, demanded more details on the control structure of more recent applications. This was the case for the GI application Malabar pepper, where the consultative group requested a stronger inspection structure and the inclusion of personalities from outside the Spice Board in the control organization.[117] Therefore, the State and its bodies are participating in the control as GI owners, even if this is intended to be a temporary situation.

In addition, GI ownership granted to the State can help to ensure consumer confidence in 'authentic' products without the need for sophisticated control systems. In fact, the Government is often seen

---

[116] 'Post-registration implementation is at present very low and the proprietors or users of all the registered GIs should begin to appreciate the importance of registration and takes the adequate steps to improve production, enforce quality measures': 'Interview: G.K. Muthukumaar, Senior Associate, Anand and Anand'.

[117] Letter from Spice Board to the GI Registry, 17 August 2007.

as capable, in the field of handicrafts in particular, to maintain a high standard of quality. For example, the KSHDC is prized by consumers of local handicrafts as guaranteeing authenticity. This perception cannot, however, be sufficient to ensure the system of GIs in India because consumer confidence should not be broken, and the French and European experience shows how aspects of organizational controls can be tricky. Perhaps this is solely a matter of time in India, new in the protection of GIs.

# Part III
# An Essay on the Particularism of GIs as Intellectual Right

Comparative analysis of the French and Indian regimes can help qualifying the legal nature of GIs in countries with sui generis laws and thus understanding the internationalization of the GI concept in a new country of the Old World , in order to improve the international protection of GI products at an international level.

It is generally agreed that GIs are related to the category of IPRs. However, in France, given the codification of the principle within multiple areas of law, such as consumer law, rural law and intellectual property law, other qualifications of the appellation of origin have been made by French scholars.[1] L. Lorvellec considers that

> the concept of appellation of origin is completely foreign to the idea of property, including intellectual property, it is a sign intended to inform consumers ... it is not possible to call property a right without holder and without definite object ... the AOC is part of the right to consumer's information. It defines a set of rules on the market but does not create a monopoly.[2]

---

[1] At community level, Regulation (EC) No. 510/2006 is filed under Information and Consumer Protection.
[2] Lorvellec, 'La Protection Internationale Des Appellations D'origine Contrôlées', 387.

This qualification highlights the difficulty of using the concept of property, including intellectual property, in discussions of appellation of origin. It seems useful therefore to go back to the history of the creation of the category of IPRs, which explains its imperfection. As recalled by M.A. Hermitte and N. Olszak,[3] under the old regime of the Middle Ages in Europe, industrial property[4] was not recognized as such, but was protected by special, and often precarious, privileges, for inventions and guild regulations for trademarks. The French Revolution established economic freedom, and proclaimed the fundamental value of the property right as the second most important human right after freedom. IPRs fit badly into the concept of ownership under the French Civil Code, being by nature intangible objects.

Consequently, E. Picard proposes the creation of a new legal category, at the same level as real rights (over objects) and personal rights (over persons): intellectual rights, understood as exclusive exploitation rights on intellectual conceptions.[5] This description as intellectual rights appears all the more necessary to qualify GIs, where the classical idea of property is more likely to be dismissed, especially in the light of the Indian experience which confirms the 'failure' of this concept.

A GI is a distinctive sign, 'an indication that identifies a product', but the rest of the definition, 'where a given quality, reputation or other characteristic of the good is essentially attributable to its geographical

[3] Marie-Angèle Hermitte, 'Les Appellations D'origine Dans La Genèse Des Droits De La Propriété Intellectuelle', in *Systèmes Agroalimentaires Localisées. Terroirs, Savoir-Faire, Innovations*, ed. Pascale Moity-Maïzy (Etud. Rech. Syst. Agraires Dév., 2001), 196–198; Norbert Olszak, 'La Propriété Industrielle Est-Elle Bien Une Propriété? (a Propos De L'arrêt "Bain De Champagne", Paris, 4ème Ch. A, 12 Septembre 2001, Parfums Caron C. C.I.V.C.)' (Recueil Dalloz, 2002), x.
[4] Industrial property is a sub-category of intellectual property.
[5] We note the theory of customers rights issued by P. Roubier in his book *Law of Industrial Property*, Sirey, 1952, autonomous category of the same level as the real and personal rights. The rights of customers are characterized by an exclusive monopoly. Within the category of the rights of customers, P. Roubier proposes a rights group which he calls 'intellectuals' but which include only the rights proceeding from an act of intellectual creation, excluding logos. This doctrine raises reservations because of its foundation on the basis of industrial property rights functions and not on the content of law. Therefore, we will retain the term of intellectual rights in the broadest sense, including all intellectual conceptions conferring exclusive use, including trademarks.

origin', implies a specificity of GI, indicating the geographical origin of a product rooted in space, which clearly distinguishes it from other distinctive signs. For example, the idea of reward, usually associated with the category of patents and copyright and not with trademark, applies to GIs. The objective of rural development is another specificity that goes beyond the ideas of fair trade and consumer protection that are attached to all distinctive signs.

# 9

# An Intellectual Right Characterized by the Dismemberment of the Right to Use

## Qualification of Intellectual Property Rights Reinforced by Globalization

### The Situation in France and Europe

GIs are part of IPRs within the scope of the Paris Convention, which embraces the Lisbon Agreement. France incorporated the definition of the appellation of origin in the Code of Intellectual Property, but many of the provisions are codified in the Consumer Code and the Rural Code, reflecting the specificity of GIs in France. Reciprocally, the presence of the appellation of origin and the PGI in the Code of Intellectual Property distinguishes them from other 'official signs of quality and origin' placed under the authority of the INAO, such as those for organic farming. GI is an IPR because of the monopoly on exploitation conferred to the sign and the nature of human creation. The value of the sign is the result of human creation. All geographical signs are not GIs, only those which designate a product of human creation born in a given place. Although the name itself, the object of the GI, is imposed by nature and history, it should not be considered, as S. Visse-Causse does, that 'what is missing is the original aspect of intellectual creation'.[1] Intellectual creation comes from the fact of transforming an ordinary pre-existing name into a known and famous name, a name that has new meaning, thanks to human skills.

The qualification of intellectual rights permits the consideration of a regime including very broad rights in terms of innovation while avoiding extensive qualification of ownership, a construction which from the beginning was seen as inadequate for GIs. For Mr Pleasant and Fernand-Jacq, who have studied these issues in the 1920s,[2] 'although the legal standard of property is not suitable for this right, let's simply remind that the legislator intended to protect such right with the highest protection, with the most extensive guarantees, with the most effective actions'.[3] Since then, this characterization of intellectual 'property' has been acquired by the doctrine. J. Audier places appellations of origin among the various IPRs as do Mr C. Piatti[4] and N. Olszak.

At the European level, the ECJ justified the protection of GIs by recognizing them as IPRs able to attract consumers.[5]

## Qualification Reinforced by the Indian GI

GIs have been introduced in India under the TRIPS Agreement and therefore are naturally classified as IPRs. Moreover, according to S. Visse-Causse, the more human factors are present, the more the qualification of IPRs is legitimate.[6] There is no doubt that human factors are essential in defining the link with the origin for Indian GIs.

The next step is to determine with greater sharpness the peculiarities of GIs compared to other IPRs. In the words of N. Olszak, 'against the majesty of the AOC there can be no rights for ordinary distinctive signs.... This exceptional status reveals that we are in another world'.[7]

---

[1] Visse-Causse, *L'appellation D'origine: Valorisation Du Terroir*, 208.
[2] Plaisant and Fernand-Jacq, *Traité Des Noms Et Appellations D'origine*, 54.
[3] Ibid., 53.
[4] Piatti, 'L'appellation D'origine (Essai De Qualification)', 557–581.
[5] See in particular the case Exportur, point 28 and Belgique-Espagne, point 54.
[6] Visse-Causse, *L'appellation D'origine: Valorisation Du Terroir*, 108.
[7] About a case of prior trademark limited in practice due to the existence of an AOC, Champagne in this case, see Olszak, 'La Propriété Industrielle Est-Elle

## Right in GI, Right to GI: The Subdivision of the Right to Use the GI

Despite the consensus on the classification of GIs as IPRs, many unresolved questions remain about the holders of GIs, which questions about their qualification as property. European regulation is silent on the issue of ownership of rights, as are the French laws and the Lisbon Agreement. R. Pleasant considers that the appellation of origin is different from trademark because 'it belongs to a community without personality, not to a legal entity'. For F. Pollaud-Dulian, it belongs to the 'evolutive community of local producers who meet the conditions of use' and in no case to the State.[8] According to M.C. Piatti, the appellation of origin is co-owned by the State and the producers.[9] However, according to this author, 'there is no co-ownership of the right of appellation of origin that is to say, a joint holding of all facets of the right, but two beneficiaries of different rights. Producers and processors are in a kind of dependence on the public authority that grants them use of the right they claim'.[10]

The qualification of M.C. Piatti is built from the dissociation between the 'right in' an appellation of origin and 'the right to' an appellation of origin, that operates as a subdivision of the right to use the GI proposed by J. Audier.

### A Qualification from the French Law ...

*The Content of the Qualification*

J. Audier considers that the appellation of origin is characterized by a split in the nature of the property involved, leading to a distinction between the 'right in' the appellation of origin and the 'right to' the appellation of origin. In 1993, J. Audier wrote that 'Unless otherwise agreed, the public authority holds an intellectual property right in appellation of origin that it has recognized, it confers the right to use

---

Bien Une Propriété? (a Propos De L'arrêt "Bain De Champagne", Paris, 4ème Ch. A, 12 Septembre 2001, Parfums Caron C. C.I.V.C.)', 1894.
[8] Pollaud-Dulian, *Droit De La Propriété Industrielle*, 728.
[9] Piatti, 'L'appellation D'origine (Essai De Qualification)', 581.
[10] Ibid., 564.

that appellation of origin for groups of people in the conditions it determines'.[11] Then, J. Audier qualifies the right to the appellation of origin a 'right to use, intangible heritage'.[12] The holder of the appellation of origin is the public authority, the word holder being used without being specifically qualified. Extending this reasoning in Europe, N. Olszak considers that the holder of PDO/PGI is now the EC. N. Olszak especially notes the novelty of the European form of ownership, despite the fact that all GIs remain truly national, but he does not dispute the right of a public authority to hold this property, stating that 'the State ownership in principle guarantees the stability and the duration of geographical indications'.[13] These qualifications, however, were issued before the French reform of 2006 which provided for the withdrawal of the role of public authorities in France and before the internationalization of GIs following the TRIPS Agreement.

*Its Relevance after TRIPS and French 2006 Reform*

In recent writings, J. Audier is updating his qualification of the appellation of origin under the experience of WTO members: 'Applicants for GI registration (producer groups or government entities) are entitled to the right in the GI so that all producers have the right to the GI'.[14] The public authority would no longer automatically be the holder of the right in the appellation of origin which may well be to the benefit of producer groups, the principle being that the holder of the right on GI is the GI applicant.

In France since the 2006 reform, the applicant for the AOC or PGI is the defence and management organization, with legal personality, who in France has the right in the appellation. The right in the GI, for the benefit of the GI applicant, also has a long history in countries that

---

[11] J. Audier, 'De la nature juridique de l'appellation d'origine', *Bulletin de l'OIV*, 1993, pp. 21–37. Cf. aussi: M.C. Piatti, 'L'appellation d'origine (essai de qualification)', *RTD Com*, no. 3, juillet 1999, pp. 557–581.

[12] Jacques Audier, 'De La Nature Juridique De L'appellation D'origine', *Bulletin de l'O.I.V.*, no. 743–744 (1993): 34.

[13] Olszak, *Le Droit Des Appellations D'origine Et Des Indications De Provenance*, 95–97.

[14] Jacques Audier, 'Passé, Présent Et Avenir Des Appellations D'origine Dans Le Monde: Vers La Globalisation', *Bulletin de l'O.I.V.*, no. 929–931 (2008): 425.

protect GIs through the system of certification marks, such as the United States. Thus, the owner of French appellations of origin and PGIs registered in the United States as certification marks is not the State agency, INAO, but the applicant group, such as, for example, the Inter-professional Committee of Champagne.

## ... Which Seems to Apply to Indian Law

The Indian GI Act is characterized by the coupling of the proprietor and user of the GI. The Indian qualification of authorized user reinforces the qualification proposed by Audier of a right of use conferred to the producers and a right in the GI conferred to the GI applicant, with the additional qualification of the 'right in the GI' as a property right. But in India, many GIs have been applied for by the State or its bodies, which corresponds to Audier's pre-2006 qualification, where he stated that the public authority holds an IPR in appellation of origin that it has recognized. Still this right in the GI granted to the public authority is not provided for by the Indian GI Act but is the consequence of practice. The Indian legal framework therefore offers the scholar a chance to test in vivo the qualification separating the right in the GI from the right to the GI and to assess its relevance. The implementation of the Indian GI Act shows the perverse effect of this principle of subdivision of rights when the GI is understood as a property right: the risk of the supremacy of property right over the right of use, leading to the absence of registered users, especially since the benefit of the right of use is subject to certain conditions that may make it difficult to access.

# The Conditions for Exercising the Right to Use

## Registration of Producers in India versus the Control of Producers in France

J. Audier qualifies the 'right to' the appellation of origin as the right to use the appellation. This right of use is subject to compliance with the GI specifications. However in some countries, formalities can go beyond this requirement. In around 10 WTO members, the right to use GIs also requires the authorization or registration of users.[15]

In India, the right of use is not automatic but depends on the registration at the GI Registry. The French reform introduced a new requirement for operators to be able to use the GI although not expressed as such: the proof of capability of operators, the first step of the control mechanism, which now applies to all PDOs and PGIs. This authorization may be refused and is not automatic. In India, is the registration of users related to the verification of the capability of producers to meet the conditions of the GI specifications? It seems so, because the application for registration of producers as authorized users describe how the manufacturer makes the product and comprises the whole statement of case of said GI. It therefore appears that the right to use the GI in France and in India is conditioned by the validation a priori of the skills of producers: the check of capability of operators in France and the registration of producers as authorized users in India. This 'barrier' is thus not unique to India and is found in French law, even if in that case the barrier is more hidden.

However, the same authorities that authorize the use of the GI differ in India and in France. Indeed, in France, the capability of operators is now checked by the independent control body, whereas in the past, when it was planned, it was placed under the direct responsibility of INAO, which was at that time the holder of the right in the appellation of origin. The intervention of an independent third party is the cornerstone of the reform in France, supposed to avoid any conflict of interest. But in India, the registration of producers as authorized users requires the consent of the GI owner, a configuration that can be compared to the old French situation which has already shown precisely its limits. Is this potential conflict of interest between the GI owner and the GI user the reason there are so few registered users in India? And if so, how can one solve this issue?

### Right to Use Untapped in India: The Concept of Ownership Should Be Removed

Given the lack of authorized users registered in India, several solutions are possible. One proposal would be that producers may apply for

---

[15] Ibid., 425.

registration in a simplified manner, without requiring the consent of the owner. To raise awareness among producers and encourage them to register, the IPAB to publish about the GI application in the Land Acquisition Act, that is in a newspaper having good circulation in the locality and in the language of the territory, and affixture of public notice in prominent places in the territory. Only then, the artisans will know that a GI has been applied for in respect of the goods that they are creating.[16] This suggestion is interesting because it builds similarities between intellectual property and real property. But this strengthens the concept of GI as a property right, which cannot be compared to real property right.

Another way would be to remove that requirement, but doing so also risks strengthening the belief that to be authorized to use the GI would require to be a proprietor of the GI, a stance that might weaken the legal nature of GIs as a right of use. The many oppositions regarding the applicant and the way in which co-applicants have become co-owners of GIs in India seem to demonstrate that risk. The collective nature of GIs is not satisfied if each producer needs to be the co-owner of the GI to be authorized to use it. Of course, if registration of GIs is on behalf of associations, their members seem to be the natural GI users, but the non-member producers would be excluded. This situation differs from the French experience where, before the reform, even if only one producer group was originally responsible for the AOC application, all producers, including non-members, could use it. So there was no situation of several associations being co-applicants. Even if the mechanism of co-ownership is used in India to include all producers, there will always be a risk of excluding a legitimate 'owner'.

It seems that the problem is the qualification of property of the Indian GI Act which is considered sacrosanct and interpreted in the same way as for trademarks and patents, negating the benefit of the provisions conferring rights to GI users (right to use but also right of action for infringement...). One solution could be the removal of the concept of ownership, maintaining only the right to use as in the case of the European regulation. Indeed, French doctrine and jurisprudence have never

---

[16] GI Payyanur Pavithra ring, OA/2/2010/GI/CH and M.P. Nos. 1/2010 & 269/2012 in OA/2/2010/GI/CH, 14 November 2012.

ceased to affirm the unavailability of the appellation of origin, which is considered 'not subject to private appropriation'. Similarly, the Indian GI Act establishes the inalienability of the GI which cannot be the object of any assignment, licence, mortgage or guarantee. This provision is very similar to case for certification marks, which cannot be sold or transmitted without the favourable opinion of the Registrar of Trademarks. Aside from that, certification marks hold a much more different position than that given to individual trademarks, which suggest to exclude them from the ordinary categories of trademarks, in the case of GIs, no favourable opinion of registrar can depart from the aforementioned rule. What is, then, the interest in giving a property right which cannot be used in the same way as other similar rights, particularly due to the restrictions on its transfer and disposal? Indeed, inalienability takes away one of the core of property rights, that is, right to convey/transfer property.

Let's start from this essential concept of inalienability. GIs are usually names of places, or for a few exceptions, non-geographical names referring to a geographical place, used by everyone in the place. This is why they are inalienable and unavailable. Place names are common things, that is to say, things whose use is common to all, such as air or sea. Article 714 of the French Civil Code defines *choses communes* as 'things that belong to no one and whose use is common to all', noting that 'mandatory rules govern how to enjoy them'. In other words, it is something that the sovereign authority decides to allocate for use by the public under rules of use determined by the authority. The names of places, or by extension names, that refer to them are with no doubt *choses communes*. Does this mean that GIs are *choses communes*? C. Le Goffic retains the category to describe the appellation of origin in what is an interesting demonstration in many ways.[17] We need to analyze if GIs meet the various elements of the definition of *choses communes:* first their inalienable character, which is well suited to GIs, and second their common use to all under restrictions imposed by the public authority. The second element concerns the right to use the geographical name, the *choses communes*, which needs to be analyzed in details.

---

[17] Caroline Le Goffic, *La Protection Des Indications Géographiques En France, En Europe Et Aux Etats-Unis*, vol. Thèse (Paris: Le droit des affaires, Propriété intellectuelle, IRPI, Litec, 2009), 272 et suiv.

# 10
# A Collective Right to Use Tinted with Public Law

According to N. Olszak, the French appellation of origin is a collective public sign.[1] The collective nature of GIs is also present in other IPRs such as collective marks or in collective works protected under copyright. However, the concept of collective right in GIs is specific, to be interpreted in the light of the principle of inalienability of place names, that can be used by all producers in the area who comply with the rules born in this place. This specificity is reflected in the obligation that the applicants represent GI producers/operators, a salient feature of the new French regulations and an essential requirement in India.

## The Collective Nature of GIs, a Universal Reality

The European Commission announced in its summary of the contributions to the Green Paper that 'any new system should preserve the link with the region of production and the collective nature of geographical

[1] Norbert Olszak, 'L'appellation D'origine, Un Bien Sublime?', in *Etudes Offertes Au Doyen Philippe Simler* (LITEC Dalloz, 2007), 777–788.

indications'.[2] The collective nature of GIs is considered as important as the link between the product and its origin is found in all systems of GI protection. The foundations have been enriched with the experience acquired for over a century to reach a concept of collective right specific to GIs: the representation of producers by the GI applicant.

## Collective Enjoyment, Individual Exercise

### Collective Right of Use

The shared modes of production developed over time contributed to the collective creation of the reputed product This principle was stated very early when discussing the French law of 1919 which defines the appellation of origin, the proposed right of individual ownership was rejected in favour of the concept of collective right, used by all.[3]

The right to use granted by the GI is for the benefit of several persons, not limited to one person. Such persons may be designated in the GI application. The Lisbon Agreement requires that the international application contains the holders of the right to use the appellation of origin, designated collectively or, where collective designation is not possible, by name. It is the same for GIs applications in India, which contains a statement which may include a collective reference to all producers concerned. The assistant registrar for GIs in his order has reaffirmed the collective aspect of Indian GIs.

### Collective Right to Sue

The collective aspect of GIs is found in the persons authorized to take legal action to defend the title. In France, under the 1919 Act, it was the unions.[4] The jurisprudence has followed this qualification, including in the United Kingdom, where in the course of 'passing off' action, the

---

[2] 'Communication De La Commission Au Parlement Européen, Au Conseil, Au Comité Économique Et Social Européen Et Au Comité Des Régions Sur La Politique De Qualité Des Produits Agricoles'. Ibid., 12, voir commentaire de Ruzek, 'La Stratégie Communautaire De Protection Des Indications Géographiques En Question', 1–9.
[3] *Une Réussite Française: L'appellation D'origine Contrôlée*, 20.
[4] Olszak, *Appellations D'origine Et Indications De Provenance* (*Indications Géographiques*), Section 179.

judges decided it was irrelevant that the persons entitled to describe their product by the name Champagne are actually a group of people producing a product in a given place and are not an individual. This decision thus recognized a collective right to take legal action to defend the use of the geographical name.

*Individual Exercise of the Right to Use*

N. Olszak recalls that the right to use the appellation of origin is an individual exercise of a collective right because the AOC exists only thanks to the action of individuals, whether corporations or actual persons.[5] This exercise is formalized by the capability of individual operators in France and by the registration of individual producers in India.

## The Representation of Producers, the Specific Character of the Collective Right

*A Similar Concept under French and Indian Laws...*

Before the 2006 reform in France, there was no legal requirement for the representation of producers by the organization in charge of drafting the specification. Several associations of producers could coexist for the same appellation of origin. Even the formation of an association was not mandatory, but the French reform of 2006 establishes precisely the obligation of one single defence and management organization for an AOC or a PGI to which all operators shall adhere, with the principle of fair representation of all the operators of the sector.

In India, the law specifically provides that the applicant shall represent the interests of producers, a feature that was not required by the definition of the WIPO Model Law on which the Indian Act was drafted nor by the TRIPS Agreement.

*Applied in Different Ways...*

However, India and France are implementing the shared concept of representation of producers/operators in different ways. In India, it seems to be a functional representation, part of the objectives that the applicant shall meet, but it does not hold consistently in practice due

---

[5] Olszak, *Le Droit Des Appellations D'origine Et Des Indications De Provenance*, 83.

to the lack of mandatory organic link between the producers and the applicant. In France, since the 2006 reform, there is an organic representation of operators by the defence and management organization which can be described as optimal as all within a single AOC/IGP are ex officio members of a single organization and should be represented fairly.

In both cases, the objective of such an obligation is the guarantee that the specification meets the interests of all operators within the community. Depending on the degree of their representation, the producers are more or less involved in the drafting of the GI application comprising the technical specification. In France, the obligation to represent producers offsets the withdrawal of the role of the INAO, public authority, in the definition of the content of GI specifications meant to take into account the general interest.

The obligation to represent the interests of producers characterizes the specific collective nature of GIs. In contrast, collective marks do not require such representation.

## Variations of the Nature of Public

*GI Specification Examined by INAO in France and by the GI Registry in India*
In France, before 2006, the nature of public law of the appellation of origin was based on the State intervention in the definition, management and protection of the appellation of origin.[6] Although since the reform more private actors are involved, it is nonetheless true that the role of INAO goes well beyond the role of National Institute of Intellectual Property (NIIP) for the examination and registration of trademarks, including collective marks and certification marks. In fact, regarding GIs, the public authority carefully examines the use of the name, the product's history, the environmental characteristics, the product and the specialized knowledge used by producers, not just the availability of the sign as it is the case in trademark law. The GI is not only a distinctive sign; it is a distinctive sign whose use is conditioned upon compliance with rules examined by the public authority.

The Indian GI Registry identically conducts substantive examination of GI applications. The role of the Indian government in the validation

---

[6] Piatti, 'L'appellation D'origine (Essai De Qualification)', 569.

of a 'standard' is considered a specific criterion of GIs compared with the certification mark regulations for which content is at the sole discretion of the owner of the trademark and is not examined.[7] So this is a specific criterion to GI sui generis laws.

Is the French INAO of the same nature as the Indian GI Registry? The easy temptation is to say yes, but the strong presence of producers in the bodies of INAO responsible for assessing the link with the origin creates a certain contrast to the case of members of the consultative group in India, who are usually experts from public research institutions or universities.[8] M.A. Such a strong presence of professionals in the committees of INAO is a risk of neo-corporatism. In the post-reform context where the specifications are further developed by the profession, one can indeed wonder whether so large a presence of producer interests in INAO is legitimate, considering the necessary role of the State.

*The State Filing GIs Applications in India*

The implementation of Indian law is characterized by the presence of the State as proprietor of GIs. In some other countries, appellations of origin or GIs are a property of the State, but they are rare: for example, Cuba, Guatemala, Mexico, Panama and Peru.[9]

However in India, the property vested in the State is not enshrined in the GI Act but results from practice. The State itself has some reluctance to call itself the proprietor, preferring instead the role of a guardian or facilitator. In a somewhat vague comment of the GI Act, GIs are defined as a public property, but is it in the sense of ownership of the State or in the sense of something not appropriated?

In addition, the State status as a proprietor of rights also occurs in countries using the certification marks system. Many GIs protected under the collective certification mark in the United States are registered

---

[7] According to the presentation of V. Ravi, OMPI and S. Balganesh.
[8] V. Ravi, drafter of the GI Act, wishes to reinforce the role of the consultative group who shall be also competent for the objections.
[9] Jacques Audier, 'Mondialisation Et Indications Géographiques: Applications Nationales De L'accord Adpic, Section 3 Indications Géographiques', *Propriétés Intellectuelles*, no. 26 (2008): 9.

in the name of public authorities.[10] For example, the GI 'Certified 100% grown in Idaho Potato' is a certification mark registered in the name of the state of Idaho, specifically in the name of 'Potato Commission, State agency, Idaho'.[11] The State intervention in the definition of the GI application seems to be a salient feature beyond sui generis systems.

*The Role of Public Authority in the Mechanism of International Protection*

The Lisbon Agreement is based on the relay of applications via the competent authority of the country, the State. It is a mechanism that differs from those applicable to other IPRs. The protection of PDO/PGI at the European level is also due to the action of the member states, which transmit PDO/PGI applications to Brussels and act as the only appropriate party to resolve objections.

However, France is part of the Lisbon Agreement and a member of the EU, which is not the case for India. Blocked negotiations on the establishment of a multilateral register are such that it is unlikely that this element of public law will be recognized as a feature of GIs, including within the sui generis systems.

A large number of bilateral agreements are signed by States that include a list of GIs to be protected by each signatory party. This is not practised for other IPRs: is it an element of public law? Considering that the list annexed to the agreements on GIs is decided by the sovereign state, the answer is yes.

*GIs, Part of National Heritage?*

GIs are often referred to as national heritage. J. Audier agreed that GIs are part of national heritage because of their recognition which is generally

---

[10] Le Goffic, C. (2009). *La protection des indications géographiques en France, en Europe et aux Etats-Unis* (Paris: Le droit des affaires, Propriété intellectuelle, IRPI, Litec).

[11] Trademarks no. 3 530 137 et 3530136 for identical logos with different colours. Trademark no. 2914309 for a little different logo 2934385, 2406487 2403069 1735559. A côté des marques de producteurs privés: 2972018 Registration Date 19 July 2005 Owner (registrant) Clement Enterprises 2191792 Registration Date 29 September 1998 Owner (Registrant) George Mac Western Speciality, Inc. Dba Great Mountain West Supply Corporation Utah.

under the jurisdiction of the State.[12] N. Olszak believes that appellations of origin should be specifically protected as they are part of our heritage.[13] This is a fundamentally political idea, specific to sui generis systems. M.-H. Bienaymé extends this concern globally in the hope that the policy of protection of GIs under the WTO succeeds as a tool to preserve the sustainability of the cultural heritage of the world.[14] In India, GIs concern products that are considered as national heritage and that are protected by the State.

*Control in France and in India*
According to N. Olszak, 'GIs are a quality guarantee as to the nature of the goods'.[15] The quality is guaranteed by control system, an essential and very organized tool in France. Despite the decline of the State in the controls in France, the entire system is under its control with the approval of the controlling bodies and control schemes for each GI by INAO.

In India, regulatory control of the certification bodies by the public authority does not exist. However, GI user registration is done at the GI Registry, a public authority that has the power to intervene, unlike the recognition of users of the collective mark, which is under the sole authority of the owner of the mark.

*The State Capable of Prosecution*
Specific to the European and the French law, continued with the 2006 reform, is the ability of the State to pursue in justice, as is the ex-Officio protection provided by the EU Regulation 1151/2012. This is not the case elsewhere and cannot be considered an element of public law of the GI.

*GI as Imprescriptible in France, Limited in Time in India*
In France, unlike other IPRs which are conferred for a limited period of time, the appellation of origin can never be regarded as generic in

---

[12] Audier, 'De La Nature Juridique De L'appellation D'origine', 27.
[13] Olszak, 'La Propriété Industrielle Est-Elle Bien Une Propriété? (a Propos De L'arrêt "Bain De Champagne", Paris, 4ème Ch. A, 12 Septembre 2001, Parfums Caron C. C.I.V.C.)', 1894.
[14] Bienaymé, 'L'appellation D'origine Contrôlée', 424.
[15] Olszak, 'La Politique Communautaire Des Signes De Qualité Et D'origine'.

nature and therefore fall into the public domain. However, this perpetual and imprescriptible character of the appellation of origin is not explicitly incorporated into the European regulations, which on the contrary provides for a procedure to cancel the registration of GIs in the event the European Commission or any individual or entity believes that the conditions of the specifications of the product are no longer met.[16]

Imprescriptibility is not a principle of Indian law; the GI is valid for a period of 10 years, renewable indefinitely. However, this is one of the elements V. Ravi, editor of the GI Act, proposes to remove.

## Private/Public Dualism of the GI

Being a right to use which benefits producers/operators, the private nature of GI is indisputable and articulates with its public nature. This public/private duality is implemented in distinctly different time sequences in India and in France.

### The Private Nature of GIs

The private nature of GIs is widely acknowledged. The use of the appellation of origin by producers makes it a private right.[17] The internationalization of GIs by the TRIPS Agreement strengthens the private nature of GIs, which are a tool available to private individuals who wish to use it to promote their products.

A contrario, does the absence of GI use by producers in India mask its role as a private right to make it only a public right? This question seems relevant for products which are not exploited or in decline. In the case of other products, it is only a matter of time delay.

### The Implementation of Public/Private Dualism: Differences between India and France

Is the Indian situation, with its lack of GI users, permanent or temporary? Can't it be explained by the low capacity of producers in claiming their right to use the GI? Even if this lack of use is temporary, in India, the intervention of public authority in the registration of GIs comes before the intervention of private producers who can ask to be registered

---

[16] Art. 12 Regulation 510/2006.
[17] Piatti, 'L'appellation D'origine (Essai De Qualification)', 560.

as authorized users only after the GI has been registered. It is contrary to the French situation, where such will is first expressed privately, before the intervention of public authority. The choice of producers to use the GI instrument is prior to the recognition of the appellation of origin or its registration by the State.[18] In India, the product is certainly born from the creativity of the producers, but the whole approach to protect the name as a GI results from the intervention of public authority. It is only later that the question of the participation of producers to the system emerges. This difference between France and India is due to the mode of creation of legal frameworks: in India, the GI Act is the result of TRIPS Agreement obligations, while in France, the legal framework is the result of strong demand from wine producers represented by J. Capus since the beginning of the 20th century. Even if India and France are both Old World countries, they can still be distinguished according to the seniority of the existence of the legal instrument. India can be called a new country of the Old World.

## Conclusions on the Legal Nature of GIs

The comparison between the legal regimes of appellation of origin and the French PGI on one side and the Indian GI on the other side yields a number of similarities.

GIs are distinctive signs and constitute part of the range of intellectual rights. Not able to be appropriated in France, they are inalienable in India, where they are nevertheless appropriated. The experience of registered proprietors is a failure in India, and the model of property as understood in the Civil Code cannot be applied to the GI. The duality of rights in versus rights to GI therefore leaves room for the sole right to a GI, which is a right of use. The collective nature of the right to GI is essential and is institutionalized by the obligation of producers' representation required by French law and Indian law, constituting it as a collective right of use.

The sign protected as a GI, the place name, can be described as a *chose commune* because the place names can be used by all the inhabitants of

---

[18] Ibid., 560.

a place. Is this name still a *chose commune* thing when it becomes a GI and, indeed, a signal for the market? C. Le Goffic deduced the qualification of the appellation of origin as a *chose commune* based upon the observation of the 'common use' by any operator in the hands of whom the goods covered by an appellation of origin are circulating, noting that the freedom of use of common things may be subject to an authorization that is intended to preserve it, the 'overriding mandatory rules'. So for this author, 'the appellation of origin is a *chose commune*, not subject to appropriation, subject to a non-exclusive individual right to use by all operators marketing complying wines'.

The qualification of *choses communes*, subject to a right of use regulated by mandatory rules, raises several questions. First, it appears that the use of the sign is regulated for the sole benefit of a particular collective, the group of operators complying with the specifications. This is a division of the *chose commune* (commons), with use restricted to a certain group. Here the commons is the name of the place, whose use is common for all residents. There is a subdivision of the *chose commune* which may be the object of a particular use for a certain group of people who do not use it to designate a place any more, but instead to identify a product from this place. Indeed, it appears that the place name which is used by all is not comparable to the place name which has become a GI. The exclusive right to collective use is given to operators because the name is a different thing when it becomes a GI. The creation of a product in a place justifies assignment of the value of this commons to a particular group. GIs are no longer the *chose commune* but one of its potential utilities, this subdivision. This particular use is framed by rules.

In France, these rules are set by producers who propose the content of the GI specification. The GI specifications are the rules of use. Following the substantive examination, the public authority can certainly change the content of GI application but has to respect the choices of the community of producers. The rules governing the use of the name are thus defined by the specifications and not by the public authority, although INAO comprises a majority of representatives of the profession. However, these rules are controlled under the supervision of the public authority that ensures compliance with the rules, even if the specific guarantee of the State is attenuated. Then, GIs are not themselves the *choses communes*, because their use is not regulated by the 'overriding mandatory rules', which is a condition of the definition of a commons in the French Civil Code. GI is a right to use the *chose commune*, that is, the geographical name. The public authority guarantees the exclusive use of the name to producers under various conditions developed by producers and accepted by the public authority. The GI would be a collective exclusive right to use a *chose commune* reserved for a group of people because of the reputation of their creation, and guaranteed or affected by public authority.

In India, the idea that GI itself is a *chose commune* is attractive because it refers to the quality of the State as the guardian. It would legitimize the State's role as drafter of the contents of the specification, in its function of enactor of mandatory rules, without depriving the producers or the uses given them by the monopoly. It is nevertheless true that the policing of GI, as enacted by the State, should be based on the wishes of the producers, although at the moment, unlike in France, their desires are not taken into account in the process. Still, if we consider this intervention of the State as temporary, the principle of the GI Act is that the rules of use are determined by the producers and therefore, as in France, GI is not itself a *chose commune* but the right to use a *chose commune*.

# General Conclusion

Modern India, as a WTO member, has chosen to comply to the TRIPS Agreement obligation to protect GIs with a sui generis legal framework. One of the most unique features of GI in post-TRIPS India is the broad scope of protection that includes all kinds of products as soon as they exhibit some 'uniqueness', including handicraft. The Indian tradition of GIs on handicrafts questions the validity of GIs for products whose reputation, quality or characteristics are based on the geographical environment that essentially comprises human factors, with hardly any or no natural factors included. Ancient and shared knowledge forms the basis of GIs which, to be acceptable, should be sophisticated, should not only rely on the creation of designs and should be correctly mapped. France, on the other hand, had created a sophisticated system of protection of appellation of origin based on the concept of *terroir* which is particularly suited to wines and spirits, which has subsequently been applied to all agricultural products. Even the European PGI, which offers a more flexible link between the product and its geographical origin, remains confined to agricultural products due to the predominance of natural factors, although its definition, which is more aligned to the TRIPS Agreement, opens new ways to describe a link to the origin.

The innovative experience in countries recently implementing GI laws, such as India, has influenced the European and French conceptions. On 17 March 2014, France has adopted a law protecting GIs for non-agricultural goods,[1] to be registered by the French National Institute of Industrial Property. In France, many traditional handicraft goods in revival after a long time of disappearance are expecting a lot from the new law, whereas in India, handicrafts are still a major industry, although in decline.

---

[1] LOI n° 2014-344 du 17 mars 2014 relative à la consommation.

However, practice in France, Europe and India shows that handicraft products may involve natural factors, be it raw materials or elements of its active environment during the transformation process and, on the other hand, the reputation of the agricultural products or foodstuff may result from the know-how that is always characterized by its remarkable history. It is thus necessary to remove the product's categorization actually provided by the TRIPS Agreement which distinguishes between wines, spirit and other goods and also provided by the new law in France and Europe, where the proposal of the EU report on GIs for non-agricultural goods is to set up a specific law for GIs for non-agricultural goods, registered by the European Office in charge of trademarks.

A change of paradigm is therefore urgently required, as is the implementation of a global system for protecting the link to the geographical origin, based on the concepts of natural *and/or* human factors, replacing an approach based merely on product categorization.

The concepts of human and/or natural factors should help determine the strength of the link with the origin, with the hypothesis that human factors taken alone confers a weaker link to the origin than a combination between human and natural factors.

The large range of products designated by GIs reintroduces the idea of distinguishing legal categories based on the strength of the link to the origin, and not according to product categorization. It conducts to propose the internationalization of the principle of two levels of geographical references, as it exists in Europe, depending on whether there are only human factors or a combination between human and natural factors. In Europe, the identical protection afforded to the PDO and PGI despite their objectives being clearly distinct can be questioned. It remains to imagine the two levels of protection associated, provided that the standard level of protection of the TRIPS Agreement is insufficient, and appears below the rights conferred to trademarks, which prohibit identical use of the sign subject to the trademark on similar products with no need to prove the risk of public confusion.

This distinction between PDO and PGI makes sense in Europe, the birthplace of the appellation of origin; it may seem abstract to countries such as India, which are not members of the Lisbon Agreement and therefore not very permeable to the category of the appellation of origin. But the revision of the Lisbon Agreement to introduce the concept of

GIs next to the one of appellation of origin might open this vision of two levels of geographical references beyond Europe.

Traditional knowledge must be protected by an ad hoc law, as the law on GIs only protects the name. GIs could be considered only if the services originate locally and demonstrate their specificity to a local root. Regarding the protection of traditional knowledge that cannot be located and, therefore, cannot be the base for a GI registration, the European 'traditional specialty guaranteed' (TSG) is worth mentioning. TSG corresponds to a traditional product which, thanks to its raw materials, composition or method of production and/or processing, guarantees a specificity of the product that clearly distinguishes it from other similar products in the same category. These include the famous example of Jamon Serrano or the more recent Neapolitan Pizza. TSG does not refer to a geographical origin but is intended to protect the traditional composition of a product or a traditional production method. The registration of a TSG does not necessarily protect the name alone, but also the acronym TSG and the community symbol. Thus, in the context of opposition proceedings, the name reservation may be challenged if it appears that the name is used by opponents in a lawful, recognized and economically significant manner for agricultural products or foodstuffs.

This category could validly be applied to traditional Indian goods whose production is not precisely localized. However, the protection conferred is relatively low if the only benefit is that exclusive right to use the logo TSG, which explains its minimal success in Europe. Although not internationalized, could such an instrument be useful in India? The TSG is reminiscent of certification marks on Indian traditional manufacture such as 'handloom' and whose interest is real. In any case, it is a relevant instrument in the event that there is no link to a place.

These considerations have an impact on the international protection of GIs. For example, can Indian GIs claim protection under the European regulation? First, because of the scope of European regulation, limited to agricultural and food products, two-thirds of the Indian GIs are excluded from the European protection. In this regard, given the assumption of the validity of GI for handicraft products, it appears urgent for Europe to take up the issue of expanding the scope of GIs to all products in order to avoid disputes before the Dispute Settlement Body of the WTO.

The confrontation between traditional India and globalized India, rich in terms of the dynamics of the GI tool introduced by the WTO and used for protecting traditional products, also manifests itself in the government's application of GIs. The traditional role played by the Indian state has left its mark, by granting rights over GIs to the State or to the applicants supported by the State. This interventionist concept of the role played by the State is against the recent tendency reinforced by the 2006 French reform where the State takes a backseat in the protection of GIs in France. GIs protection in India is a top-down State-driven process, whereas in Europe it is a bottom-up producer-driven process. Then the other question is whether Indian GIs registered by government agencies or by the government are in conformity with European rules which provide that only one group of producers or processors may file a GI. The difference in nature of GIs between France and India is here precisely revealed. For example, does the Tea Board meet this definition? The recent application for a PGI for Darjeeling, filed by the Tea Board, has been accepted by the European Commission without this element apparently being subject to any objection. It is likely, that implicitly, the European Commission has not focused on the legal status of the applicant but has sought to extract the elements to judge whether the producers and processors were behind the application. This would mean that the Commission has assessed if the applicant, the Tea Board, represents the interests of producers! This confirms that the Indian practice of the State filing GIs should be interpreted as justified by its role of representation of producers, not as a throwback to an interventionist State which would grant licences to use the GIs as at the time of the 'License Raj'. This presence is not in itself inconsistent with economic liberalization in India.

However, France/Europe and India' legal frameworks share many common features, such as the substantive examination of the content of GI applications by the public authorities, and the collective use by all those who comply with the GI specification. Therefore, this research, which deals an experimental tool capable of evolution, argues that GI is an intellectual right on a distinctive sign, and more precisely a collective exclusive right to use a *chose commune* which is reserved for a group of persons as a reward of the reputation they have built over time, reservation guaranteed or affected by the public authority.

The government intervention in the examination of the conditions of GI applications, which is essential and gives the GI the nature of a regulated right to use, seems to justify the principle of dependence between the GI of the country of origin and the GI of the foreign country because it is difficult to see how the public authorities of third countries could make such an examination of the link to the origin by principle of locality. The recognition of customary use of the name could only be the responsibility of local authorities. Thus, the European Commission should necessarily trust the Indian State, which decided that Darjeeling was a GI, to make its own decision. And yet, this is a product known in Europe.

Beyond these legal twists and turns, there remains the question of economic and cultural efficiency of the legal framework in India. Are GIs strong enough to meet the hopes that India has in the system? Will they allow on the one hand for improvement in the living conditions of producers and on the other to maintain practices that seem destined to disappear, such as hand-weaving? The GI Act does allow for the documentation of traditional knowledge, and the ability to inventory assets, in ways that fit within the meaning of welfare legislation, but that is not enough: Indian producers must insist upon access to their right to use, an intellectual right which should be as much or more of the focus than the property right. This is an issue which goes far beyond geographical indications.

# Bibliography

1er Congrès De L'origine, Tenu En Pays D'auge À Deauville Du 25 Au 27 Juin 1948. Caen: BNICE et INAO, 1992.

Achoth, L. 'Report on Surveys on Coffee Holdings and Coffee Market Chain in India in Relation to Mould Contamination in Coffee'. Bangalore: Coffee Board of India, 2005.

Addor, Felix, and Alexandra Grazzioli. 'Geographical Indications beyond Wines and Spirits, a Roadmap for a Better Protection for Geographical Indications in WTO/TRIPS Agreement'. *The Journal of World Intellectual Property*, 5, no. 6 (2002): 865–897.

Agostini, Eric. 'Nullité De La Marque Utilisant Une Appellation D' Origine Pour Des Produits Ne Relevant Pas De L'aire Géographique Précise De Cette Appellation'. *Recueil Dalloz*, (1995): 58.

Akhileshwar, Pathak. 'Law, Liberalisation and Globalisation in India: Just a Game of Chance?' *IIMA Working Papers, Indian Institute of Management Ahmedabad*, 12, no. 3 (2003): 22.

Amilien, Virginie. 'A Propos De Produits Locaux'. *Anthropology of Food*, no. 4 (2005): 1–9.

Anvar, Shabnam Laure. 'Semences Et Droit: L'emprise D'un Modèle Économique Dominant Sur Une Réglementation Sectorielle'. Université Paris I Panthéon-Sorbonne, 2008.

Assayag, Jackie. *La Mondialisation Vue D'ailleurs, La Couleur Des Idées*. Paris: Editions du Seuil, 2005.

Astier, Alexandre. *Petite Histoire De L'inde*. Edited by Eyrolles Pratique. Paris: Editions Eyrolles 2007.

Audier, Jacques. 'De La Nature Juridique De L'appellation D'origine'. *Bulletin de l'O.I.V.*, no. 743–744 (1993): 21–37.

———. 'Indications Géographiques: Le Virus "Générique"'. *Propriétés Intellectuelles*, no. 8 (2003): 252–260.

———. 'Mondialisation Et Indications Géographiques : Applications Nationales De L'accord Adpic, Section 3 Indications Géographiques'. *Propriétés Intellectuelles*, no. 26 (2008): x.

———. 'Passé, Présent Et Avenir Des Appellations D'origine Dans Le Monde: Vers La Globalisation', *Bulletin de l'O.I.V.*, no. 929–931 (2008): 405–435.

Audier, Jacques. 'Réflexions Juridiques Sur La Notion De Terroir'. *Bulletin de l'O.I.V.*, no. 747–748 (1993): 423–437.

'Avis Sur La Mise En Œuvre De La Réforme Des Signes D'identification De La Qualité Et De L'origine Des Produits Agricoles Et Agroalimentaires'. 46. Paris: Conseil National de l'Alimentation, 2008.

Balganesh, Shyamkrishna. 'Systems of Protection for Geographical Indications of Origin: A Review of the India Regulatory Framework'. *The Journal of World Intellectual Property*, 6, no. 1 (2003): 191–205.

Barham, E. 'Translating Terroir: The Global Challenge of French AOC Labeling'. *Journal of Rural Studies*, 19, no. 1 (2003): 127–138.

Barham, E. and Sylvander, B. *Labels of Origin for Food: Local Development, Global Recognition*. Wallingford, UK: CABI, 2011.

Bérard, Laurence, and Philippe Marchenay. *Les Produits De Terroir, Entre Cultures Et Règlements*. Paris: CNRS Edition, 2004.

———. 'Local Products and Geographical Indications: Taking Account of Local Knowledge and Biodiversity'. *International Social Science Journal*, 58, no. 187 (2006): 109–116.

———. 'Produits De Terroir Et Enjeux Européens: Une Approche Anthropologique'. In *Les Produits Agroalimentaires Régionaux: Approches Théoriques Et Résultats D'études*, edited by Lucie Sirieix, Fatiha Fort and Hervé Remaud, 16–24. Montpellier: Cahiers de Recherche MOISA No. 1, 2001.

———. *Produits De Terroir: Comprendre Et Agir*. Bourg-en-Bresse: CNRS, 2007.

Bienaymé, Marie-Hélène. 'L'appellation D'origine Contrôlée'. *Revue de Droit Rural*, no. 236 (1995): 419–424.

Blakeney, Michael. 'Geographical Indications and TRIPS'. Quaker United Nations Office, 2001.

Boillot, Jean-Joseph. *L'économie De L'inde*. Paris: La Découverte, 2006.

Bonet, Georges. 'Des Cigarettes Aux Parfum, L'irrésistible Ascension De L'appellation D'origine Champagne Vers La Protection Absolue'. *Propriétés Intellectuelles*, no. 13 (2004): 853–862.

Boquérat, Gilles. 'Le Swadeshi À L'épreuve De L'ouverture'. In *De La Mondialisation Au Développement Local En Inde*, edited by Frédéric Landy and Basudeb Chaudhuri, 27–41. Paris: CNRS Editions, 2002.

Bowen, Sarah. 'Development from Within? The Potential for Geographical Indications in the Global South'. *The Journal of World Intellectual Property*, 13, no. 2 (2010): 231–252.

Boze, Jean Christophe. 'L'affaire Bronco En Californie: Pas De "Napa" Sur L'étiquette Sans Raison De Napa Dans Le Vin'. *Revue de Droit Rural*, no. 333 (2005): 22–25.

Capus, Joseph. *La Genèse Des Appellations D'origine Contrôlées*. Paris: INAO, 1947.

Casabianca, François, Bertil Sylvander, Y Noël, C Béranger, JB Coulon, Georges Giraud, Gilles Flutet, François Ronçin, and E Vincent. 'Terroir Et Typicité:

Propositions De Définitions Pour Deux Notions Essentielles À L'appréhension Des Indications Et Du Développement Durable'. *Terroirs Viticoles*, 2, no. Actes du VIème Congrès international des terroirs viticoles (2006): 544–551.

Chakravarty, Sumit, Gopal Shukla, and Suman Malla and C P Suresh. 'Farmers' Rights in Conserving Plant Biodiversity with Special Reference to North-East India'. *Journal of Intellectual Property Rights*, 13, no. May (2008): 225–233.

Chandola, Harsh V. 'Basmati Rice: Geographical Indication or Mis-Indication'. *The Journal of World Intellectual Property*, 9, no. 2 (2006): 166–188.

Chandran, Sajeev, Archna Roy, and Lokesh Jain. 'Implications of New Patent Regime on Indian Pharmaceutical Industry: Challenges and Opportunities'. *Journal of Intellectual Property Rights*, 10, no. July (2005): 269–280.

Charlier, Christophe, and Mai-Anh Ngo. 'An Analysis of the European Communities: Protection of Trademarks and Geographical Indications for Agricultural Products and Foodstuffs Dispute'. *The Journal of World Intellectual Property*, 10, no. 3–4 (2007): 171–186.

Chaturvedi, Sachin. 'India, the European Union and Geographical Indications (GI): Convergence of Interests and Challenges Ahead'. 2002.

Chengappa, P.G. 'Institutional Aspects of Agricultural Marketing in India'. In *Institutional Change in Indian Agriculture*, edited by Suresh Pal, Mruthyunjaya, P. K. Joshi and Raka Saxena, 331–348. New Delhi: National Centre for Agricultural Economics and Policy Research, 2003.

'Communication De La Commission Au Parlement Européen, Au Conseil, Au Comité Économique Et Social Européen Et Au Comité Des Régions Sur La Politique De Qualité Des Produits Agricoles'. 16: Commission des Communautés Européennes.

Das, Kasturi. 'International Protection of India's Geographical Indications with Special Reference to "Darjeeling" Tea'. *The Journal of World Intellectual Property*, 9, no. 5 (2006): 459–495.

———. 'Prospects and Challenges of Geographical Indications in India'. *The Journal of World Intellectual Property*, 13, no. 2 (2010): 148–201.

de Sainte-Marie, Christine. 'De La Provenance À La Gestion De L'origine Géographique: La Requalification De La Clémentine De Corse'. In *Les Produits Agroalimentaires Régionaux: Approches Théoriques Et Résultats D'études*, edited by Lucie Sirieix, Fatiha Fort and Hervé Remaud, 51–60. Campus Ensa–Inra de Montpellier: Cahiers de Recherche MOISA, 2001.

Debrez, Anne F. 'Les Tendances Jurisprudentielles Des Délimitations Des Appellations D'origine Contrôlées Viti-Vinicoles'. *Recueil Dalloz*, (2005): 282.

Delfosse, Claire. 'La France Fromagère'. *Thèse pour le nouveau Doctorat, sous la direction de M. GILBANK, Université de Paris I Panthéon-Sorbonne*, (1992): 163–202.

Derruppe, Jacques. 'Appellations D'origine, Indication De Provenance'. In *Répertoire De Droit International*. Encyclopédie Dalloz.

Escudero, Sergio. 'International Protection of Geographical Indications and Developing Countries'. 1–57: South Centre, TRADE Working Papers, 2001.
Evans, G. E., and Michael Blakeney. 'The Protection of Geographical Indications after Doha: Quo Vadis?' *Journal of International Economic Law*, 9, no. 3 (2006): 575–614.
Fish, Allison. 'The Commodification and Exchange of Knowledge in the Case of Transnational Commercial Yoga'. *International Journal of Cultural Property*, 13, no. 2 (2006): 189–206.
François, Renaud. 'Les Dénominations Génériques'. 130: Université Robert Schuman de Strasbourg, 2002.
Gangjee, Dev. 'Melton Mowbray and the GI Pie in the Sky: Exploring Cartographies of Protection'. *Intellectual Property Quartely*, no. 3 (2006): 291–309.
Gangjee, D. *Relocating the Law of Geographical Indications*. Cambridge: Cambridge University Press, 2012.
Ganguli, Prabuddha. *Gearing Up for Patents, the Indian Scenario*. Hyderabad: Universities Press (India), 1998.
Garcia, C., S. Bhagwat, J. Ghazoul, K. M. Nanaya, C. Nath, C. G. Kushalappa, Y. Raghuramulu, R. Nasi, and P. Vaast. 'Biodiversity Conservation in Agricultural Landscapes: Challenges and Opportunities of Coffee Agroforestry in the Western Ghats, India'. *Conservation Biology*, x, no. x (2009): x–xx.
The Geographical Indication of Goods (Registration and Protection) Act, 1999, Bare Act with Short Comments Professional Book Publishers, 2005.
Gervais, D. *The TRIPS Agreement*. London: Sweet & Maxwell, 2003.
Gervais, Daniel J. 'Traditional Knowledge: Are We Closer to the Answers? The Potential Role of Geographical Indications'. *ILSA Journal of International and Comparative Law*, 15, no. 2 (2009): 551–567.
Gonzales_Vaqué, Luis. 'Indications Géographiques Et Appellations D'origine: Interprétation Et Mise En Oeuvre Du Nouveau Règlement No. 510/2006'. *Revue du Droit de l'Union Européenne*, no. 4 (2006): 795–813.
Gopalakrishnan, N.S., Prabha, S. Nair, and Aravind K. Babu. *Exploring the Relationship between Geographical Indications and Traditional Knowledge, an Analysis of the Legal Tools for the Protection of Geographical Indications in Asia*. Vol. August Geneva: ICTSD Programme on IPRs and Sustainable Development, International Centre for Trade and Sustainable Development, 2007.
Gopalan, Raguvaran, and Sindhu Sivakumar. 'Keeping Cashmere in Kashmir: the Interface between GI and TK'. *Journal of Intellectual Property Rights*, 12, no. November (2007): 581–588.
Graefe zu Baringdorf, Friedrich-Wilhelm. 'Rapport Sur La Proposition De Règlement Du Conseil Relatif À La Protection Des Indications Géographiques Et Des Appellations D'origine Des Produits Agricoles Et Des Denrées Alimentaires': Commission de l'agriculture et du développement rural, 2006.
Guennif, Samira, and Julien Chaisse. 'L'économie Politique Du Brevet Au Sud : Variations Indiennes Sur Le Brevet Pharmaceutique'. *Revue Internationale de Droit Economique*, XXI, no. 2 (2007/2): 185–210.

'Guide Du Demandeur D'aoc/Aop'. 42: INAO, 2009.
'Guide Du Demandeur Igp'. 66: INAO, 2009.
Handler, Michael. 'The WTO Geographical Indications Dispute'. *Modern Law Review*, 69, no. 1 (2006): 70–80.
Hermitte, Marie-Angèle. 'Les Appellations D'origine Dans La Genèse Des Droits De La Propriété Intellectuelle'. In *Systèmes Agroalimentaires Localisées. Terroirs, Savoir-Faire, Innovations*, edited by Pascale Moity-Maïzy, 195–206: Etud. Rech.Syst. Agraires Dév., 2001.
'Hon'ble Union Minister of Commerce & Industry Thiru Murasoli Maran Inaugurated Modernised Patent Office in Chennai'. In *Press Releases*: Patent Office India, 2001.
Hughes, Justin. 'The Spirited Debate over Geographic Indications'. *Law Review*, (2003): 101.
'Interview: Gk Muthukumaar, Senior Associate, Anand and Anand'. *The Financial Express*, 7 January 2009.
IP/C/W/386. 'Incidences De L'extension De L'article 23'. In *Communication de l'Argentine, de l'Australie, du Canada, du Chili, d'El Salvador, des États-Unis,du Guatemala, de la Nouvelle-Zélande, du Paraguay, des Philippines et du Taipei chinois*, 8 novembre 2002.
Jena, Pradyot R., and Ulrike Grote. 'Changing Institutions to Protect Regional Heritage: A Case for Geographical Indications in the Indian Agrifood Sector'. *Development Policy Review*, 28, no. 2 (2010): 217–236.
Jena, P.R. and Grote, U. 'Impact Evaluation of Traditional Basmati Rice Cultivation in Uttarakhand State of Northern India: What Implications Does It Hold for Geographical Indications?' *World Development*, 40(9) (2012): 1895–1907.
Josling, Tim. 'The War on Terroir: Geographical Indications as a Transatlantic Trade Conflict'. *Journal of Agricultural Economics*, 57 (2006): 337–63.
Kailasam, K. C. *Law of Trademarks and Geographical Indications*. New Delhi: Wadhwa and Co., 2003.
Kamperman Sanders, Anselm. 'Incentives for and Protection of Cultural Expression: Art, Trade and Geographical Indications'. *The Journal of World Intellectual Property*, 13, no. 2 (2010): 81–93.
Khilnani, Sunil. *L'idée De L'inde*. Paris: Fayard, 2005.
Kieffer, Simone. 'Un Nouveau Statut Pour L'inao Qui Devient "L'institut National De L'origine Et De La Qualité"'. *Revue de Droit Rural*, 349 (2007): x.
Kumar, Ashwani. The Minister of State in the Ministry of Commerce and Industry (Shri Ashwani). 'Lok Sabha Unstarred Question No 3824 to Be Answered on 16.05.2006 G I Certificate', edited by Government of India Ministry of Commerce and Industry, 2006.
'L'inde Agricole : Entre Forces Et Faiblesses'. 7: Momagri, Mouvement pour une organisation mondiale de l'agriculture, 2008.
*La Blanchisserie De La Rivière Sauvagean Et Le Blanchiment Des Toiles À Cholet.* Cahors: Association des Amis du Musée du Textile Cholerais, REMPART, 1992.

'La Réforme Des Signes De L'identification De La Qualité Et De L'origine'. INAO, 2007.
Langford, Jean. *Fluent Bodies: Ayurvedic Remedies for Postcolonial Imbalance.* Durham: Duke University Press, 2002.
Le_Goffic, Caroline. *La Protection Des Indications Géographiques En France, En Europe Et Aux Etats-Unis.* Vol. Thèse. Paris: Le droit des affaires, Propriété intellectuelle, IRPI, Litec, 2009.
———. 'Le Parmesan, C'est Râpé! (Commentaire De L'arrêt De La Cjce Du 26 Février 2008)'. *Propriété industrielle*, no. 7 (2008): 1–5.
———. 'Retour Sur Le Cas Du "Champagne Soviétique" (Commentaire De L'arrêt De La Cour D'appel De Paris Du 25 Avril 2007)'. *Propriété industrielle*, no. 4 (2008): 18–22.
Liebl, Maureen, and Tirthankar Roy. 'Handmade in India'. In *Poor People's Knowledge: Promoting Intellectual Property in Developing Countries*, edited by J. Michael Finger and Philip Schuler, 53–73: World Bank/Oxford University Press, 2004.
Lightbourne, Muriel. 'Of Rice and Men, an Attempt to Assess the Basmati Affair'. *The Journal of World Intellectual Property*, 6, no. 6 (2003): 875–893.
'Livre Vert Sur La Qualité Des Produits Agricoles: Normes De Commercialisation, Exigences De Production Et Systèmes De Qualité'. 24. Bruxelles: Commission des Communautés Européennes, 2008.
Lorvellec, Louis. 'La Protection Internationale Des Appellations D'origine Contrôlées'. In *Ecrits De Droit Rural Et Agroalimentaire*, 385–398. Paris: Dalloz, 2002.
———. 'La Protection Internationale Des Signes De Qualité'. In *Ecrits De Droit Rural Et Agroalimentaire*, 399–416. Paris: Dalloz, 2002.
Mahias, Marie-Claude. 'Les Sciences Et Les Techniques Traditionnelles En Inde'. *L'Homme*, 37, no. 142 (1997): 105–114.
Marchenay, Philippe, and Marie-France Lagarde. *A La Recherche Des Variétés Locales De Plantes Cultivées.* Paris: BRG et Page PACA, 1987.
Marette, Stéphan , Roxanne Clemens, and Bruce A. Babcock. 'The Recent International and Regulatory Decisions about Geographical Indications'. *Midwest* 37, January 2007.
Marie-Vivien, Delphine. 'From Plant Variety Definition to Geographical Indication Protection: A Search for the Link between Basmati Rice and India/Pakistan'. *The Journal of World Intellectual Property*, 11, no. 4 (2008): 321–344.
———. 'The Protection of Geographical Indications for Handicrafts: or How to Apply the Concepts of Natural and Human Factors to all Products'. *The WIPO Journal*, 4(2) (2013): 191–203.
Marie-Vivien, D., Garcia, C.A., Kushalappa, C.G. and Vaast, P. 'Trademarks, Geographical Indications and Environmental Labeling to Promote

Biodiversity: The Case of Agroforestry Coffee in India', *Development Policy Review*, 32, no. 4 (2014): 379–398.

Milbert, Isabelle. 'L'impact Des Changements Culturels Et Économiques Sur Les Comportements Alimentaires : Le Cas De L'inde'. *Economie Rurale*, 190 (1989): 46–49.

Mishra, Jai Prakash. 'Intellectual Property Rights and Food Security'. *The Journal of World Intellectual Property*, 4, no. 1 (2001): 5–25.

Nagarajan, S. 'Geographical Indications and Agriculture-Related Intellectual Property Rights Issues'. *Current Science*, 92, no. 2 (2007).

Nair, Latha_R, and Rajendra Kumar. *Geographical Indications, a Search for Identity*. Delhi: LexisNexis Butterworths, 2005.

New, William. 'Modalities Drafted for WTO Geographical Indications, Biodiversity Amendment'. *Intellectual Property Watch*, 15 July 2008.

Ngo, Mai-Anh. *La Qualité Et La Sécurité Des Produits Agro-Alimentaires*: L'Harmattan, 2006.

O'Connor, Bernard. *The Law of Geographical Indications*. London: Cameron May, 2004.

Olszak, Norbert. 'Actualité Du Droit Des Signes D'origine Et De Qualité (Appellations D'origine, Labels)'. *Propriété Industrielle*, 6 (2006).

———. *Appellations D'origine Et Indications De Provenance (Indications Géographiques)*: Répertoire pénal Dalloz, 2008.

———. 'L'appellation D'origine, Un Bien Sublime?' In *Etudes Offertes Au Doyen Philippe Simler*, 777–788: LITEC Dalloz, 2007.

———. 'La Politique Communautaire Des Signes De Qualité Et D'origine'. In *Congreso internacional sobre el desarrollo sostenible*. Burgos, 2008.

———. 'La Propriété Industrielle Est-Elle Bien Une Propriété? (a Propos De L'arrêt "Bain De Champagne", Paris, 4ème Ch. A, 12 Septembre 2001, Parfums Caron C. C.I.V.C.)'. 1894–1896: Recueil Dalloz 2002.

———. 'La Réforme Des Aoc Et Les Libertés. Note Sous Ce, Ord. Réf., 12 Février 2007, No. 301131, Association Sopravit Et Autres *Gazette du Palais, Spécial Droit agraire*, 227 (2007): 9–14.

———. *Le Droit Des Appellations D'origine Et Des Indications De Provenance*. Paris: Tec&Doc, 2001.

———. 'Le Goût Des Vins Aop Et Igp: Description Et Contrôle Des Caractéristiques Orga-Noleptiques'. *Revue de Droit Rural*, no. 371 (2009): x.

———. 'Les Nouveaux Règlements Européens Sur Les Appellations D'origine Et Indications Géographiques Protégées Et Les Spécialités Traditionnelles Garanties'. *Revue de Droit Rural*, no. 343 (2006): x.

Panini, M N. 'Trends in Cultural Globalisation'. *Economic and Political Weekly*, 34 no. July 31 (1999): 2168–2173.

'The Patents (Amendment) Act 2005'. In *Gazette of India*, 2005.

Patnaik, P. 'Manmohan Singh and Colonialism'. *People's Democracy*, July 17 2005, 3.

Piatti, M.-C. 'L'appellation D'origine (Essai De Qualification)'. *Revue trimestrielle de droit commercial*, Juillet (1999): 557–581.
Pingali, Prabhu, and Yasmeen Khwaja. 'Globalisation of Indian Diets and the Transformation of Food Supply Systems'. Paper presented at the 17th Annual Conference Indian Society of Agricultural Marketing, Hyderabad, 5–7 February 2004.
Plaisant, Marcel, and Fernand-Jacq. *Traité Des Noms Et Appellations D'origine*. Paris: Librairie Arthur Rousseau, 1921.
Pollaud-Dulian, Frédéric. *Droit De La Propriété Industrielle*. Paris: Montchrestien, 1999.
Profeta, Adriano, Richard Balling, Volker Schoene, and Alexander Wirsig. 'The Protection of Origins for Agricultural Products and Foods in Europe: Status Quo, Problems and Policy Recommendations for the Green Book'. *The Journal of World Intellectual Property*, 12, no. 6 (2009): 622–648.
Racine, Jean-Luc. 'L'inde Émergente, Ou La Sortie Des Temps Postcoloniaux'. *Hérodote, La Découverte*, 120 (2006): 28–47.
———. 'L'inde Et L'ordre Du Monde'. *Hérodote*, 108 (2003): 91–112.
Rangnekar, Dwijen. 'Geographical Indications and Localisation: A Case Study of Feni'. 64: CSGR Report, 2009.
Rangnekar, D. and S. Kumar. 'Another Look at Basmati: Genericity and the Problems of a Transborder Geographical Indication'. *The Journal of World Intellectual Property*, 13, no. 2 (2010): 202–230.
Rao, C Niranjan. 'Geographical Indications in Indian Context: A Case Study of Darjeeling Tea'. *Economic and Political Weekly*, 15 October 2005 (2005): 4545–4550.
Rochard, Denis. *La Protection Internationale Des Indications Géographiques*. Paris: Presses Universitaires de France, 2002.
Roncin, François, and François Boulineau. 'Valorisation Des "Légumes De Terroir" Par Les Signes Officiels D'identification De La Qualité Et De L'origine (Aop-Igp), Comment Est-Ce Réalisable ?', Angers 7–9 September 2005.
Ruet, Joël. 'Réformes Et Nouvelle Économie Politique En Inde'. *Critiques internationales* 3, no. 32 (2006): 189–207.
Ruzek, Vincent. 'La Stratégie Communautaire De Protection Des Indications Géographiques En Question'. *Revue de Droit Rural*, no. 373 (2009): 1–9.
Saha, Tushar Kanti, and Nalin Bharti. 'Beyonds Wines and Spirits: Developing Countries'gi Products and Their Potential in WTO Regime with Special Reference to India'. *Journal Of Intellectual Property Rights*, 11, no. March (2006): 89–97.
Samaddar, S.G., and A.B. Samaddar. 'Koma Chaul: A Potential Candidate for Geographical Indication'. *Journal Of Intellectual Property Rights*, 15, May (2010): 2214–2219.
Schmidt-Szalewski, Joanna. 'La Protection Des Noms Géographiques En Droit Communautaire'. *La Semaine Juridique Entreprise et Affaires*, 44, no. 703 (1997): 1–7.

Schmidt-Szalewski, Joanna. 'Protection Communautaire Des Dénominations Géographiques'. *Propriété industrielle*, 6, no. Juin (2009).
Sen, Amartya. *The Argumentative Indian: Writings on Indian Culture, History, and Identity*. London: Penguin, 2005.
Singh, B.P. *L'etat Et Les Arts En Inde*. Paris: Editions Karthala, 1999.
Sridhar, Madabhushi. 'Gi for Tirupathi Laddu: Whose Interests Protected?' *Sinapse, an intellectual property rendez-vous*, 16 March 2010.
Srivastava, Suresh C. 'Geographical Indications and Legal Framework in India', *Economic and Political Weekly*, (2003): 4022–4033.
Sylvander, Bertil, Gilles Allaire, and Giovanni Belletto. 'Les Dispositifs Français Et Européens De Protection De La Qualité Et De L'origine'. Paper presented at the Symposium international 'Territoires et enjeux du développement régional', Lyon, 9–11 mars 2005.
Taraporevala, V.J. *Law of Intellectual Property*. Mumbai: Inkwell Printers, 2005.
Téchoueyres, Isabelle, and Virginie Amilien. 'Produits Locaux Entre Nature Et Culture : De La Ferme Voisine Au Terroir. Entretien Avec Laurence Bérard'. *Anthropology of Food*, no. 4 (2005).
Thomas, Frédéric, and Dao The Anh. 'Qualités Et Origine Au Vietnam: L'épineuse Question De L'administration De La Preuve Entre Qualité Et Origine'. 17. Paris: Conférence 'Localiser les produits : une voie durable au service de la diversité naturelle et culturelle des Suds ?' UNESCO, 2009.
TN/C/W/25. 'Questions Relatives À L'extension De La Protection Des Indications Géographiques Prévue À L'article 23 De L'accord Adpic Aux Produits Autres Que Les Vins Et Spiritueux'. In *Note du Secrétariat*, 18 mai 2005.
*Une Réussite Française: L'appellation D'origine Contrôlée*. INAO, 1985.
Vaidyanathan, A. 'India's Agricultural Development Policy'. *Economic and Political Weekly*, 35, no. May 13 (2000): 1735–1741.
Venkatesan, V. 'Bittersweet Status: The Grant of G.I. Status to Tirupati Laddu Is Criticised as Being against the Spirit of the Geographical Indications of Goods Act, 1999'. *Front Line*, 26, no. 21 (2009): 1–3.
Vidal, Denis. 'In Search of Basmatisthan: Agro-Nationalism and Globalisation'. In *Globalizing India, Perspectives from Below*, edited by Jackie Assayag and Chris Fuller, 47–65. London: Anthem Press, 2005.
Visse-Causse, Séverine. *L'appellation D'origine: Valorisation Du Terroir*. Paris: adef-Association des Etudes Foncières, 2005.
Watal, Jayashree. *Intellectual Property Rights in the WTO and Developing Countries*. 2nd ed. New Delhi: Oxford University Press (India), 2005.

# Index

Agricultural and Processed Food Products Export Development Authority (APEDA), 18, 20, 123–124, 134, 213–216
agricultural goods in India, GIs, 110
  colonial history, reputation created by, 125–133
  delimitation of geographical area issue, 134–136
  registered products, 111
  reputation based on plant varieties, 111–125
Agricultural Products Quality Control Act, 154
agricultural regulation, 165
agricultural surplus, xxi
agricultural universities, 195–196
Agriculture and Processed Food Products Export Development Authority (APEDA), 192
agriculture, essential constituent of Indian economy, 16
Allahabadi Surkha Amrood Utpadak Welfare Association, 189
alleppey, meaning of, 90
All India Agarbathi Manufacturers' Association (AIAMA), The, 181–182
All India Rice Exporters Association, 214
Andhra Pradesh Handicraft Development Corporation, 194
Andhra Pradesh Technology Development & Promotion Centre (APTDC), 186
Apex Cooperative Societies, 185, 194
appellation Huile d'Olive de Nyons, 31

appellation morbier, definition of, 30
appellation of origins (AOC), France, 2, 7, 32–36, 49, 95, 99, 136, 160. *See also* Geographical indication (GI)
  contemporary history of, 25
  definition of, 7n13, 29
  exceptions procedures for, 173–174
  identical procedure for all products, 31–32
  Law of 1 August 1905, 26
  Law of 1919, 26–27
  Law of 1927, 29
  Law of 1955, 29
  Law of 1957, 28
  modern regime for protection of, xx
  natural and human factors, combination of, 29–31
  previous approval procedure of, 168–169
  product characteristics, 27
  strong protection of, 55–60
appellation Olive de Nyons, 31
applicant kind and the product type, 198–199
'applicant–proprietor/authorized user pair,' the, 201–210
  the applicant/proprietor, 201–204
  the registered authorized user, 204–210
applicant–proprietor, producers represented by, 210–231
application for registration of GIs, 51–52
Aranmula Kannadi GI, 78
Aranmula metal mirror, 71

## Index

Aranmula Viswabrahmana Kannada Nirman Society, 188
area of origin, definition of, 25
Assam tea, 191
associations and cooperatives members, 222–224
authority, definition of, 201
automatic protection, 145–146
Ayurvedic treatment, 108

Banyuls (decree of 18 September 1909), 26
Basmati Export Development Foundation (BEDF) laboratory, 123
Basmati Growers Association (BGA), 122–124
Basmati rice, xvii, xxii, 9, 17–21, 111, 120–125, 134
Benares silk, 199
Bharatiya Janata Party (BJP), 47
Bikram Yoga style, 109
biocentre, 198
biological diversity, 13
bio-piracy, 46

Caravan, 16
certification body, 171
certification marks system, 6
Chamba Rumal GI, 77–78
Champagne (decree of 17 December 1908), 26
Chamundi Silks Textiles Ltd, 224
Chanderi Development Foundation, 189
Chanderi sari, GI, 103
Chhattisgarh Hastshilp Vikas Board, 193
Choovatta Valappil Tharavad Dharmadaiva Paripalana Trust, 224
chowka, 75
Clairette de Die (decree of 21 April 1910), 26
co-applicants, inclinations of, 199

Code of Intellectual Property, 247
Coffee Board Research Institute, 127, 130, 190, 192, 211, 237
Coir Industry Act, 1953, 192
collective marks system, 6
collective right to sue, 256–257. *See also* Geographical indication (GI)
Commodity Boards, 190–192
Company Act of 1956, 183, 193
competent authority, 201
Competition Act of 2002, 183
Comté, definition of, 30
Confederation of Indian Industry (CII), 76, 186
  in economic development of India, 185
  establishment, 185
Consumer Code and the Rural Code, 247
Controller General of Patents, Designs and Trademarks, The, 180
Coorg green cardamom, GI, 133, 135, 192
Craft Development Institute (CDI), 196, 219–222
Crafts Council of India, 187
cultural differences between old and new world countries, 4–10
cultural identity, xx, xxii–xxiv, 48, 234

Darjeeling Planters Association, 191
Darjeeling tea, 21–24, 46, 50, 125–126, 191
Darjeeling Tea Association (DTA), 191
Decree-Law of 1935, 175
Department of Handloom and Textiles, Government of Tamil Nadu, The, 198
Department of Horticulture, Government of Karnataka, The, 197–198

Department of Science, Technology
& Environment, Government
of Goa, The, 198
Department of Sericulture, 183
Design and Technical Development
Centre, 187
designation of origin, definition of, 33
designation of services by GIs, 107–109
Development Commissioner for
Handicraft, 1950, 196
Directorate of Handicrafts & Cottage Industries, 185
Dispute Settlement Body (DSB) of
WTO, 63, 150–154
Doha Declaration, 155
*dorukha-tanka*, 77

EUCJ, 33–34, 62–63, 174
Europe
situation in, 247–248
state role in protection of GIs in,
147–149
European Commission, 34, 41, 49,
64, 94, 97, 101, 138, 148–149,
151–154, 166, 174, 255, 262,
269–270
European Commission's Directorate-General for Agriculture, 6
European Community (EC), xxi,
6n11
European Court of Justice (ECJ),
34–35
European migrants, 4
European Regulation 2081/92, 147
European Regulation No. 510/2006,
151
European Union (EU), 6n11, 8, 11,
13, 43
provisions for GI from foreign
countries, 151–153
provisions, new, 169–170
Export (Quality Control and Inspection) Act, 120
Exportur case, 38, 169

Federation of Aroma/Agarbathi
Manufacturing Enterprise
(FAME), 222
Federation of Indian Micro and
Small & Medium Enterprises
(FISME), 178
France
application for GI registration in,
160–166
control in, 261
producers in, 251–252
role of producers' organizations
after 2006, 163–166
role of the state in scrutiny,
166–177
action for infringement, 174–177
GI application examination, 166–168
supervision of control
mechanisms, 168–174
situation in, 247–248
state role decline in, 159
Free Trade Agreement, 153–154
French Civil Code, 244
French GIs, nature factors
predominance of
necessity of localization of raw
material for AOC, 92–93
raw material source, 93–97
French law of 1919, 256
French Law on consumption, xxiv
French Law, qualification from,
249–251
French National Institute of Industrial Property, 266
French reform of 2006, 171–173

GATT, 6, 10, 47, 150
genetic resources, 12–13
geographical environment, 7n13,
29–30, 32, 50, 52–53
geographical indication (GI), xxii,
xix–xx, 23–24, 32, 39, 43,
106–107. *See also* Appellation
of origins (AOC), France act,

Indian of 1999, xxii, 1, 13–14, 44–48, 142, 251
ambivalence of the applicant of, 200–231
applicant supported by the state, 182–190
applications, examination of, 166–168
collective nature of, 255–263
consequences for international governance of, 154–158
definition of, xvii, 7n14
designation of all products through, 49–51
dual purpose of, 234–238
ex officio protection of, 174–175
extension of additional protection, 7–8, 11–12, 66, 105
in France
appellation of origin (see Appellation of origins [AOC], France)
link to origin through local varieties and breeds, 136–142
in India, 178
analysis of, xxiii
control in, 261
fight against counterfeiting of products, 17–24
fragmentation of national identity, 14
link to origin based on local knowledge, 97–106
nature of products, 69
for non-agricultural products, xxiii
parliamentary debates on GI Act, 45–48
preamble of GI Act, 45
protection against traditional products decline, 15–17
protection of GIs prior to Act, 44–45, 65–68

qualification reinforced by, 248
registered in name of state, xxiv, 14
registered products, 70
registration of producers in, 251–252
right to use untapped in, 252–254
state filing GIs applications in, 259–260
use to protect products, 2
internationalization at WTO, 3–13
legal nature of, 263–265
legal rules protecting, xviii
legal tool, 81
in the name of state, registration of, 190–198
origin of legal protection, 1
particularism of, 243–245
post-TRIPS Agreement, 1
promotion in France and Europe, xxi
protection through bilateral agreements, 153–154
registration by producers, 160–166
Registry, xxv, 47–48, 50, 85
rift between new and old world countries, 10–13
right in, 249–251
rights conferred in France, Europe and India, 55–68
risk of bias of, 238–241
specification drafting, 163–165
state role in protection of, 147–149
principle of equivalence, 148
principle of reciprocity, 148
state role in GIs compared to IPRs, 148–149
transmission of objections, 149
sui generis laws, 259
transfer to an association, 188–189
Geographical Indications of Goods (Protection and Registration) Act (GI Act) of 1999, xx, 49

Geographical Indications of Goods (Registration and Protection) Rules, 2002, The, 49
geographical origin, xvii, xviii, xxi, xxiii, 2, 7, 41, 49–50, 53
  acquiring of significance in market, 18–19
GI-able, 48
globalization, xviii–xix, 15, 17
Goa Cashew Feni Distillers & Bottlers Association, 198
Government enterprises, for marketing of handicrafts, 193–194
Government of the States of the Union, The, 197–198
Government of the Union of India, The, 196–197
green paper, 255
Green Revolution, 16
gross domestic product (GDP) of India, xxii
guild trademarks, xviii

handicraft GIs, India, 15–16, 110
  ancient and sophisticated know-how, 70–81
  lack of precision in geographical areas delimitation, 86–87
  safeguarding the interest of specific communities, 81–83
  vs French GIs, absence of natural factors
    clay influence, 92
    high-quality raw material importance, 88
    minor influence of soil and climate, 91
    origin of raw material, 89–91
    river water influence, 91–92
  written proof on ancient history, 83–86
handloom park, Pochampally, 186
heritage weaves, 183

homogeneity, concept of, 30

Ikat, meaning of, 75
Indian Agricultural Research Institute, 121
Indian Council for Agricultural Research, 122–123
Indian state
  autonomous organizations of, 193–194
  interventionism of, 178–179
  role of the state in scrutiny, 180–181
  support to the applicant, 181–190
  rationale for the ubiquity of, 231–241
    disadvantaged producers, 231–238
    risk of bias of GI registry, 238–241
indigenous plant varieties, 113–120
initial evaluation trial (IET), 122
intangible heritage, 250
intellectual property, 147
Intellectual Property Appellate Board (IPAB), 73, 180, 202
intellectual property facilitation (IPF), 178
intellectual property rights (IPRs), 3–4, 48, 101, 106, 247–248
international bureau, 146
International Organization for Standardization (ISO), 81
international protection, mechanism of, 260
Jammu and Kashmir Handloom Co-Operative Societies Union, 220
jasmine rice, 19
joint proposal, 156
*Journal of Geographical Indications*, xxv
Kalamkari GI, 76–77

Index 285

Kancheepuram silk saris, 46, 72, 74, 84, 217
Kani shawl GI, 71, 86
Karimnagar Silver Filigree Handicrafts, 186
Karnataka Silk Industries Corporation (KSIC), 183
Karnataka Soaps & Detergents Ltd (KSDL), 183–184
Karnataka State Handicraft Development Corporation (KSHDC), 193
Kashmir Handmade Pashmina Promotion Trust (KHMPPT), 219–220
Kashmir pashmina, 89
Kasmati trademark, 17, 19–20
Kerala Ayurveda, GI, 108
Konark stone, 88
Kondapalli Bommalu artisans, GI, 82
Kondapalli Bommalu, GI, 73, 84
Kondapalli Wooden Toys Manufacturers Mutually Aided Purchase, 186
Kota Doria Development Hadauti Foundation, 190
Kovai Kora cotton saris GI, 71, 84

label rouge, 163
Laguiole cheese, xviii
Lanco Institute of General Humanitarian Trust, 186
Land Acquisition Act, 253
legal differences between old and new world countries, 4–10
legal nature of applicant, 201–202
Lisbon Agreement for the Protection of Appellations of Origin and Their International (1958), 3, 7n13, 30, 33, 39, 55–56, 60–61, 101, 105–106, 145–147
additional protection in TRIPS Agreement, 8

authorities of the countries, role, 146–147
automatic protection, 145–146
local association, 189
local usage, 28
Lucknow chikan craft, GI, 199

Maharaja of Mysore, 183
Maran, Murasoli, 48
middle class of India, benefit from opening of foreign capital, xxii
monsooning process, 127
motif creation, 74–78
Multifiber Agreement (2005), 15
Mutually Aided Cooperative Welfare Society, 186
Mysore Agarbathi, GI, 79–80, 182
Mysore Central Food Technological Research Institute, 79
Mysore Powerloom Silk Manufacturers Cooperative Society, 225
Mysore Sandal Soap Factory, 183
Mysore sandal soap, GI, 81
Mysore silk, GI, 89–90, 183

National Bank for Agriculture and Rural Development (NABARD), 186
National Committee for Appellations of Origin of Cheeses, 29
National Committee for Appellations of Wines and Spirits, 161, 175–176
National Committee of Appellations of Origin of Cheeses, 176
national heritage, 260–261
National Institute of Appellations of Origin (INAO), 28, 43, 56, 95, 97, 174
National Institute of Fashion Technology, 187
National Institute of Intellectual Property (NIIP), 258

National Institute of Interdisciplinary Science and Technology (NIIST), 230
National Institute of Origin and Quality, France, 6
National treatment obligation, 150
nation building phase in India, 14
nature of public, variations of, 258–262
Navara rice, 187
new world countries, xx, 4, 146. *See also* Geographical indication (GI); Old world countries
Nilgiri tea, 191
non-agricultural GIs, 70
non-productive government enterprises, 218–219
non-traditional products GIs, 80–81
northern countries, 4

Office for the Harmonization in the Internal Market (OHIM), 104
official control, 170
Official Journal of the European Union (OJEU), 167
old world countries, xx, xxiv. *See also* Geographical indication (GI); New world countries
  GI an intellectual property right backed by, 3–4
  India as new country of, 13–24
Open Source Yoga Unity (OSYU), 109
origin-based products, xix
Orissa Ikat GIs, 75–76
Orissa Pattachitra, GI, 74
Orissa State Cooperative Handicrafts Corporation, 185

Palakkadan Matta Farmers Producer Company Ltd, 188, 223
Palakkadan Matta rice, 187
Paris Convention (1967), 8, 247

Paris Convention on the Protection of Intellectual Property (1883), 3
parmesan, 174–175
Parthasarathy Handicraft Centre, 188
pashmina shawls of Kashmir, 46
Pashmina Weavers Union, 220
patent information centres (PIC), 195
Pavithra Ring, 73
Payyanur Pavithra Ring Artisans and Development Society, The, 182, 223
permitted use, 207
*phylloxera* crisis, 25
Pipli appliqué work, GI, 185
Pipli handicrafts, 83
plant variety(ies), 111–125
Pochampally Handloom Tie & Dye Silk Sarees Manufacturers' Association, 185–186
Pochampally Handloom Weavers Cooperative Society, 185
Pochampally Ikat Foundation, 186
Pochampally Ikat GIs, 75–76, 85, 107, 185
pre-reform situation, in France, 168–169. *See also* France
pre-WTO system, state role in Lisbon Agreement system, 145–147
  authorities of the countries, role, 146–147
  automatic protection, 145–146
primary cooperatives, 185–187. *See also* Geographical indication (GI)
Primary Handicrafts Cooperative Societies. *See* Primary Handloom Weavers' Cooperative Societies
Primary Handloom Weavers' Cooperative Societies, 185
principle of equivalence, 148
principle of producers' organizations, 161–163

Index   287

principle of reciprocity, 148
private/public dualism, of geographical indication, 262–263
producer(s), 201
  representation of, 257–258
  representation of the interests of, 202–203
  state's ambivalent representation of, 211–213
producers' associations, 181–182
product compliance certificate (CCP), 163
products from India, competition from foreign products, 15
proprietor, required consent of, 204–207
prosecution, the state capable of, 261
protected designation of origins (PDOs), 2, 32–38, 41, 49–50, 55–57, 92–93
  examination of, 166–167
  registered in EU, 42
  rural code provisions for, 58–60
  strong protection of, 60–65
protected geographical indication (PGI), xxiii, 2, 22, 33, 49–50, 55–57, 93–97, 137
  definition of, 38, 40
  erstwhile certification of, 169
  examination of, 166–167
  geographical origin of, 37–38
  human factors, importance of, 38–43
  rejection of PGIs for, 43
  rural code provisions for, 58–60
  strong protection of, 60–65
public interest, representatives of, 224–227
Punjab Small-Scale Industries and Export Corporation, 194, 233
Puri Creative Handicraft Cooperative Society, 185

registered authorized user, 204–210
registered proprietor, 200
Reliance Industries Ltd, 227
religious organization
  controversy over, 228–231
  state participation in, 184 (*see also* Geographical indication [GI])
reserves, 157
Rio Convention on Biodiversity, 13
Roquefort, 31

Scotch Whisky Association, 44
Seed Act of 1966, 120, 122
self-sufficiency, xix
shahtoosh shawls, 219
signatory countries, 145
Silk Weavers' Cooperative Societies, 72
single industrial producer, objections against, 227–228
Societies Act of 1973, 189
sole private producer, 182
Southern countries, 4
Special Union, countries of, 146
Spice Board, 135, 192
stakeholders, 66, 107, 146, 165–166, 176, 190, 203, 210–211, 216
state agencies, for intellectual property, 195
state, associations supported by, 185
state cooperatives, 194
state's intellectual property agencies, legitimacy of, 219
statutory Commodity Boards, 190–191
Swadeshi movement, xix

Tea Board of India, 21–22, 24, 67, 191
Technology Information, Forecasting and Assessment Council (TIFAC), 186, 195

terroir products, concept of
  cultural dimension of, 36
  definition of, 37
  origin of, 35
  rejection for PGIs, 43
  social composition of, 36
Texmati trademark, 17, 19–20
Third World countries, xxii
Tirumala temple, 184
Tirumala Tirupati Devasthanam (TTD), 184
Tirupati laddu, GI, 79
Trade and Merchandise Act of 1958, 44–45
Trademark Act of 1999, 45
trademark law, influence of, 207–208
Trade-Related Aspects of Intellectual Property Rights (TRIPS) Agreement, xxiii, xvii, xix, 1, 4, 10, 39, 43, 45–46, 49, 51, 68, 101, 107, 150. *See also* Geographical indication (GI)
  Article 22.1 of, 7
  Article 22.2 of, 8
traditional knowledge (TK), 106–107
traditional specialty guaranteed (TSG), 268
transmission of objections, 149
*Travels in India* (Jean-Baptiste Tavernier), 86

uniqueness, concept of, 51–55. *See also* Geographical indication (GI)

United Nations Industrial Development Organization (UNIDO), 189–190
United States Patent and Trademark Office (USPTO), 18, 22–23
US Federal Trade Commission, 18–19
Uttar Pradesh Diversified Agriculture Support Project, 189

village cooperatives, 185

weaving plant, establishment of, 183
widespread plant varieties, 113–120
Wildlife Trust of India, 219
WIPO Model Law, 257
World Intellectual Property Organization (WIPO), 1, 39, 49, 106–107
World Trade Organization (WTO), 13, 63, 105
  agreement on Trade-Related Aspects of Intellectual Property Rights (TRIPS), xxiii, xvii, xix, 1, 6
  impact on the role of the state
    consequences for international governance, 154–158
    DSB decision, 150–154

yarn spinning, 74
yoga, 108–109

zari, 72

# About the Author

**Delphine Marie-Vivien** is a researcher in law with CIRAD, a French research centre tackling international agricultural and development issues (UMR Innovation, Montpellier, F-34398 France). She is a graduate in Chemistry and Intellectual Property Law. After two years as patent engineer in the oil industry, she joined CIRAD, and worked for five years on intellectual property and genetic resources issues in agriculture. She was a visiting researcher at the National Law School of India University, Bengaluru, India, between 2005 and 2008, to conduct her PhD research. Her thesis, defended in Paris, was entitled 'The Law of Geographical Indications in India Compared to French, European and International Laws'. After three years in South Korea, since 2012 she is based in Vietnam, working on research projects regarding the protection of geographical indications in South-East Asia. She can be reached at delphine.marie-vivien@cirad.fr.